P9-EDL-417

The Internet
QuickStart

Mary Ann Pike
Tod G. Pike

PTC LEARNING RESOURCES CENTER

The Internet QuickStart

Copyright © 1994 by Que® Corporation.

All rights reserved. Printed in the United States of America. No part of this book may be used or reproduced in any form or by any means, or stored in a database or retrieval system, without prior written permission of the publisher except in the case of brief quotations embodied in critical articles and reviews. Making copies of any part of this book for any purpose other than your own personal use is a violation of United States copyright laws. For information, address Que Corporation, 201 W. 103rd Street, Indianapolis, IN 46290.

Library of Congress Catalog No.: 94-65325

ISBN: 1-56529-658-3

This book is sold *as is*, without warranty of any kind, either express or implied, respecting the contents of this book, including but not limited to implied warranties for the book's quality, performance, merchantability, or fitness for any particular purpose. Neither Que Corporation nor its dealers or distributors shall be liable to the purchaser or any other person or entity with respect to any liability, loss, or damage caused or alleged to be caused directly or indirectly by this book.

96 95 94   4 3 2

Interpretation of the printing code: the rightmost double-digit number is the year of the book's printing; the rightmost single-digit number, the number of the book's printing. For example, a printing code of 94-1 shows that the first printing of the book occurred in 1994.

Publisher: David P. Ewing

Associate Publisher: Corinne Walls

Managing Editor: Anne Owen

Marketing Manager: Ray Robinson

About the Authors

Mary Ann Pike has a B.S. in electrical engineering and an M.A. in professional writing from Carnegie Mellon University. She has experience in software design and development, and is currently working part-time as a technical writer at the Software Engineering Institute at Carnegie Mellon University.

Tod Pike is a graduate of Carnegie Mellon University, where he first became acquainted with the Internet. He has experience in UNIX system administration and TCP/IP network management. Currently working at the Software Engineering Institute, he can be reached on the Internet at `tpike@pittslug.sug.org`.

Publishing Manager
Thomas H. Bennett

Acquisitions Editors
Thomas F. Godfrey III
Nancy Stevenson

Product Development Specialist
Steven M. Schafer

Production Editor
Susan Shaw Dunn

Editors
Susan Ross Moore
Danielle Bird

Technical Editors
Ellen Riddle
Sue Clark
Jerry L. Dunn

Book Designer
Amy Peppler-Adams

Cover Designer
Dan Armstrong

Production Team
Stephen Adams
Angela Bannan
Cameron Booker
Teresa Forrester
Karen Dodson
Joelynn Gifford
Dennis Clay Hager
Carla Hall
Joy Dean Lee
Jamie Milazzo
Tim Montgomery
Aren Munk
G. Alan Palmore
Nanci Sears Perry
Caroline Roop
Dennis Sheehan
Amy Steed
Michael Thomas
Mary Beth Wakefield
Sue VandeWalle
Donna Winter
Robert Wolf

Indexer
Charlotte Clapp

Composed in *Stone Serif* and *MCPdigital by* Que Corporation.

Acknowledgments

The authors would like to thank all of those who contributed to the success of this project:

- The Internet users who volunteer their efforts to maintain some of the lists of useful information to be found on the Internet, including Jonathan Kamens, Scott Yanoff, Gene Spafford, David Lawrence, and Stephanie Da Silva.

- Rusty Williams and the people of Delphi Internet Services Corporation, who provided a connection to Delphi.

- Steve Dennett and the other members of Prodigy Services Company for providing a connection to Prodigy and cheerful technical assistance.

- The people of CompuServe, Inc. for providing a connection to CompuServe.

- The people at America Online, Inc., who provided a connection to America Online.

- The staff at Que, who provided us with guidance and encouragement and put a lot of hard work into this project, especially Tom Bennett, Tom Godfrey, Steve Schafer, and Susan Dunn.

Trademark Acknowledgments

All terms mentioned in this book that are known to be trademarks or service marks have been appropriately capitalized. Que cannot attest to the accuracy of this information. Use of a term in this book should not be regarded as affecting the validity of any trademark or service mark.

Contents at a Glance

Table of Contents

2 A Brief Background on the Internet   33

Part II How to Use the Internet   57

3 Levels of Internet Access   59

10 Selected USENET Groups   247

Introduction

The Internet is a worldwide computer network that gives you access to many different resources. Although some providers can give you an account on the Internet, it isn't necessary to have an Internet account to get access to its many resources.

A number of commercial on-line services now provide some level of access to the Internet. *The Internet QuickStart* gives you step-by-step instructions on how to access the Internet from CompuServe, Prodigy, America Online, and Delphi. *The Internet QuickStart* also gives step-by-step instructions for using a UNIX account that is directly connected to the Internet, and gives you information about how to access some of the most useful Internet resources.

Who Should Use This Book?

If you already have an account with one of the commercial on-line services (CompuServe, Prodigy, America Online, or Delphi), *The Internet QuickStart* will show you how to use that account to access the resources of the Internet. If you are new to the Internet and have access to a UNIX Internet account, this book also will show you how to use some common UNIX applications to access Internet resources.

What Can the Internet Do for You?

The Internet comprises thousands of host computers and millions of users all over the world. When you are connected to the Internet, you can access a number of different resources:

- You can send electronic mail to anyone connected to the Internet (including those who are connected through the commercial on-line services).

- You can retrieve files (programs or data files) from any host on the Internet that makes them available.

- You can participate in discussion groups on thousands of different topics.

- You can use applications that allow you to search the Internet for resources that are of interest to you.

- You can connect to bulletin board systems around the world that give you access to different types of program and data files.

How This Book Is Organized

The Internet QuickStart gives you three different types of information: some background information about the Internet, step-by-step instructions on how to access the Internet from some of the popular on-line services, and descriptions of some of the more useful resources available on the Internet.

Part I, "An Internet Overview," includes chapters 1 and 2. These chapters give you an overview of what the Internet is, what resources are available, and general information about how to access those resources:

- Chapter 1, "Introducing the Internet," discusses what makes up the Internet and what resources are available. General information is given about Internet e-mail, discussion groups, file transfers, information retrieval, and host resources.

■ Chapter 2, "A Brief Background on the Internet," defines some of the jargon you see used on the Internet, and gives some background information about the Internet. Internet e-mail and host addresses also are explained, as are some of the cultural aspects of participating in Internet discussion groups.

Part II, "How to Use the Internet," includes chapters 3 through 8:

■ Chapter 3, "Levels of Internet Access," discusses the different Internet resources accessible from the different on-line services, and compares these to the Internet resources accessible from a UNIX account directly connected to the Internet. There is also some discussion of other ways of accessing the Internet.

■ Chapter 4, "Using the Internet via CompuServe," tells you how to send e-mail to the Internet from CompuServe. Also explained is how to transfer files and locate information on the Internet through the e-mail interface.

■ Chapter 5, "Using the Internet via Prodigy," tells you how to send e-mail to the Internet from Prodigy. Also explained is how to transfer files and locate information on the Internet through the e-mail interface.

■ Chapter 6, "Using the Internet via America Online," discusses how to use America Online's various Internet interfaces to send e-mail, participate in discussion groups, transfer files, and locate information. (At the time this book was written, AOL's Internet interface was limited to e-mail and mailing list participation.)

■ Chapter 7, "Using the Internet via Delphi," discusses how to access the different Internet services that Delphi offers. These services include e-mail, discussion groups, file transfers, information lookup, and connecting to host resources.

■ Chapter 8, "Using the Internet via a UNIX System," discusses how to access various Internet services from some of the more common interfaces available on UNIX systems. These services include e-mail, discussion groups, file transfers, information lookup, and connecting to host resources.

Part III, "A Resource Guide to the Internet," includes chapters 9 through 12. These chapters contain lists of various useful Internet resources and information about how to access them. These resources include discussion groups, file repositories, bulletin board systems, and on-line information systems:

- Chapter 9, "Software and Files (ftp and Gopher Sites)," discusses some of the major file repositories on the Internet. A number of the very large sites are discussed, as are some specialized sites that are grouped by topic.

- Chapter 10, "Selected USENET Groups," contains brief descriptions of a subset of the more useful USENET news groups (similar to forums on other on-line services). The news groups are grouped by topic.

- Chapter 11, "Mailing Lists," contains the description of a large subset of the many thousands of e-mail discussion groups available on the Internet. The mailing lists are grouped by topic.

- Chapter 12, "Other Internet Resources," talks about some of the more useful resources you can find on the Internet, including on-line library catalogs, on-line journals and newsletters, bulletin board systems that have useful information for particular topics, and on-line books.

Where to Find More Help

After you familiarize yourself with the resources discussed in this book, you may be interested in learning more about the Internet or in finding even more resources to use.

Que Corporation has several other books about the Internet, including *Using the Internet*, Special Edition, which provides a comprehensive look at the Internet (its development, legal considerations, choosing an Internet provider, etc.), and *The Internet Resource Quick Reference*, which contains more complete lists of mailing lists, USENET news groups, Internet service providers, and other Internet resources.

The on-line services themselves often provide information about the accessing the Internet and using Internet resources. Prodigy, America Online, and Delphi all have forums devoted to the Internet. They provide Internet experts who monitor the discussions and answer questions about how to find and access Internet resources.

Conventions Used in This Book

Throughout the book you will find special features that help emphasize important information. Each chapter contains notes and cautions that provide additional information and warnings about problems you may encounter. Sections called "If you have problems" try to help you determine why a particular action did not work as expected. When a new term is introduced, a definition for the term appears in the margin near the term.

This book also uses the following special typefaces:

Typeface	Meaning
Special font	Represents system and screen messages, Internet addresses, and directories
Boldface type	Represents words and commands that you type

Part I
An Internet Overview

Chapter 1

Introducing the Internet

The Internet is a worldwide network connecting thousands of individual computers. The Internet gives you access to many different resources that you can take advantage of. The resources typically available to you are electronic mail, USENET discussion groups, information retrieval systems, file uploading and downloading, and a few other host resources. The sections in this chapter introduce these resources and give you general information about them.

Part II, "How to Use the Internet," gives instructions for using the Internet resources available from the various on-line service providers listed in that section. Part III, "A Resource Guide to the Internet," provides lists of specific Internet resources that you can access.

What Is the Internet?

The Internet network was initially developed by the U.S. government as an experiment in computer networking. Because of the manner in which it developed, the major sites on the Internet (until recently) have been academic and government organizations. Within the last few years, however, a number of commercial sites have been connected to the Internet, and more are connecting every day.

Because it's called *the Internet*, it sounds as though it's one big, organized communications network. In reality, the Internet is many thousands of small networks that connect to a central backbone network over which the smaller networks communicate. No central authority runs the Internet. At the time of publication of this book, the Internet backbone was under the direction of the National Science Foundation, but current plans are to turn the backbone management over to a commercial network provider within the next five years.

The Internet is managed by the people who use it. People who are very active in the Internet community volunteer their time to direct the technical and administrative development of the Internet. The cooperative interaction of the early academic and government research agencies connected to the Internet fostered the development of a community atmosphere that still exists to a great extent on the Internet.

Most Internet users are expected to be reasonable people who will respect the privacy of others' property and contribute to the good of the Internet community. Many people on the Internet volunteer their time and computer resources to maintain lists of resources, administer mailing lists, and provide files that can be retrieved by anyone with access to the Internet. A real sense of community exists among those who interact over the Internet.

The individual Internet hosts can be any type of computer, from UNIX workstations to VMS machines to PCs to Macintoshes. The only requirement is that they use the TCP/IP communications protocol to connect to the Internet, since the Internet is TCP/IP based. These hosts provide the many resources available on the Internet. This chapter will talk about some of the most useful of these resources. Chapter 2, "A Brief Background on the Internet," will discuss more about the history of the Internet, its jargon, and its culture.

Electronic Mail and Mailing Lists

E-mail
Electronic message sent from one computer user to another.

One of the primary uses of the Internet is *electronic mail* (*e-mail*). By using the Internet, you can send a message to a user on another computer almost anywhere in the world, as long as his/her network has an e-mail gateway to the Internet.

General E-Mail Concepts
You can compare electronic mail to regular postal mail. The *header lines* of an e-mail message are like the information you put on the envelope when you send a postal mail message—they tell the computer where to

deliver the message, and to whom, just as the address you put on an envelope tells the post office who is supposed to get your postal mail, and where they live.

E-mail header lines specify who you are sending the mail to (the *destination* header lines), who the mail is from (the *originator* header lines), and other information about the message, such as the time and date it was sent, and information about the subject of the message.

The program you use to send the mail generates most of the header information automatically. You don't need to worry about what the header information means (just as you don't need to know what happens to your letter after you drop it in a mail box), but you do need to understand how to address your mail so that it reaches your destination. Mail addresses are discussed in more detail in Chapter 2, in the section "Internet Addresses."

Following the header lines in your e-mail message is the *message body*, which contains the actual message you are sending. The message body is analogous to the information you put inside the envelope. And just as the post office doesn't care what's in the letter you send, the contents of your e-mail message doesn't matter to the mail software; the message shows up in the recipient's mail box.

The best way to understand what an e-mail message looks like is actually to look at one. You can see that the header lines include one starting with `To:`, which indicates who is going to receive the message. The line starting with `From:` tells you who sent the message. The `Subject:` line tells you what the message is about. Other header lines also appear, but you don't really need to understand the information they contain. They can be useful, though, to a systems administrator who's trying to figure out a problem with the mail software.

```
Received: from localhost by smallcorp.com (5.65/3.00)
               id AA04639; Mon, 29 Nov 93 11:20:18 -0500
Message-Id: <9311291620.AA04639@smallcorp.com>
To: tpike@bigcorp.com
Subject: Thanks!
Date: Mon, 29 Nov 93 11:20:17 EST
From: Joe User <juser@smallcorp.com>

Thanks for the help with the problem last week!

                          Joe
```

General Mail Software Features

The people who provide your Internet access will have software that lets you use Internet e-mail. Take a minute to learn about some common features of the mail software you may use; this discussion will give you an idea of how you can use this software to communicate with e-mail effectively.

All e-mail software will let you read mail that is sent to you, although different software does it in different ways. Some e-mail software is *character-oriented* (that is, it doesn't use graphics and can work on any kind of terminal), whereas other software is graphical (that is, it needs some kind of graphics software, such as Microsoft Windows, to run). Your mail messages will be displayed differently depending on the type of software used. Character-oriented e-mail software usually prints your messages on-screen, pausing every screen so that you can read the contents. Graphical e-mail software often displays your message in a window.

Your e-mail software will enable you to manage the mail messages you have received. It will let you remove mail messages you no longer are interested in. Many e-mail software packages also allow you to move a mail message into different folders so that you can categorize your messages in a convenient way.

All e-mail software also allows you to send messages to other people on the Internet. You can send messages in several different ways; creating the mail message is slightly different, depending on what command you used to do so.

The easiest way to send a mail message is to reply to a message that you have received. Sending a reply is so easy because you don't have to figure out how to address the message—instead, the e-mail software will use the address of the person who sent you the message as the destination address for the new message. All you need to do is to type the message you want to send, and your job is done.

Caution
Don't forward a message unless you have permission from the sender. Forwarding a message without permission isn't only rude, quite often it's against the law.

Another common feature of most e-mail packages is the capability to forward a message to another user. Forwarding is handy if you have received a message that you think would be of interest to someone else; you just tell the program who to send the message to, and off the message goes. Some systems enable you to put a brief introductory message before the forwarded material.

Names and Addresses

By now, you are probably impatient about finding out how to address your mail to another user. The idea of an e-mail address isn't hard to understand if you think of the analogy of addressing a postal mail message, but e-mail addresses are a little more cryptic.

User name
ID that a person uses to log in to his Internet host account.

An e-mail address tells you who to send the mail to and where to send it, just as a postal address does. The first part of the e-mail address is the *user name*, which is analogous to the name of the person who is to receive the postal message. If the user's name is John Smith, for example, he may log in to the computer as `jsmith`, `john_smith`, or maybe even `js`. Generally, whatever name he uses to log in is the one to send mail to.

Host name
Unique name that identifies a particular Internet host.

The second part of the e-mail address is the *host name*, which is like the postal address of the user. This name is usually the name of the computer that the user logs in to so that he can read his mail. So if user John Smith logs in to the machine `bigmachine.bigcorp.com` using the login name `jsmith`, his e-mail address will be `jsmith@bigmachine.bigcorp.com`. The "at" symbol (@) is used to separate the user name from the host name in the e-mail address.

The concept of how hosts are named on the Internet is explained in Chapter 2, "A Brief Background on the Internet," but the preceding paragraphs should give you a general idea of how to address your Internet e-mail.

Other E-Mail Services

A fact of life on the Internet is that not everyone has the same types of services available. Almost everyone has access to e-mail, however, and so many services on the Internet are available through e-mail. Although these services aren't as convenient through e-mail as through their normal interface, they are usable. Some of the Internet services that you can access through e-mail are ftp, archie, and WAIS. These services will be described in later sections of this chapter, and instructions on using them from different on-line services will be given in Part II of this book.

Mailing Lists

One common use of electronic mail is when a group of people with a common interest want to exchange messages with each other. One way of doing so would be for each person in the group to keep track of who is on the list, so that when they wanted to send a message to the group, they would send the message to each person individually. As you can imagine, the process of keeping track of every person who shares the interest of the group can get cumbersome quickly, especially if the group is large.

Mailing list
A service that easily allows a group of people to exchange mail on a particular topic.

The idea of a *mailing list* was developed to fix these problems with group communication. With a mailing list, one person at a central site maintains the list of people who are in the group. A mail nickname (or alias) is set up so that when a group member sends a message to the alias, the message is sent to everyone who is in the group. The advantage of this centralized approach is that only one person (the *list maintainer*) needs to know who is on the list; the maintainer takes care of adding and removing people from the list.

The centralized mailing list has some disadvantages, however. If the central machine is unavailable (it has a hardware problem, for example), the whole mailing list can't be used. Also, if the list maintainer goes on vacation (or gets married, or is busy), being added to or removed from the list can take a while. (Some lists, however, are managed with software that can handle administrative requests automatically, so no human overseer is necessary.) On the whole, though, the mailing list is a very successful service on the Internet.

So successful are mailing lists that you can find a list for almost every topic you can imagine. Everything from accordion music to zoology is discussed on mailing lists. Mailing lists are popular because they are specific to a particular topic and are easy to set up (given a willing list maintainer). A list of some of the available Internet mailing lists is given in Chapter 11, "Mailing Lists."

Although all mailing lists serve the same purpose—to distribute mail messages to a group of people—you should be familiar with a few different types of lists.

Moderated Mailing Lists

One type of mailing list is the *moderated list*. With a moderated list, messages sent to the mailing list address don't immediately go to the group. Instead, the message is sent to the group moderator, who decides whether the message is appropriate for the group. Generally, when you join a moderated mailing list, you will receive a note telling you what criteria the moderator uses to decide whether an article is appropriate.

In many cases, a mailing list is moderated because the people who belong to the group want to keep the group focused on a particular topic. They may want to discuss a topic without having arguments or side topics intrude into the discussion, or they may want to cut down on the volume (number of mailings) generated by the list by removing redundant messages. For whatever reason, a mailing list is moderated by group choice.

Mailing List Digests

In some cases, a mailing list may have too many messages for group members to read comfortably. Sometimes, this condition is temporary when a popular new topic of discussion is brought up, but sometimes the mailing list is just too popular. In these cases, the mailing list sometimes will be condensed into digest form. With a digest, individual messages to the group are collected into one large message. For example, a mailing list may be set up to send a digest message every day. So if the list receives 10 messages in a day, a single large message will be sent out that holds all 10 individual messages.

The advantage of the digest lists is that most mail software can process one large message more easily than many small ones. Most people also find reading through one long message at a predetermined time easier than many messages that appear randomly during the day.

LISTSERV Mailing Lists

LISTSERV
A software package that automates the maintenance of a mailing list.

Many mailing lists on the Internet are set up using the *LISTSERV* package (or another similar package) because it makes the list maintainer's job much easier. If you want to be added to one of these mailing lists, for example, you send a mail message to the LISTSERV address for the mailing list. In the message body, you put the LISTSERV command `subscribe`, usually followed by your e-mail address or real name.

Each LISTSERV server may have different commands available, so you can ask the server for help. If you send a message with the command `help` in the message body, the server will send you a message with a list of the commands it understands.

The list of mailing lists in Chapter 11 provides the e-mail address for the maintainer of the list. If the mailing list uses one of these automated packages, this fact is noted.

USENET Discussion Groups

So far, this chapter has discussed how you can use e-mail to communicate with an individual or (by using mailing lists) groups of specific individuals. Now you'll look at a system that allows you to communicate unrestricted with many people—USENET and netnews.

News group

Discussion group for a particular topic.

USENET—short for "users' network"—is made up of all the machines that receive network *news groups*. The network news, commonly referred to as *netnews*, is the mechanism that sends individual messages (called *articles*) from your local computer to all the computers that participate in USE-NET. Anyone who receives the news groups can read and reply to the articles you submit.

Note: *USENET isn't specifically an Internet service. The news articles, however, are usually transmitted over the Internet, and many sites on the Internet carry at least some of the news groups.*

Although you don't have to understand the exact details of how USENET works, a broad outline will help you understand what makes USENET a very powerful means for reaching a great deal of people. The basic idea with USENET is that when you post an article, the article is stored on your Internet service provider's machine (or in some cases, your PC, if you can compose articles off-line), and then sent to other computers that have agreed to exchange netnews articles with your service provider. These machines, in turn, send your article to other machines, who send it to others. This process continues until your article has reached every computer that participates in USENET. Because each machine can send articles to many other machines, your article can reach the majority of USENET computers within a few hours.

When your article is on a computer system's disk, the user of that computer can read your article by using news-reading software. Like the software that allows you to read your electronic mail, the news-reading software lets you read articles, post new articles, reply to articles, and perform other functions. Common news reader functions are covered later in the section "General News Group Activities."

Understanding News Articles

A news article is very similar to an e-mail message. It has some information at the top of the article in the header lines and the content of the article in the message body. Just as in an e-mail message, the header lines give information to the netnews software to allow it to put the article in the right news group or groups (an article can appear in more than one group at the same time—this is called *cross-posting* the article) and to identify the sender of the article.

The message body of the article contains the information that the sender of the article wrote. Sometimes, if the author is responding to a previous news article, he/she will quote material from the original article to help illustrate a point. (See the section "USENET Etiquette" in Chapter 2 for some general guidelines to use when reading and posting articles to USENET news groups.)

Signature
A witty comment or information about the author.

In many cases, the article ends with a *signature*. Many news readers allow you to set up a file that contains your signature; the contents of this file automatically are tacked to the end of each article you post.

To give you a better idea of what a netnews article looks like, the following is a sample article:

```
Newsgroups: comp.sys.mac.hardware
Path: bigcorp.com!tgp
From: tgp@figcorp.com (Tod Pike)
Subject: Re: recent prices
Message-ID: <1993Nov30.134422.4009@bigcorp.com>
Sender: netnews@bigcorp.com (Netnews)
Date: Tue, 30 Nov 1993 13:44:22 EST
Lines: 10


Recent prices should be posted to this news group soon - keep
an eye out!

                              Tod Pike
-------------------------------------------------------------
To reach me, send mail to tgp@bigcorp.com
Disclaimer: I don't speak for the boss!
```

In this example, the first line (starting with the word Newsgroups) indicates in which news group the article is posted. The line starting with From gives the author of the article; the line starting with Subject gives the topic of the article. The rest of the header lines (everything up to and including the line Lines) give additional information about the article. Following the first blank line is the message body. The line of dashes and all remaining lines is the user's signature.

News Groups and Topics

The information carried by USENET is divided up into news groups. Each news group is devoted to a particular topic, although the discussion in these groups can be far-reaching. Like Internet mailing lists, a news group exists for almost every topic you can imagine; many large USENET sites carry well over 5,000 news groups!

To get an idea of how discussion happens in news groups, you may think of USENET as a large building, and each news group is a room in that building. Each room has a name on the door and a brief description of the discussion topic in that room.

In some rooms, you may find a small number of people politely discussing a serious topic. You can come in, ask a question, and join in the discussion.

Note: *USENET doesn't involve live exchanges; it's more like sending e-mail to and receiving e-mail from a large number of people.*

In other rooms, you may find a loud, raucous group of people discussing a heated topic. Each person is shouting out his opinion loudly, with little regard for the shouting of the people around them. If you try to enter the conversation, you find that your opinions are ignored, or that you are insulted.

On USENET, both scenarios happen every day—sometimes in the same news group at different times!

How News Groups Are Organized. News groups are named in a hierarchical manner. The name of a news group is made up of several words separated by periods—for example, comp.sys.mac.hardware. In a news group name, the words on the left-hand side of the name are the most general—they specify the hierarchy that the group belongs in. As you move along the name to the right, the words become more and more specific about the topics the group discusses.

For example, in the valid news group name `comp.sys.mac.hardware`, the first word, `comp`, gives the hierarchy; groups under `comp` are for discussions about computers. The next word, `sys`, indicates that the group discusses computer systems, as opposed to languages or editors. The next word, `mac`, tells you that the group discusses Macintosh computer systems. The final word, `hardware`, lets you know that the group talks about hardware issues relating to Macintosh computer systems.

The left-most word in the group name defines the so-called *top-level hierarchies*. In the current scheme of USENET are seven main top-level hierarchies. These hierarchies are listed in the following table, with a description of the topics discussed in groups under them.

Hierarchy	Description
comp	Computer-related topics
rec	Recreational topics
sci	Topics related to sciences
soc	Social issues
news	Topics of interest to people who run USENET sites
talk	Conversational topics, often controversial
misc	Miscellaneous topics not covered elsewhere

In addition to these hierarchies are a few other hierarchies, listed in the following table. Most of these were created in response to a specific need or to discuss a topic of limited interest. The system that you use to read netnews may not have any of these hierarchies, but most of the major Internet service providers will carry them.

Hierarchy	Description
alt	A hierarchy with relaxed rules for creation of groups
vmsnet	Devoted to systems running the VMS operating system from Digital Equipment Corporation
bionet	Devoted to biological sciences
k12	Devoted to education in grades kindergarten through 12

General News Group Activities. Your service provider will have software that you can use to access the USENET news groups (there may be more than one interface available). Similar to the software that allows you to read your e-mail, your news-reading software lets you perform several different functions. Although the exact method you use to perform these functions depends on the software available on your Internet service provider, this section will give you a broad outline of what you can expect to do. The exact details of performing these functions are outlined in Part II, "How to Use the Internet."

The most basic function a news reader can provide is to enable you to read the articles in a news group. Many news readers will present a list of the articles in the group, showing some information from the headers of the article (usually the subject and author). This way, you easily can pick the articles you want to read. Some news readers present the articles in the order that the local system received them (*not always* the order in which they were posted), whereas others present the articles grouped together by a common subject. The latter approach, used in a *threaded* news reader (because you can follow the thread of a conversation), can make finding all the discussion on a particular topic easier.

After you read an article, almost all news readers remember that you have the article. This way, when you start up the news reader the next time, you won't see the article again. Some news readers allow you to mark all the articles in a group as being read (even though you haven't actually seen them). This capability can be useful if, for example, you have returned from a vacation to find that several hundred articles have been posted to a news group. At these times, rather than try to catch up on all the articles, just marking all the old articles as being read and then starting to read new articles as they arrive on your system may be better.

The second most important function of a news reader is to allow you to post articles. Most news readers allow you to post an entirely new article to a group or to reply to an article you are reading. Just as in your e-mail software, the reply function uses the information in the article you are reading (such as the subject and news groups the article is in) and allows you to compose your reply to the article. Whether you are posting a new article or a reply to a current article, your article will go out to the rest of the USENET sites.

Caution
Be careful when replying to an article, either publicly or privately via e-mail. Make sure that you are doing what you want! If you meant to reply privately to the author of a message but accidentally post the reply to the news group, the mistake can be embarrassing.

If you are reading an article and want to reply privately to the author of the article (rather than publicly in the news group), most news readers enable you to send a reply message via electronic mail directly to the author of the message. This reply message appears to the author of the news article just like a normal mail message.

Some news readers have other functions that allow you to save a news article in a file for future reference, or to search the articles in a news group for those matching a topic you are interested in. But the functions mentioned earlier in this section (reading articles, posting a new article, posting a follow-up article, replying to the author via e-mail) are common to all news readers; you should read the instructions for the news reader provided by your Internet site for information on other features it may have.

Transferring Files with ftp

ftp
A program that allows you to transfer data between different computers on a network.

You already have seen how you can use e-mail to send a message over the Internet. Suppose, however, that you want to get a file (such as a program or document) from one place to another on the Internet. You could send the file in an e-mail message, of course, but a much better method of moving files exists—the *file transfer protocol (ftp)* service. This service is designed to allow you to connect to a computer on the Internet (using an ftp program on your local machine), browse through the programs available on that computer, and then download or upload files.

Note: *Unlike e-mail, ftp allows you to transfer text and binary (program, graphics, etc.) files. You must explicitly tell ftp that you are transferring binary files, however.*

Understanding Client/Server Services

The ftp service is an example of a client-server system. In this kind of system, you use a program on your local computer (called a *client*) to talk to a program on a remote computer (called a *server*). In the case of ftp, the server on the remote computer is designed to let you download and upload files, but many other services are available on the Internet. Some of these, such as Gopher and archie, are discussed later in the section "Gopher, archie, and Other Information Retrieval Systems."

For a computer system to let you connect to it using an ftp program, the system must have an ftp server running on it. The administrators of the machine must set up this machine and decide which files and information will be made available on the ftp server.

Anonymous ftp

One common type of ftp server is an anonymous ftp server. With this kind of server, you can connect and download or upload files without having an account on the machine. If the ftp server isn't anonymous, when you connect to the server you must provide a user name and password, just as though you were logging in to the machine. On an anonymous ftp server, you use the special user name anonymous when you connect. This anonymous user name lets you log in by providing any password you want (often, the server asks you to enter your Internet mailing address as your password).

Note: *If you want to retrieve files from a machine that doesn't have an anonymous ftp server, you must have an account that you can log in to on that machine.*

Anonymous ftp servers are one of the major means of distributing software and information across the Internet. A large amount of software—often provided free of charge—is available on anonymous ftp servers. Software is available for many different types of computer systems, such as UNIX, IBM PC, and Macintosh systems.

Connecting to ftp Servers

The exact method you use to connect to an ftp server depends on the software provided by your Internet service provider, but this section gives you an outline of what to expect. Exact details of how to use ftp on your Internet service provider are given in Part II, "How to Use the Internet." In general, though, you use the ftp command on your local machine and give the machine that you want to connect to. For example, on a UNIX system, if you want to ftp to the machine rs.internic.net (a site that has many documents related to the Internet), you would use the command ftp rs.internic.net.

When you connect to the ftp server, you are prompted for a login name. If you have an account on the ftp server machine, you can use your

1

account name; if this is an anonymous ftp site, use the login name anonymous. After the account name, you are prompted for a password. Naturally, if you logged in using your account name, you will use your account's password here. If this is an anonymous ftp site, you can use anything for the password, but by convention you should use your e-mail address for the password. This way, the ftp site maintainer can keep track of who has been using the server and contact people who have downloaded files.

Most ftp programs have similar commands. Some of the most useful ones are as follows:

Command	Purpose
ls	Lists files in the current directory
dir	Lists files, with more information
get	Downloads file to your machine
put	Uploads file from your machine
cd	Changes directory
bye	Logs off from the ftp server
help	Displays a help message
binary	Tells the ftp server that you will be downloading a binary file

Your ftp program, of course, may have other commands available or use different names for these commands.

Locating Files

Most ftp sites don't have a listing of all their available files, although some do. Generally, the only way to locate a file or find interesting files is to use the dir or ls commands to list the contents of the directories, and the cd command to move into directories under the one you are in.

Because the file and directory names are in whatever form used by the machine the ftp server is on, what you see when using the dir or ls commands varies depending on the type of system you connect to.

If the server is running on a UNIX system, for example, the file names will appear in upper- or lowercase, and can be of any length. If you want to download a file, you must be sure to type the file name exactly as it appears when you do an `ls` or `dir`.

Note: *While using ftp, using the exact case when changing directories is also important.*

On some machines (especially the very large archive sites), the site maintainers keep an index of available files with brief descriptions of what they are. These indexes make finding useful files much easier. When you enter a directory, you should look for a file called INDEX (in upper- or lowercase letters). You also should look for a file called README (readme, read.me, or whatever). These README files are generally descriptions of the contents of the directories, or information about the server system. You always should download the README files and read the contents—the files are put there for a reason.

Postmaster

An address to which you can send questions when you don't have a user's address at a site.

If you have a question about an ftp server or about the contents of the files there, you should send an e-mail message to the *postmaster* of the ftp machine. For example, if you connect to the machine `rs.internic.net`, you should send e-mail to the address `postmaster@rs.internic.net`. Some ftp servers have a different person to contact; in this case, the name of the contact person will appear when you connect to the machine, or will be in a README file in the first directory you see when you connect.

Downloading and Uploading Files

After you find a file that you are interested in, you can download the file to your service provider account, or your local PC, if your provider allows you to do so automatically. You should be aware of several things before you download the file, however. First, use the `dir` command on the file and make a note of the size of the file you want to download. Make sure that the system you are downloading to has enough space to store the file; you may have to leave the ftp program and remove some files before you can download the file.

Binary file

A file with characters that can't be printed or displayed, such as programs and picture or sound files.

You also should check whether the file you are interested in downloading is a *binary file*. If you want to download a binary file, you must tell the ftp program to do so. (Most programs have a `binary` command to do so.) If you aren't sure whether the file is binary, you should tell your server that it is; you can transfer non-binary files in binary mode without problems.

If you have problems...	If the file is very large, and the ftp server is slow or the Internet connection is slow (the machine is in Europe or Asia, for example), transferring the file may take several minutes. If the Internet connection is very slow, the download may stop and you will be logged out; in this case, you should try again. In general, transferring large files after normal work hours is a good idea, because the system and network load is lighter.

You probably won't upload many files to Internet ftp sites. Unless you are doing development of a useful utility program that you want to make available to others, you won't find much of an opportunity to do uploads. On most anonymous ftp sites that allow uploads, you will see a directory called `incoming`, which is set up to be a place where uploads should go. If you place a file in the area for uploads, you should upload a short description of what the file is, or send an e-mail message to the site maintainer to explain what you uploaded.

Gopher, archie, and Other Information Retrieval Systems

One of the most frustrating problems with the Internet is the difficulty of finding information such as ftp sites, host resources, sources of information, and so forth. Imagine if you went into your local public library and found that rather than the books be arranged on shelves according to a book classification scheme, the books are piled all over the floor. Rather than use a central card catalog, the librarians placed notes on some of the piles stating what people had found in that pile. This scenario is how the Internet has been for most of its existence; many resources are available, but no way to easily locate them.

Information retrieval systems are being explored as a way to locate information resources on the Internet. Although a complete central list of all the resources on the Internet still doesn't exist, the various information retrieval systems go a long way toward making it easy to find a resource.

Several different information retrieval systems now in use on the Internet allow you to search for information in different ways. This section will give a brief overview of how these systems work and what information they are designed to handle. The chapters in Part II, "How to Use the Internet," will give detailed information on how to use these information retrieval systems on the various Internet providers.

Locating Programs with archie

archie

An application that allows you to search easily for information at anonymous ftp sites on the Internet.

telnet

A program that allows remote login to another computer.

archie was the first of the information retrieval systems developed on the Internet. The purpose of archie is simple—to create a central index of files that are available on anonymous ftp sites around the Internet. To do so, the archie servers connect to anonymous ftp sites that agree to participate and download lists of all the files on these sites. These lists of files are merged into a database, which users can then search.

You can access the archie databases in several different ways. (For ease of access on the Internet, several different sites have archie databases; they all contain the same information.) Your site can provide an archie client, which makes the database search simple, or you can use the *telnet* program to connect to one of the archie machines and search the database there. See the section "Connecting to Host Resources by Using telnet" later in this chapter for more information on how to use telnet.

After you connect to one of the archie database machines (through a client program or through telnet), you can search the database for a program or file. Because the database knows about only the names of the files, you must know at least part of the file name you are looking for. For example, if you are looking for a program that compresses files (makes them smaller), you search the database for the word *compress*. The archie program will return the location of all the files with that name.

Now, this search returns only those files called exactly compress, so it wouldn't return the location of a file named uncompress (which will undo the work of the compress program). archie, however, lets you search on a string that is anywhere in the file name. If you tell archie to do a substring search, it will look for your search string anywhere in the file name. Similarly, you can tell the archie program to match the file name even if it has different capitalization that your search string.

The archie server will return to you the machine name and location of the files that match the string you are searching for. This allows you to use the ftp program to connect to the machine and download the file to your local machine. The main limitation of archie is that you must know at least something about the name of the file to search for it; if you don't have any idea what the file is called (for example, you want a program that searches for viruses on your machine and don't know that it is called scanv), you may have to try several searches using different strings before you find something that looks useful.

Another limitation of archie is that not all sites on the Internet that have anonymous ftp participate in the archie database. So if a file you would be interested in is at a site that doesn't participate in the archie database, you wouldn't be able to find that file with archie. Even given these limitations, archie is a very useful tool for locating files for downloading through ftp.

Locating Files Using Gopher

Gopher

An application that allows you to access publicly available information on Internet hosts that provide Gopher service.

Gopher is another information retrieval system, but it's set up very differently than the archie service. Sites on the Internet that want to distribute information through the Gopher system set up and run Gopher servers that allow people with Gopher clients to display and download files and directories.

Gopher's functionality is very similar to ftp's, but the Gopher system presents the directories on the server as menus on-screen; you can move into a directory by typing the number of a menu item (or, if your client allows it, by using your mouse to select a menu item). Displaying or downloading a file is also as easy as selecting an item from a menu. This ease of use, plus the capability to put descriptive titles on the menu items, makes Gopher a much easier method of browsing files than simply using ftp.

One big advantage of the Gopher system is that you can include menu items on a server that will move the user to another server on another machine on the Internet if selected. For example, one menu item on machine A's Gopher server may say Connect to Machine B Gopher. When that menu item is selected, your Gopher client will connect to machine B's Gopher server, just as though you had connected to it when you ran the Gopher client.

This capability to link Gopher sites together makes hopping from site to site, examining what each site has available, and then moving to other interesting Gopher sites very easy. Also, when a new Gopher site becomes available on the Internet, the administrators send a mail message to the maintainers of the Gopher software (at the University of Minnesota) to have their site included in the master list of all Gopher sites worldwide. Many organizations run Gopher servers; universities and colleges, companies, and government agencies all have information available through Gopher.

Note: *The Gopher maintainers run a Gopher site (located at the machine* `boombox.micro.umn.edu`*) that lists all the known Gopher sites and lets you connect to them. This site gives you a great starting place to browse through all the Gopher sites so that you can discover the wealth of information available on the Internet. Although many interesting Gopher sites are listed in Part III, "A Resource Guide to the Internet," the main Gopher site at* `boombox.micro.umn.edu` *is always the best place to begin exploring the information on Gopher.*

With all the Gopher sites available, though, locating a site that carries the information and files you want may be hard. What you would like to do is search the Gopher sites for a document you want. A service called Veronica is available to do this. You can search the Veronica database—built by scanning the Gopher menus on servers around the world—by selecting `Search Gopherspace using Veronica`, which is found on the Gopher site `gopher.tc.umn.edu`.

Locating Documents Using WAIS

WAIS

Wide Area Information Servers, a system for searching and retrieving documents from participating sites.

Although Gopher is a good tool to use for exploring the files and systems available on the Internet, what if you wanted to find all documents available on a particular subject? *WAIS* (pronounced "ways") is a system that allows you to search for your subject through documents on servers all over the world.

The heart of the WAIS system is the use of client software running on your local computer that lets you ask for information in simple, English-like language. The client takes your question and sends it to the WAIS server you select. The server takes your question and searches all the documents it knows about for the information you want. If it finds documents that match your question, it returns indexes to these documents, which you then can use to download the documents and display them on your local system.

One key feature of the WAIS system is the capability of a WAIS server to have indexes that actually point to other WAIS servers. A central site on the Internet maintains indexes to all known WAIS servers on the Internet; you can use this central site as a starting point for your searches. For example, say that you want to find all the times that President Clinton mentioned the city of Atlanta, Georgia, in his speeches.

When you start up your WAIS client, set your search database to be `directory-of-servers`, located on the machine `quake.think.com`. If you search for *president clinton* in this database, it will return (among others) a database named `clinton-speeches`. You now can use this database to search for *atlanta*. This search returns some number of documents, and the first ones are the ones that best match your question. These speeches, when retrieved, are the ones that mention Atlanta, Georgia.

Locating Information with World Wide Web

World Wide Web

A hypertext-based system that allows browsing of available Internet resources.

Yet another means of locating information on the Internet is the *World Wide Web* (WWW) system. The World Wide Web is an attempt to connect all the other information retrieval systems together so that you can use one client program to get information from archie, Gopher, and WAIS servers, as well as WWW servers.

The basic idea of the World Wide Web system is the creation and use of documents that have links to other documents. Depending on the WWW client you use (displaying on a terminal using printing characters or on a window system such as Microsoft Windows), the links in a WWW document are displayed with an index number next to them, or highlighted in some way. You can access these links to other documents by typing the index number or clicking the highlighted text (if the client supports the use of a mouse). The system will then download the document you want and display it on your system. This document also may have links to other documents, and so on.

WWW is somewhat like Gopher in that you can connect to a local WWW server or to the main server on the machine `info.cern.ch`, which gives information about how to access other WWW servers. If you don't have a local WWW server to try, starting with the main server is a good idea; this server has a large amount of information about how to use WWW effectively.

So, to find information about a particular topic with a WWW client, you can connect to the main server at info.cern.ch. This server has a document that lists all the available WWW servers by the type of information they hold. You can read through this document until you find a server with information on the topic that interests you. You can then select this server and go to its initial page, which will display information about all the documents available on the topic. Some documents available on WWW are searchable, so you can find information easily.

One main advantage of the WWW clients (especially the graphical ones) is that they easily allow you to browse documents of different types. If a document contains a sound recording or a picture, the WWW client will automatically retrieve the sound or picture and play or display it for you (if the computer or terminal that you are using supports sound and graphics). Also, the WWW client lets you access Gopher, archie, and WAIS servers automatically without running a new program. This capability makes your life a little easier if you are searching for information without knowing what type of server it is on.

Note: *Many WWW servers aren't available yet. WWW is a relatively new system and doesn't have as many sites supporting it as Gopher and WAIS. WWW is certainly catching on, and should be as popular as the other information retrieval systems soon.*

For examples and exact details on how to use WWW on your Internet provider, see Part II, "How to Use the Internet," and the chapter specific for your provider.

Connecting to Host Resources by Using telnet

Just as a computer system can run an ftp server to allow you to transfer files, a computer on the Internet can run other servers to let you do other things when you connect. A wide variety of these services (called *host resources*) are available on the Internet, and they provide everything from information about agriculture to space research. Some of these host resources are similar to bulletin board systems, with which you may be familiar . But rather than dial into one of these systems using a telephone line and modem, you can connect to these systems over the Internet by using telnet.

1

Using telnet to Connect to Host Resources

A telnet connection allows you to type commands to the remote machine just as though you had a terminal hooked right into it. You probably are already familiar with the idea of a terminal program—if you have a modem connected to a personal computer that you use to dial into computer systems, you use a terminal program to talk to the modem and remote system.

Just as you use a local ftp program to connect to an ftp server on another machine on the Internet, you use a telnet program on your local machine to talk to the telnet server on another machine anywhere on the Internet. The main difference between ftp and telnet is that when you connect to the remote machine with ftp, the ftp server lets you do only things connected with transferring files. When you connect to a machine using telnet, what you see really depends on what the host resource provides. You may see a bulletin board menu system, a simple command-line interface, or informational messages before you type anything. It all depends on what the resource expects.

How you use the telnet program to connect to host resources depends on the software your Internet provider has. On most systems, you use the `telnet` command and give the name of the host you are going to connect to. For example, the command `telnet psupen.psu.edu` connects you to a site with agricultural information.

After you connect to the host, you are asked to provide an account name and password. For most host resources given in this book, a special account name and password for the host resource are listed; this information is provided with the description of the host resource.

In some cases, you will use a slightly different form of the telnet command. With this form, you give a port number after the host you are connecting to—for example, `telnet downwind.sprl.umich.edu 3000`. The port number indicates that you want to connect to a special program rather than the login program—in this case, one that gives you the weather in different cities in the United States. Quite often, when you connect to a server with this form of the telnet command, you don't need to provide an account name and password.

Locating Host Resources

Locating the various machines on the Internet that provide these host resources can be difficult, because no central directory lists them all. First, you should consult the lists in Part III, "A Resource Guide to the Internet," where quite a few interesting host resources are listed. Another good resource is the USENET news group `alt.internet.services`. A regular post made to this group is the Updated Internet Services List, which summarizes many host resources.

You also can use the ftp program to download this list. You can connect to the site `rtfm.mit.edu` and download the file `/pub/usenet/news.answers/internet-services/list`.

Summary

The Internet comprises more than a million host computers throughout the world. Many of these hosts provide open access to resources (files, programs, and so forth) that can be used by anyone connected to the Internet. Even if your provider has limited connection to the Internet, the most basic Internet service (e-mail) gives you access to other useful Internet services (such as ftp, archie, and WAIS). The chapters in Part II discuss what Internet services are available from some commercial on-line service providers.

Chapter 2

A Brief Background on the Internet

As the Internet has grown over the years, a number of terms have sprung up that you likely will see referenced as you explore the Internet. This chapter explains the terms and gives a little background on them, where appropriate.

This chapter also explains what makes up an Internet address and how the address space is partitioned. You also will learn about some of the social aspects of the Internet.

Internet Terminology

As you read documents and participate in conversations on the Internet, you may come across terms that you are unfamiliar with. This section explains some of the most common terms you may encounter.

Term	Definition
account	A user ID and disk area restricted for the use of a particular person, usually password protected.
ACM	Association for Computing Machinery, a professional society for people connected with the computer industry.
address	See *e-mail address* and *host address*.
alias	A short name used to represent a more complicated one, often used for mail address or host domain names.

(continues)

Term	Definition
analog	A form of electronic communication using a continuous electro-magnetic wave, such as television or radio. Any continuous wave form, as opposed to digital on/off transmissions.
archie	An application that allows you to search easily for information at anonymous ftp sites on the Internet.
archive	A repository of files available for access at an Internet site. Also, a collection of files—often a backup of a disk, or files saved to tape to allow them to be transferred.
ARPA	Advanced Research Projects Agency, the government agency that originally funded the research on the ARPANET (became DARPA in the mid '70s).
ARPANET	An experimental communications network funded by the government that eventually developed into the Internet.
article	Message submitted to a USENET news group. Unlike an e-mail message, which goes to a specific person or group of persons, a news group message goes to directories (on many machines) that can be read by any number of people.
ASCII	Data that's limited to letters, numbers, and punctuation.
ATM	Asynchronous Transfer Mode, a developing technological advance in communications switching. This technology uses hardware switches to create a temporary direct path between two destinations so that data can be exchanged at a higher rate.
AUP	Acceptable use policy, the restrictions that a network segment places on the traffic it carries.
backbone	The major communications lines of a network.
bandwidth	The maximum volume of data that can be sent over a communications network.
bang	A slang term for an exclamation point.
bang address	A type of e-mail address that separates host names in the address with exclamation points. Used for mail sent to the UUCP network, where specifying the exact path (host by host) of the mail is necessary. The address is in the form of *machine!machine!userID*, where the number of machines listed depends on the connections needed to reach the machine where the account user ID is.
BBS	An acronym for *bulletin board system*, a system that allows people to connect to a computer to upload and download files and leave messages for other users.
binary	Data that may contain non-printable characters, including graphics files, programs, and sound files.

2

Term	Definition
bit	The basic unit of digital communications. There are 8 bits in a byte.
BITNET	Because It's Time Network, a non-TCP/IP network for small universities without Internet access.
bounce	An e-mail message that you receive that tells you an e-mail message that you sent wasn't delivered. Usually contains an error code and the contents of the message that wasn't delivered.
bps	Bits per second, units of measure that express the speed at which data is transferred between computers.
bridge	A device that connects one physical section of a network to another, often providing isolation.
BTW	By The Way, an ;abbreviation often used in on-line conversations.
byte	A digital storage unit large enough to contain one ASCII character. Compare to *bit*.
CIX	Commercial Internet eXchange, a consortium of commercial providers of Internet service.
client	User of a service. Also, often refers to a piece of software that gets information from a server.
compress	A program that compacts a file so that it fits into a smaller space. Also can refer just to the technique of reducing the amount of space a file takes up.
CNRI	Corporation for National Research Initiatives, an organization formed to foster research into a national data highway.
CREN	Corporation for Research and Educational Networking, an organization formed by the joining of two different educational networks to enhance the capabilities of the two networks.
CPSR	Computer Professionals for Social Responsibility, an organization that encourages socially responsible use of computers.
cyberspace	A term used to refer to the entire collection of sites accessible electronically. If your computer is attached to the Internet or another large network, it exists in cyberspace.
DARPA	Defense Advanced Research Projects Agency (originally ARPA), the government agency that funded the research that developed the ARPANET.
dedicated line	See *leased line*.
dialup	A type of connection where you use a modem to connect to another computer or an Internet provider over phone lines.

(continues)

Term	Definition
digest	A type of mailing list where a number of messages are concatenated and sent out as a single message.
digital	Type of communications used by computers, consisting of individual "on" and "off" pulses.
DNS	See *Domain Name System*.
DOD	Department of Defense, a U.S. government agency that originally sponsored the ARPANET research.
domain	Highest subdivision of the Internet, for the most part by country (except in the United States, where it is by type of organization, such as educational, commercial, and government). Usually the last part of a host name; for example, the domain part of ibm.com is .com, which represents the domain of commercial sites in the United States.
Domain Name System	The system that translates between Internet IP address and Internet host names.
dot address	See *host address*.
download	Bring a file from another computer to yours.
ECPA	Electronic Communications Privacy Act, a law that governs the use and restrictions of electronic communications.
EDUCOM	A non-profit consortium of educational institutions that helps introduce electronic information access and management into educational organizations.
EFF	Electronic Frontier Foundation, an organization concerned with the legal rights and responsibilities of computer usage.
e-mail	An electronic message delivered from one computer user to another. Short for *electronic mail*.
e-mail address	An address used to send e-mail to a user on the Internet, consisting of the user name and host name (and any other necessary information, such as a gateway machine). An Internet e-mail address is usually of the form *username@hostname*.
emoticon	See *smiley face*.
encryption	The process of scrambling a message so that it can be read only by someone who knows how to unscramble it.
ESNET	The Department of Energy's network.
EtherNet	A type of local area network hardware. Many TCP/IP networks are EtherNet-based.

Term	Definition
expire	Remove an article from a USENET news group after some specified interval.
FAQ	Frequently Asked Question document (often pronounced "fak"), containing a list of commonly asked questions on a topic. Most USENET news groups have a FAQ to introduce new readers to popular topics in the news group.
FARNET	A group of networks interested in promoting research and education networking.
feed	Send USENET news groups from your site to another site that wants to read them.
finger	A program that provides information about users on an Internet host (possibly may include a user's personal information, such as project affiliation and schedule).
flame	Communicate in an abusive or absurd manner. Often occurs in news group posts and e-mail messages.
ftp	A program that allows you to transfer data between different computers on a network.
FWIW	For What It's Worth, an abbreviation often used in on-line conversations.
FYI	For Your Information, often an abbreviation used in on-line conversations. An FYI is also a type of Internet reference document that contains answers to basic questions about the Internet.
gateway	A device that interfaces two networks that use different protocols.
gigabit	Very high-speed (1 billion bits per second) data communications.
gigabyte	A unit of data storage approximately equal to 1 billion bytes of data.
Gopher	An application that allows you to access publicly available information on Internet hosts that provide Gopher service.
GUI	Graphical user interface, a computer interface based on graphical symbols rather than text. Windowing environments and Macintosh environments are GUIs.
headers	Lines at the beginning of an e-mail message or news group post that contain information about the message: its source, destination, subject, and route it took to get there, among other things.

(continues)

Term	Definition
hosts	Individual computers connected to the Internet; see also *nodes*.
host address	A unique number assigned to identify a host on the Internet (also called *IP address* or *dot address*). This address is usually represented as four numbers between 1 and 254, separated by periods—for example, 192.58.107.230.
host name	A unique name for a host that corresponds to the host address.
hypertext	An on-line document that has words or graphics that contain links to other documents; usually, selecting the link area on-screen (with a mouse or keyboard command) activates these links.
IAB	Internet Architecture Board, a group of volunteers who work to maintain the Internet.
IEEE	Institute of Electrical and Electronics Engineers, the professional society for electrical and computer engineers.
IETF	Internet Engineering Task Force, a group of volunteers that helps develop Internet standards.
IMHO	In My Humble (or Honest) Opinion, an abbreviation often used in on-line conversations.
Internet	The term used to describe all the worldwide interconnected TCP/IP networks.
Internet Society	See *ISOC*.
InterNIC	The NSFNET manager sites on the Internet that provide information about the Internet.
IP	Internet protocol, the communications protocol used by computers connected to the Internet.
IP address	See *host address*.
IRC	Internet Relay Chat, a live conferencing facility available on the Internet.
ISO	International Standards Organization, an organization that sets worldwide standards in many different areas. For example, the organization has been working on a network protocol to replace TCP/IP (this isn't widely supported, however).
ISOC	Internet Society, an educational organization dedicated to encouraging use of the Internet.
kill file	A file used by some news reader software that allows you automatically to skip posts with certain attributes (specific subject, author, and so on).

Term	Definition
knowbots	Knowledge robots, programs that automatically search through a network for specified information.
labels	The different components of an Internet host name.
leased line	A dedicated phone line used for network communications.
local	Pertaining to the computer you are now using.
lurking	Observing but not participating in an activity, usually a USENET news group.
Lynx	A character-oriented interface to the World Wide Web (WWW).
mailing list	A service that forwards to everyone on a list an e-mail message sent to it, allowing a group of people to discuss a particular topic.
mail reflector	Software that automatically distributes all submitted messages to the members of a mailing list.
man *command*	A UNIX command that provides information about the UNIX command entered in the parameter *command*. (*man* is short for manual entry.)
MBONE	Multicast backbone, an experimental network that allows live video to be sent over the Internet.
Merit	Michigan Educational Research Information Triad, the organization that initially managed NSFNET.
MILNET	The DOD's network.
MIME	Multipurpose Internet Mail Extensions, an extension to Internet mail that allows for the inclusion of non-textual data such as video and audio in e-mail.
moderator	A person who examines all submissions to a news group or mailing list and allows only those that meet certain criteria to be posted. Usually, the moderator makes sure that the topic is pertinent to the group and that the submissions aren't flames.
modem	An electronic device that allows digital computer data to be transmitted over analog phone lines.
Mosaic	A graphical interface to the World Wide Web (WWW).
Netfind	A service that allows you to try to look up an Internet user address.

2

(continues)

Term	Definition
netiquette	Network etiquette conventions used in written communications, usually referring to USENET news group posting, but also applicable to e-mail.
netnews	A collective way of referring to the USENET news groups.
network	A number of computers physically connected to enable communication with one another.
news groups	The electronic discussion groups of USENET.
NIC	Network Information Center, a service that provides administrative information about a network.
nodes	Individual computers connected to a network; see also *hosts*.
NREN	National Research and Education Network, a proposed nationwide high-speed data network.
NSF	National Science Foundation, current supporter of the main Internet backbone in the United States.
NSFNET	Network funded by the National Science Foundation, now the backbone of the Internet.
OTOH	On The Other Hand, an abbreviation often used in on-line conversations.
packet	The unit of data transmission on the Internet. A packet consists of the data being transferred with additional overhead information, such as the transmitting and receiving addresses.
packet switching	The communications technology that the Internet is based on, where data being sent between computers is transmitted in packets.
parallel	Means of communication in which digital data is sent multiple bits at a time, with each simultaneous bit being sent over a separate line.
PDN	Public data network, a service such as Sprintnet that gives access to a nationwide data network through a local phone call.
POP	Point of Presence, indicating availability of a local access number to a public data network.
post	Send a message to a USENET news group.
postmaster	An address to which you can send questions when you don't have a user's address at a site.

2

Term	Definition
protocol	The standard that defines how computers on a network communicate with one another.
provider	Some who sells—or gives away, in some cases—access to the Internet.
remote	A host on the network other than the computer you now are using.
router	Equipment that receives an Internet packet and sends it to the next machine in the destination path.
RFC	Request For Comments, a document submitted to the Internet governing board to propose Internet standards or to document information about the Internet.
serial	Means of communication in which digital data is sent one bit at a time over a single physical line.
server	Provider of a service. Also, often refers to a piece of hardware or software that provides access to information requested from it. See also *client*.
shell	An interactive command interpreter, usually on the UNIX operating system.
signature	A personal signoff used in e-mail and news group posts, often contained in a file and automatically appended to the mail or post. Often contains organization affiliation and pertinent personal information.
site	A group of computers under a single administrative control.
smiley face	An ASCII drawing such as :-) (look at it sideways) used to help indicate an emotion in a message. Also called *emoticon*.
subscribe	Become a member of a mailing list or news group; also refers to obtaining Internet provider services.
TCP	Transmission control protocol, the network protocol used by hosts on the Internet.
telnet	A program that allows remote login to another computer.
thread	All messages in a news group or mailing list pertaining to a particular topic.
toggle	Alternate between two possible values.
traffic	The information flowing through a network.
UNIX	An operating system used on many Internet hosts.

(continues)

Term	Definition
upload	Send a file from your computer to another.
USENET	A collection of computer discussion groups that are read all over the world.
user name	The ID used to log in to a computer.
UUCP	UNIX-to-UNIX Copy Protocol, an early transfer protocol for UNIX machines that required having one machine call the other one on the phone.
uudecode	A program that lets you construct binary data that was uuencoded.
uuencode	A program that lets you send binary data through e-mail.
virus	A computer program that covertly enters a system by means of a legitimate program, usually doing damage to the system; compare to *worm*.
VMS	An operating system used on hosts made by Digital Equipment Corporation.
WAIS	Wide Area Information Servers, a system for searching and retrieving documents from participating sites.
WHOIS	A service that lets you look up information about Internet hosts and users.
worm	A computer program that invades other computers over a network, usually non-destructively; compare to *virus*.
WWW	World Wide Web, a hypertext-based system that allows browsing of available Internet resources.

Background of Some Internet Terms

A number of Internet terms relate to the evolution of the Internet. Although these terms are defined briefly in the previous table, they are discussed in more detail in the following sections to provide you with some historical information about the Internet.

Internet History

The U.S. Advanced Research Projects Agency (ARPA) began to explore the feasibility of distributed computing in the early 1960s. ARPA realized that a number of military and research sites around the country would benefit

2

greatly if they could share resources such as computers, data, research results, and expensive scientific instruments. To facilitate this sharing, ARPA initiated a project to design a network to connect these sites. One goal of this project was to design a network that wouldn't be impaired seriously if physical sections of the network were lost. The ARPANET began as an experiment to see what type of network designs would work, how robust they would be, and how much information they could transfer.

One of the major developments to come out of the ARPANET research was the development of a new type of network protocol. Today's Internet uses the transmission control protocol/Internet protocol (TCP/IP) developed through ARPANET research.

The networking protocol developed for the ARPANET involved a new technology known as *packet switching*. In a packet-switched network, rather than use a dedicated line connecting the sending and receiving computers, small packets of information (containing the data being sent and information about its source and destination) are sent over a common transmission line, allowing many packets with many different destinations to flow through the same network. This way, the network can be designed with multiple physical paths between any two machines on the network, and can allow the flexibility for an individual data packet to use any of those paths. Machines called *packet-switching nodes* positioned throughout the network take care of choosing the best path for each data packet at that particular time (depending on how heavy traffic is on certain network segments, hardware problems on a segment, and so forth).

The ARPANET was formed when the first four sites—the Stanford Research Institute, the University of California at Santa Barbara, the University of California at Los Angeles, and the University of Utah—were connected together in September 1969. The ARPANET was unveiled to the public in October 1972 at the first International Conference on Computers and Communications in Washington, D.C. The demonstration was a tremendous success, encouraging more research sites to connect to the ARPANET.

By 1981, still only 213 hosts were connected to the ARPANET. Growth continued rapidly from that point, however, with 2,308 hosts connected in 1986, and approximately 1.5 million hosts worldwide in 1993.

During the early 1980s, all the network segments that made up the ARPANET were converted to the TCP/IP protocol, and the ARPANET became the backbone of the new Internet. In 1986, the National Science Foundation funded a backbone network (NSFNET) to connect the major NSF-funded supercomputer centers around the country. This network became the new backbone network for the Internet. The NSFNET was more appropriate for this task than the ARPANET because it was designed to be an operational network rather than the experimental network that the ARPANET was.

Until now, the NSF has directly funded the operation of the NSFNET backbone. For the future, the NSF is planning to have providers of the backbone service directly charge all who use it (allowing commercial and private customers greater access to the facilities). The NSF would then provide the researchers they fund with enough money to pay the providers directly for their Internet access.

Internet Management

No one individual or organization "owns" the Internet, in the usual sense of the word. Although the backbone in the United States is funded by the NSF, regional and international segments of the network have their own funding and administration. But any network connected to the Internet agrees to the decisions and standards set forth by the Internet Architecture Board (and anyone who is willing to help may participate in the process of devising and setting standards). In 1979, the researchers who were involved in developing the Internet protocols formed an informal committee known as the Internet Configuration Control Board to guide the technical evolution of the Internet. In 1983, the ICCB was reorganized and the new organization christened the Internet Activities Board (IAB). The Internet Activities Board has since been renamed the Internet Architecture Board.

The IAB consists of researchers and professionals who are interested in the technical development of the Internet. They coordinate the design, engineering, and management of the Internet. The IAB has two subgroups: the Internet Engineering Task Force (IETF) and the Internet Research Task Force (IRTF). Each task force consists of a number of working groups, which are made up of professionals who have an interest in a particular area of Internet operation and who volunteer their time to further the development of the Internet.

The IETF working groups help explore current trouble areas in Internet operations and solutions for these problems. They also recommend standards and provide forums for discussing ideas of interest to the Internet community. The IRTF looks at the long-term usage of the Internet and explores the development of new technology that can be used to improve the Internet.

The reports of the IAB are made public through the publication of Request For Comment (RFC) documents. Some RFCs document Internet standards, but many are meant to introduce new ideas and stimulate discussion about future developments on the Internet. Past and current RFCs can be found at the sites identified in Chapter 9.

Looking Ahead

In late 1991, President George Bush signed into legislation the High Performance Computing Act, which provided, in part, for federal support of research into and implementation of a nationwide high-speed computing network known as the National Research and Education Network (NREN). The legislation provides that the NREN be a collaboration between government and industry, and not dampen the motivation for commercial development of similar networking technology and services. The government, recognizing that access to information will be a key to future economic and technological development, wants to encourage the distribution of the technology necessary to build a national data superhighway.

Eventually, everyone should have access to the information superhighway, just as most people have telephone lines coming into their homes. The superhighway will provide access to retail merchants, information services (such as on-line magazines and newspapers), commercial databases, public information (such as library holdings), and many other services. Some of these features are already available through commercial on-line services such as CompuServe, Prodigy, and America Online, but the potential for information access through a common network is almost unlimited. Social forums also could provide access to millions of people around the world, allowing people to find out information about other cultures and exchange information about topics of common interest.

Allowing access to a common network could facilitate the concept of telecommuting (working at home, using the network to access information, having video conferences, and so on) and teleschooling (having students attend classes remotely using a two-way live video conference, in addition to video broadcasts and on-line multimedia information and exercises). Companies could take customer complaints and inquires by e-mail and distribute marketing materials and product updates on-line. All financial transactions could take place on-line, with paper money becoming almost unnecessary. Eventually, the information superhighway could change the structure of society completely.

Internet Addresses

Internet addresses are the key to using the Internet. You use mail addresses to send messages to other Internet users, and you use host addresses (or host names) to retrieve files and connect to hosts that provide Internet services. The following sections discuss what makes up an Internet address and how to find someone's e-mail address.

What Is a Host Name?

Host names are found in e-mail addresses and also are used when connecting to Internet hosts to use Internet services (such as WWW) or to retrieve files. A host name contains the domain name in addition to a name identifying the particular host and any subdomain it may be associated with at its Internet site.

A host name is made up of several words separated by periods. You can examine these words to find out information about the host. A unique domain name, such as delphi.com, identifies all Internet sites. The domain name consists of several pieces that identify the organization and the domain hierarchy to which it belongs.

As an example, look at the host name bigmachine.bigcorp.com. The rightmost word, com, specifies the domain of the machine. In this case, the word com means that the machine belongs to a commercial entity— a company of some kind. Some other domains are edu for educational institutions, mil for military sites, and gov for sites that are part of the government. Also, each country connected to the Internet is assigned a domain; for example, fr is the domain name for France.

Working to the left in the host name, you come to the word `bigcorp`. This part of the host name defines the institution that owns the machine. When an institution connects to the Internet, it must register its domain name with the Internet registration services. In this case, the domain name `bigcorp.com` has been registered to a fictional company called Big Corporation (this name can be used only for machines connected to Big Corporation's network). Examples of real-life institution names (including the domain name) are `ibm.com` for International Business Machines, `mit.edu` for the Massachusetts Institute of Technology, and `nasa.gov` for the National Aeronautics and Space Administration.

Any words to the left of the institution name are assigned within the institution. Small organizations usually will have only a single word (specifying the name of an individual machine at the organization) to the left of the institution name. Sometimes, the host name for large organizations will have more words, which usually designate departments within the organization. For example, you may see a name such as `amachine.cs.mit.edu`, which indicates that the machine `amachine` is within the `cs` (probably Computer Science) department within MIT, an educational institution. With host names, the left-hand word is always the name of a machine.

What is an IP Address?

This chapter has been focusing on using host names to get access to individual hosts on the Internet. The host name is really just a convenient way for people to refer to hosts. The host name represents the IP address (or host address) of the host, which is the address that Internet software needs to get information to or from the host. The IP address is a unique number assigned to identify a host on the Internet. This address is usually represented as four numbers between 1 and 254 separated by periods—for example, 192.58.107.230.

Most software translates automatically between the host name and the IP address so that you don't have to remember what numbers represent which machine. If you need to find the IP address for a machine, you can use the WHOIS database described later in the section "The WHOIS Database."

How to Find a Person's E-Mail Address

Finding out someone's e-mail address is a common problem on the Internet. Suppose that you meet an old friend at your high school reunion. He mentions that he now works for Big Corporation and that they are connected to the Internet. You write down his Internet address on a napkin and stick it in your pocket. The following Monday, you want to send him an e-mail message to say what a good time you had, but you've already taken your suit to the dry cleaners—and left the napkin in the pocket. How do you find out his address?

Unfortunately, this question has no easy answer. The Internet doesn't have a directory of e-mail addresses that you can use to look up your friend (like a telephone directory). You can try a few things, though.

First, you often don't need to look up a person's e-mail address at all. Most often, you will be corresponding with people who already have sent you an e-mail message. If this is the case, you can use the reply function of your mail software to send a new message. Recording in a file somewhere the e-mail addresses of people with whom you regularly correspond is a good idea, however, so even if you delete all the mail messages you have received from that person, you still can send a new message. This is like keeping a personal address book.

In the situation with your friend at Big Corporation, you can't use this approach because you haven't received any mail from him yet. In this case, the first—and often easiest—thing to try is to contact the person through some other means and ask for the address. For example, if you have a telephone number for your friend (or can call the main number for Big Corporation and get it), you can call him and ask him his e-mail address. This method is effective, although it does ruin the surprise of him getting an unexpected e-mail message from you.

If you don't have another way of contacting the person you are looking for, you will have a harder time finding his e-mail address. If you know the host name for the user, or at least the organization name, you sometimes can send mail to the postmaster at that host. Every organization connected to the Internet is required to have someone who can respond to questions and problems. This user name postmaster is usually a nickname (called an *alias*) for this person. So if you want to find out the e-mail address for your friend at `bigcorp.com`, you would send a message to `postmaster@bigcorp.com` with the request.

Note: *If you send a request to the postmaster at an organization, remember to be as specific as you can in your request. Always be polite and patient. Answering questions from people on the Internet isn't usually this person's first responsibility, and the site postmaster is often very busy. Also, if the organization is very large, locating a particular user can take a while.*

The WHOIS database is another way to find e-mail addresses.

The WHOIS Database. One important service available via e-mail is the WHOIS database. The e-mail interface to the database is useful here because you can use the WHOIS database to look up e-mail addresses. When an organization becomes connected to the Internet, it must register with the Internet Network Information Center (called the InterNIC, for short). The InterNIC maintains a database of all organizations connected to the Internet, and you often can find out the organization part of a host name by searching the database.

You can use the WHOIS database by sending an e-mail message to the address `whois@whois.internic.net`. A human doesn't read this address; instead, this address causes the WHOIS server to respond automatically to your request. You send commands to the WHOIS server by putting your requests in the body of the message. Sending a message with the word `help` in the body, for example, will cause the server to send you information about how to use the server.

Suppose that you have a friend who works for International Business Machines. You want to know the domain name there so that you can send mail to the postmaster to ask how to reach your friend. You can send a mail message to the address `whois@whois.internic.net` with the command (in the message body) `whois international business machines`. Within a few minutes, you should receive a message back from the WHOIS server with the answer. The first line in the message from the server shows that the domain name for International Business Machines is, not surprisingly, `ibm.com`. Now, you can send a message to `postmaster@ibm.com` to ask about your friend. The following example shows the e-mail reply from the WHOIS server when a message requesting the domain name for International Business Machines is sent to it.

```
Return-Path: mailserv@internic.net
Received: by internic.net (4.1/SMI-4.1)
                  id AA22021; Sat, 27 Nov 93 06:18:15 EST
Date: Sat, 27 Nov 93 06:18:15 EST
From: mailserv@internic.net (Mail Server)
Message-Id: <9311271118.AA22021@internic.net>
To: tgp
Subject: Re: whois international business machines

International Business Machines (IBM-DOM)          IBM.COM
International Business Machines (NS-HST19)
NS.AIXSSC.UK.IBM.COM160.100.239.120
```

If your service provider allows you to use telnet, you can telnet to the
machine whois.internic.net to look up information about a host. The
following is an example of connecting to the server from a UNIX system.

```
% telnet whois.internic.net
Trying 198.41.0.5 …
Connected to rs.internic.net
Escape character is '^]'.


SunOS UNIX (rs) (ttyp5)

*********************************************************************************
* -- InterNIC Registration Services Center  --
*
* For gopher, type:              GOPHER <return>
* For wais, type:                WAIS <search string>
*                                <return>
* For the *original* whois type: WHOIS [search string]
*                                <return>
* For the X.500 whois DUA, type: X500WHOIS <return>
* For registration status:       STATUS <ticket number>
*                                <return>
*
*
* For user assistance call (800) 444-4345 ¦ (619) 455-4600 or
* (703) 742-4777
* Please report system problems to ACTION@rs.internic.net
*********************************************************************************
Please be advised that the InterNIC Registration host contains
INTERNET Domains, IP Network Numbers, ASNs, and Points of
Contacts ONLY. Please refer to rfc1400.txt for details
(available via anonymous ftp at either nic.ddn.mil [/rfc/
rfc1400.txt]  or ftp.rs.internic.net
[/policy/rfc1400.txt]).
Cmdinter Ver 1.3 Wed Jan  5 23:17:34 1994 EST
[vt100] InterNIC >
```

```
[vt100] InterNIC > whois is.internic.net
Connecting to the rs Database ......
Connected to the rs Database
[No name] (IS-HST)

   Hostname: IS.INTERNIC.NET
   Address: 192.153.156.15
   System: SUN running SUNOS

   Coordinator:
     Coordinator's name and e-mail address
     Coordinator's phone number

   Record last updated on 23-Mar-93.

Would you like to see the registered users of this host? n
Whois: <Enter>
[vt100] InterNIC > exit
%
```

Note: *For more specific information about using telnet from your service provider, see the chapter in Part II that discusses your service provider.*

Host Name Lookup. Each machine on the Internet has a host name and an Internet IP address. Sometimes you will have one of these pieces of information and need the other. You may have the host name for a machine, for example, but some piece of software you have requires the IP address. One mail-based server on the Internet provides a translation between these two types of addresses.

You can send a request to this server by using the resolve@cs.widener.edu address. If you send a mail message with the phrase site delphi.com in the body of the message, for example (you can use any host name instead of delphi.com), the server would return the IP address for the machine delphi.com. The reply mail message that follows shows that the address for delphi.com is 192.80.63.1:

```
Return-Path: resolve@cs.widener.edu
Received: by cs.widener.edu (4.1/SMI-4.1)
                    id AA21120; Mon, 29 Nov 93 13:24:33 EST
Date: Mon, 29 Nov 93 13:24:33 EST
Message-Id: <9311291824.AA21120@cs.widener.edu>
Return-Path: resolve-request@cs.widener.edu
From: resolve@cs.widener.edu (Address Resolver)
Subject: Response for address(es)
To: Tod Pike <tgp@bigcorp.com>
Sender: resolve@cs.widener.edu (Address Resolver)
Reply-To: resolve-request@cs.widener.edu (Resolve Maintainer)
Precedence: bulk
```

```
The address(es) for your request:
                    delphi.com              192.80.63.1
--
Contact sven@cs.widener.edu with problems or comments.
Please note: no guarantes come with this, it's just a hack.
```

Internet News Groups (USENET)

Internet news groups are on-line discussions (via posted messages) of many thousands of different topics. The section "USENET Discussion Groups" in Chapter 1 provided some general information about what news groups are and how to access them. In addition to the mechanics of reading and posting to news groups, you should be aware of some of the social aspects of participating in news group discussions.

The Culture of USENET

Because USENET reaches a large number of people (current estimates are that more than a million people read netnews), you should be prepared for somewhat of a culture shock when you begin reading netnews. USENET reaches people in all 50 states and in many countries around the world. Quite a few people reading netnews don't speak English as a native language; certainly many will have a different cultural background than you. So an article you post may seem reasonable and understandable to you, but others may completely misunderstand it. This section will try to give you an idea of the culture of USENET and what to expect when you read and post news articles.

Going back to the Chapter 1 analogy of a news group as a room with people in it, imagine walking over to a group of people and trying to understand their culture. You probably will spend a few minutes listening to the conversation and trying to understand the basic rules of the group—how the people interact, what information has been covered before you joined, and how you should enter the conversation.

In a similar way, when you decide to read a news group, you should read the group for a while—a few weeks, if you can—before you post an article to the group. This way, you can determine the tone and character of the group, what topics have been discussed recently (topics that probably won't be welcome if brought up again), and what topics are now being discussed. You may want to try to discover who the "regulars" in the group are—those who post regularly and generally are respected by the people in the group. In some cases, sending an e-mail message to one of these regular posters to ask about the culture of the group is a good idea; a person who has been participating in a group for a while can give you a good history of the group and some pointers on working effectively with the people in the group.

Many groups maintain a list of frequently asked questions, called a FAQ (pronounced "fak"), which is posted periodically to the news group (generally once a month). You may want to read a news group long enough to see the FAQ and look through it before you make your first post, or send e-mail to one of the regular posters to ask whether they know whether there is a FAQ and how to get a copy of it. This way, you may have some of your questions answered without having to waste network resources on information that's already available. The FAQ also may give you ideas of what topics would be good to discuss in the news group.

As a general rule, news groups in the `comp` and `sci` hierarchies tend to be oriented toward "serious" topics; emphasis more likely will be placed on discussing facts rather than opinions, and the group participants likely will be tolerant of new posters. On the other hand, groups in the `soc`, `alt`, `rec`, and `news` hierarchies tend to be oriented toward people's opinions on topics and more likely will be argumentative. People in these groups often will listen to the opinions of a newcomer, but be prepared to receive other people's opinions in turn.

Finally, groups in the `talk` and `misc` hierarchies definitely tend toward being argumentative. Many groups are devoted to discussing topics that generate strong opinions, and you should be ready to defend your position if you post to one of these groups. Remember, politeness and accuracy will gain you more respect than responding in kind to other people's attacks.

USENET Etiquette

One important thing to remember when communicating via USENET is that the only thing other people see from you are the words you type. If you are trying to be witty or sarcastic, the reader of your words can't see the expression on your face or hear the tone of your voice. Remembering this fact—and writing to accurately express your feelings—can avoid many misunderstandings.

You can express emotions in a number of ways in your articles. To emphasize what you are saying, you can type in all capitals (for example, THAT IS NOT TRUE!) or use asterisks around your text (for example, *do this step first*). You also can express emotions by using small text symbols called *emoticons*. The most basic of these is the *smiley*, which looks like :-). (If you turn your head sideways, you see that :-) looks like a smiling face.) The smiley is used to indicate humor or sarcasm. Many variations of smileys exist, and you will certainly run into them when reading news.

Note: *You shouldn't use all capitals in a normal post because it is considered "shouting."*

When you compose your article, make sure that your post is worded carefully, to avoid misunderstandings. Make sure that your intent is clear; remember that some people reading your post may not be native speakers of English. If you use slang or local expressions, people outside your community (or country) may not understand you.

You should read the entire article before responding to it. Reading a few other people's replies before responding is also a good idea; other people may have made the same point you want to make, and you should avoid duplicating what other people have said. In any case, if you read an article that makes you want to respond angrily, it's a good idea to wait a few hours, so that you can calm down before replying.

Some news readers allow you to quote text from the article you are responding to. You may want to quote the parts of the original text that are pertinent to your response for clarity, but delete as much of the rest of the quoted material as possible to avoid wasting network resources. Also, if a person is requesting information that may not be of general interest to the group, you should respond with e-mail to the author of the post, if possible, rather than post your reply to the entire news group.

Another thing to keep in mind when posting is that the way you format the article can make it easier to read. These are some of the guidelines you may want to follow:

- Try to keep the Subject: line of your article relatively short, but informative.

- Don't use anything but text characters. Control characters do odd things to different types of displays.

- Keep your line lengths under 80 characters, which is the maximum line length of some displays, and put a carriage return at the end of each line.

- Break up your text into medium-sized paragraphs with blank lines between them. This format is much easier to read than long, solid blocks of text.

One of the best ways to avoid problems when posting to USENET is to remember that many people read news; someone you know, such as your boss, friend, or future spouse, quite possibly may read something you post. A good rule of thumb is never post something that you wouldn't want your mother to read!

Summary

The Internet can be rather confusing to new users. It has its own jargon, like many professions or hobbies do. Learning the jargon can make the Internet less foreign. Learning something about the history and development of the Internet also can help the user understand it.

Because of the structure of the Internet, finding information about its resources can be difficult. You can find e-mail addresses for Internet users in several ways. You can find a great deal of information in the USENET news groups, but new users should take some time to learn about a news group before jumping into the discussions. With this background material, new Internet users should be a little more comfortable when exploring the Internet.

Part II
How to Use the Internet

Chapter 3

Levels of Internet Access

The Internet itself is a web of interconnected networks that all use the TCP/IP network protocol. If you have an account on a machine that's directly connected to the Internet, you likely will have access to all the Internet services described in Chapter 1. However, many other computer networks have varying degrees of access to the Internet. This chapter discusses the levels of Internet access available from some of the commercial on-line services networks. The remaining chapters in Part II describe how to access Internet services from these networks.

The commercial networks that you'll look at in this chapter are

- CompuServe

- Prodigy

- America Online

- Delphi

These services are listed in order of increasing Internet access. You'll find that the level of Internet access varies from the e-mail-only access now provided by CompuServe and Prodigy, to the almost total access planned by America Online and now available from Delphi.

Note: *The information presented here is accurate at the time of publication. Some of the on-line services are planning to add additional Internet services in the future, so you should check with your service provider to find out what is currently available.*

For comparison, this chapter also discusses access to Internet resources from a generic UNIX system and from some commercial Internet providers.

CompuServe

CompuServe was one of the first commercial networks to provide any interface to the Internet. It has a graphical user interface available for Macintosh, Windows, or DOS.

As of this writing, the only Internet service available from CompuServe is electronic mail. On CompuServe, you can send e-mail to and receive e-mail from users on the Internet. The same charges apply for sending Internet mail as for sending CompuServe mail. Also, the Internet mail you receive is charged against your account in the same way as the messages that you send.

Although the Internet interface is limited to e-mail messages, you can access some other Internet services through the e-mail gateway. Some machines on the Internet allow you to send them mail messages that tell them to use an Internet service and then return the results to you in an e-mail message. Some Internet services available by mail are archie, WAIS, and ftp. Also, some mail servers perform specific information retrieval for you; for example, you can look up e-mail addresses and host names, as described in Chapter 1. (Some of these mail servers are also described in Part III.)

Instructions on how to access Internet services through CompuServe can be found in Chapter 4.

Prodigy

Prodigy is an on-line service with a graphical user interface available for Macintosh, Windows, or DOS. As of this writing, the only Internet service available from Prodigy for Windows and DOS is sending and receiving electronic mail. (As of this writing, Internet access isn't available for the Macintosh version of Prodigy.) The same charges apply for sending Internet mail as for sending Prodigy mail. The Internet mail you receive also is charged against your account in the same way as the messages that you send. (You may get a certain allotment of messages free, depending on your payment plan.)

Although the Internet interface is limited to e-mail messages, you can access some other Internet services through the e-mail gateway. Some machines on the Internet allow you to send them mail messages that tell them to use an Internet service and then return the results to you in an e-mail message. Some Internet services available by e-mail are archie, WAIS, and ftp. Also, some mail servers perform specific information retrieval for you; for example, you can look up e-mail addresses and host names, as described in Chapter 1. (Some of these mail servers also are described in Part III.)

Prodigy also has the Internet Forum, which gives you access to a glossary of Internet terms, the Internet Forum BB (a moderated discussion group), and basic Internet information.

Instructions on how to access Internet services through Prodigy can be found in Chapter 5.

America Online

So far, America Online (AOL) is the commercial network that offers (or plans to offer) the most extensive connection to the Internet, and does it with an easy-to-use graphical interface available for Macintosh, Windows, and DOS.

AOL has a section called the Internet Center, which allows you access to a number of Internet services. The Internet Center gives you access to AOL forums dealing with a number of different Internet topics. Also, icons in the Internet center give you easy access to various Internet services.

Now, the only Internet services available are e-mail and mailing lists, but sometime this year AOL plans to offer access to USENET groups, Gopher and WAIS services, and ftp and telnet. As the time of this writing, there is no surcharge beyond your normal account charges for using any Internet services from AOL.

Instructions on how to access Internet services through America Online can be found in Chapter 6.

Delphi

Delphi is a commercial on-line network that offers a screen-oriented interface to the Internet. (This interface is text-based and accepts only input from keyboard.) Delphi can be accessed by anyone with a terminal or terminal emulator (running on a Macintosh or PC, for example) and modem.

Through Delphi, you can access most Internet services through menu selections. Delphi allows you direct access to Internet e-mail, USENET news groups, telnet, ftp, and Gopher. No direct access to archie, WAIS, or WWW is available, but you can use these services by telnetting to another Internet host that offers them.

At the time of this writing, Delphi has a monthly charge to access Internet services. This charge allows you to transfer a certain amount of data over the Internet, with surcharges for any data transfer over this amount. Regular storage charges also apply to Internet data stored on your Delphi account.

Instructions on how to access Internet services through Delphi can be found in Chapter 7.

Generic UNIX Systems

During the years in which the Internet was growing, it was used mainly as a way to connect academic and research centers, many of them doing research in the area of computer science. The most common operating system in use at these sites was the UNIX operating system, originally developed by AT&T Bell Laboratories. UNIX is still a popular operating system at many universities, and many Internet sites that offer resources run the UNIX operating system. Some commercial Internet service providers also give you access to UNIX accounts.

Most UNIX machines connected to the Internet have access to all Internet services (Gopher, WAIS, telnet, ftp, archie, WWW, e-mail, and USENET news groups). Because UNIX has been in research environments for such a long time, many applications have been developed to access the different services, especially e-mail and news groups. A particular UNIX site may have any number of different interfaces for these services.

The UNIX operating system is very complex, with cryptic commands that can be difficult for new users to master. For the most part, the UNIX system is character-based, assuming that a terminal or terminal emulator is being used to access the system. Commands are typed at a prompt; some screen-oriented interfaces that let you use the arrow keys to move around do exist (similar to the DOS environment). Some windows environments have been developed to run on top of UNIX to provide applications with graphical user interfaces, but these usually must be run on the UNIX host itself (or a special windowing-system terminal), and cannot be run by terminals connected the UNIX host.

So although a UNIX account on the Internet can usually access all the services available on the Internet, UNIX can be a difficult operating system for novice users to understand. Chapter 8 describes how to use some of the more popular Internet application interfaces available on UNIX systems.

Other Ways to Access the Internet

A number of commercial network providers offer Internet access. These providers aren't on-line services but are strictly Internet access providers. Some of them have PC or Macintosh software that gives you a graphical user interface for Internet e-mail and USENET news groups (Internet providers such as Performance Systems International and Computer Witchcraft are in this category). These providers often allow you to read and compose e-mail and USENET news group messages off-line so that you don't have to pay for large amounts of connect time while reading/ sending news and e-mail.

Some Internet providers give you an account on their machines (often UNIX), which you access using a terminal or terminal emulator (running on a Macintosh or PC, for example) and a modem. This is usually a full-access Internet account, but some providers offer limited Internet access (only e-mail and news groups, for example) for reduced fees. Also, quite a few local bulletin board systems allow you to access many Internet services through menu selections.

Discussing these other Internet providers is outside the scope of this book. However, if you are interested only in Internet access and not the other aspects of the commercial on-line services discussed in this book, you may want to explore the options offered by one of these Internet providers. (Que's *Using the Internet*, Special Edition, gives more detailed information about finding and using a commercial Internet provider.)

Summary

You can get access to the Internet in many ways. Many commercial on-line services networks now provide at least basic (e-mail) Internet access, with some of them providing direct access to a number of Internet services. The fullest Internet access comes from commercial Internet providers or from sites connected directly to the Internet (such as universities or research centers). Even if full Internet access isn't offered by the commercial on-line services networks, many Internet services can be accessed through e-mail from those networks.

Internet Access	Internet Services Available
CompuServe	E-mail (and archie, WAIS, and ftp through e-mail)
Prodigy	E-mail (and archie, WAIS, and ftp through e-mail)
America Online	E-mail, archie (through e-mail), and mailing lists
Delphi	E-mail, USENET news groups, telnet, ftp, and Gopher (archie, WAIS, and WWW through telnet)

Chapter 4

Using the Internet via CompuServe

CompuServe was one of the first nationwide commercial on-line services to offer a connection to the Internet. But at the time this book was written, the only direct Internet service that CompuServe offered was electronic mail. Although this situation is somewhat limiting, you still can access many Internet services through e-mail.

This chapter explains how to:

- Send Internet e-mail

- Locate files using an e-mail archie server

- Download files using an e-mail ftp server

- Locate information using an e-mail WAIS server

For this chapter, you should already know how to connect to CompuServe and have your CompuServe software running.

Note: *The examples in this chapter were made using the Microsoft Windows version of the CompuServe Information Manager. The examples and procedures in this chapter will work with any communications software you use to connect to CompuServe.*

Using Internet E-Mail

Sending Internet e-mail on CompuServe is done exactly the same as sending normal mail. When you specify the address where you want the mail sent, you must place the word `internet:` in front to tell CompuServe that the mail is destined for an Internet site.

Note: *Sending and receiving Internet e-mail on CompuServe carries extra charges. You should review the CompuServe charge rates before using Internet e-mail.*

Sending Internet E-Mail

To understand the process of sending Internet e-mail, you will send a message to an automatic mail server set up for this book. The address you will send the mail to is `book@pittslug.sug.org`. Follow these steps:

1. On the main CompuServe Information Manager screen, pull down the **M**ail menu and choose **C**reate Mail.

   The Create Mail window and Recipient List dialog box appear. The Recipient List dialog box allows you to type addresses or double-click an address you have saved in the address book.

The Create Mail window and Recipient List dialog box.

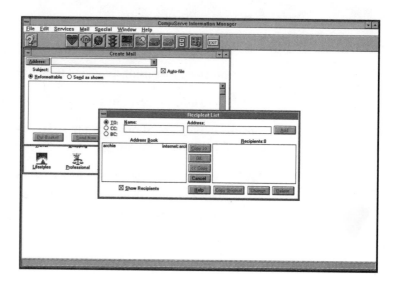

2. In the Recipient List dialog box, type **book** in the **N**ame text box. This step associates the name with the address you are sending the mail to. You can type anything here; *don't* leave this text box blank.

3. In the Address text box, type **internet:book@pittslug.sug.org**.

Fill in the **N**ame and Address text boxes

The Name and Address text boxes contain the information necessary to send the message to the e-mail server.

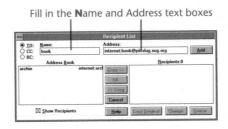

4. Choose **A**dd. The address you typed appears in the **R**ecipients list box.

The **R**ecipients list box contains the address you typed.

Recipients list

5. Choose OK. The Recipient List dialog box closes, and the address you typed appears in the **A**ddress box in the Create Mail window.

After you set up an address to send the message to, the Create Mail window shows the address.

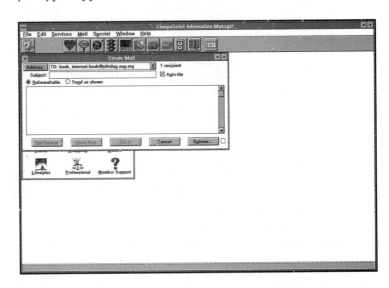

4

6. In the Subject text box, type `hello`.

7. The scroll box under the **R**eformattable radio button is the area for your message body. For this particular message, you can type anything here.

The completed mail message, ready to send out.

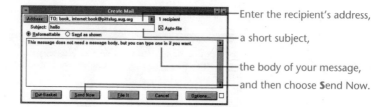

—Enter the recipient's address,

—a short subject,

—the body of your message,

—and then choose **S**end Now.

8. Choose **S**end Now to send the message. If you are already connected to the CompuServe system, your message is sent immediately. If you were creating the message off-line, CIM calls CompuServe to send your message.

CompuServe may take a few hours to process your mail and send it to the Internet host you specified.

If you have problems...

If you make a mistake in your address (for example, you typed the name of the Internet host wrong), you will get an error message saying that the message couldn't be delivered and describing the problem. If the host name is incorrect, you often get an error message such as host unknown; if you incorrectly type the name of the user you are trying to send the message to, you often get an error message such as user unknown. With either error message, you should check to make sure that the address you typed is correct.

You may also encounter other problems in sending mail from CompuServe to Internet machines. For example, the machine you are sending mail to could be unavailable, or there may be a temporary problem in the network between CompuServe and the destination machine.

In either case, the CompuServe system will try several times to deliver your message but it may eventually send you an error message saying that it could not deliver your mail. In this case, you can try to send the message again. If your mail continues to fail, you can send a message to the CompuServe staff asking for help in diagnosing the problem.

Reading Internet E-Mail

The `book@pittslug.sug.org` address that you sent a message to in the preceding section is set up to reply automatically to your message. When you connect to the CompuServe system, the system informs you if you have new mail waiting to be read. If you already are connected to the system when mail arrives for you, the system will tell you.

Note: *You must connect to CompuServe for CIM to inform you of new mail.*

Reading mail you have received from an Internet address is the same as reading normal CompuServe mail. To read your Internet e-mail, follow these steps:

1. Pull down the **M**ail menu and choose **G**et New Mail.

If you were not already connected to the CompuServe system, CIM calls the CompuServe system and connects for you.

4

The Get New Mail window appears, listing all the new mail messages you have received. Notice that the system also tells you how much reading the selected message will cost.

In the Get New Mail window, the message from the book server is highlighted.

———— Postage due

2. Double-click the line that has *Internet Quickstart* as the Name (the person who sent the message).

The mail message appears in a new window. You can scroll through the message if necessary by using the scroll bars along the sides of the window.

Reading the message from the book server in the message window.

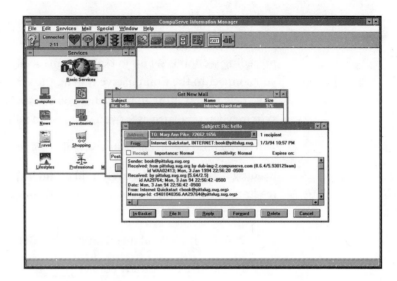

3. If you don't want to keep the message, choose **D**elete. Otherwise, you can save the message on your computer's disk by choosing **I**n-Basket.

As you can see, sending and reading Internet e-mail on CompuServe is easy.

Locating Files Using an E-Mail archie Server

archie

An application that lets you easily search for information at anonymous ftp sites on the Internet.

telnet

A program that allows remote login to another computer.

archie, as described in Chapter 1, "Introducing the Internet," is a very useful program that you can use to locate files on Internet ftp servers. Because CompuServe currently doesn't have direct access to an archie server (and doesn't let you use *telnet* to connect to a machine that does have an archie server), you must use Internet e-mail to send commands to an archie server.

For the examples in the following sections, you will use the archie e-mail server on the machine `archie.internic.net`.

Requesting an archie Help Message

The first thing you will do is ask the archie server to send you a message telling you how to use the server. To do so, send an e-mail message with the word **help** as the subject. To send this message to the archie server, follow these steps:

1. On the main CompuServe Information Manager screen, pull down the **M**ail menu and choose **C**reate Mail. The Create Mail window and Recipient List dialog box appear.

2. In the Recipient List dialog box, type **archie** in the **N**ame text box.

3. In the Address text box, type **internet:archie@archie.internic.net**.

Filling in the **N**ame and Address text boxes.

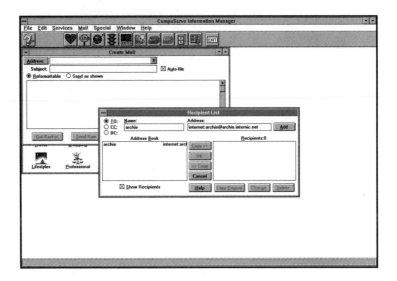

4. Choose **A**dd. The address you typed appears in the **R**ecipients list box.

5. Choose OK. The Recipient List dialog box disappears, and the address you typed appears in the **A**ddress box in the Create Mail window.

6. In the Subject text box, type a space. (CompuServe requires something in the Subject text box, but the archie server doesn't need anything in the Subject text box.)

7. In the scroll box under the **R**eformattable radio button, type **help**.

The completed mail
message, ready to
send.

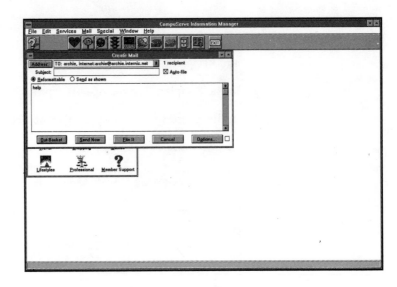

8. Choose **S**end Now to send the message.

CompuServe may take a few hours to process your mail and send it to the
archie server. Generally, the archie server will respond quickly to your
request.

Reading the archie Help Message

Reading the mail you have received from the archie server is the same as
reading mail from any other Internet host. CompuServe informs you
when you have new mail waiting to be read (if you are on-line with
CompuServe). To read the help message, follow these steps:

1. Pull down the **M**ail menu and choose **G**et New Mail.

If you were not already connected to the CompuServe system, CIM
calls CompuServe to connect and retrieve your mail.

The Get New Mail window appears, listing all the new mail messages you have received. Notice that the system also tells you how
much reading the selected message will cost.

The Get New Mail
window, with the
message from the
archie server
highlighted.

— Postage due

2. Double-click the line with *Internet:archie-errors* as the Name (the person who sent the message).

The mail message appears in a new window. You can scroll through the message by using the scroll bars, if necessary.

Reading the message from the archie server in the message window.

3. If you don't want to keep the message, choose **D**elete. Otherwise, you can save the message on your computer's disk by choosing **I**n-Basket.

Searching for a File

Request For Comments
RFC, a document submitted to the Internet governing board to propose Internet standards or to document information about the Internet.

Now you will use the e-mail archie server to search for a file. For this example, you will search for the file rfc822.txt, which is an Internet *Request For Comments* (RFC) document that explains the format of an Internet e-mail message.

To send the e-mail message to the archie server, first perform steps 1 through 5 in the earlier section "Requesting the archie Help Message" to set up the CompuServe Create Mail window with the address of the archie server. Then follow these steps:

1. In the Subject text box, type a space. (CompuServe requires something in the Subject text box, but the archie server doesn't need anything in the Subject text box.)

2. In the scroll box under the **R**eformattable radio button, type
   find rfc822.txt.

The completed
mail message,
ready to send.

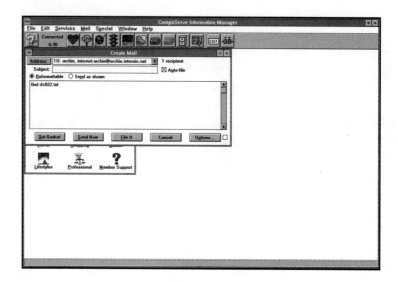

3. Choose **S**end Now to send the message.

The e-mail message is sent to the archie e-mail server. CompuServe may
take a few hours to process the mail and deliver it to the archie server.

This example shows that archie is easy to use if you know exactly the
name of the file you are looking for (for example, if you read through a
list of available RFCs for ones that were interesting). If you don't know
the exact name of the file, archie may take longer to use. archie supports
searching for parts of the file name (called *substring searching*) and searching for a file while ignoring whether the file name is in upper- or lowercase. As a result, you may come across a long list of files that match the
string you're looking for, but you may not be able to tell which file is the
one you want.

A full description of archie's features is beyond the scope of this book. If
you read the help message returned by the archie server and experiment
with the server, however, you should be able to find most of the files you
are looking for.

Reading the Results of the Search

After CompuServe informs you that you have new mail, you can read the
results of the file search. Follow these steps:

1. Pull down the **M**ail menu and choose **G**et New Mail.

   If you were not already connected to the CompuServe system, CIM calls CompuServe to connect and retrieve your mail.

   The Get New Mail window appears, listing all the new mail messages you have received. Notice that the system also tells you how much reading the selected message will cost.

The Get New Mail window, with the message from the archie server highlighted.

Postage due

2. Double-click the line with *Internet:archie-errors* as the Name (the person who sent the message).

   The mail message appears in a new window.

Reading the results of the archie file search in the message window. The message has been scrolled down to show the first file match.

Search result

3. If you don't want to keep the message, choose **D**elete. Otherwise, you can save the message to disk by choosing **I**n-Basket.

   The message you get probably will list several different Internet sites for the file rfc822.txt (the figure shows only the first one). You will use one of these sites to download the file in an example in the next section.

Downloading Files Using an E-Mail ftp Server

ftp
A program that lets you transfer data between different computers.

Because CompuServe currently doesn't have direct access to the *ftp* program, you will have to use an e-mail ftp server to download files from Internet ftp sites.

To use an e-mail ftp server, you will send an e-mail message containing commands that tell the server which ftp site to connect to, which directory the files are in, and which files to download. The e-mail ftp server processes your message and, if the commands are correct, sends the file you requested to you in an e-mail response.

In the following sections, you will use the ftp e-mail server on host `decwrl.dec.com`. The e-mail address for the server is `ftpmail@decwrl.dec.com`.

Requesting the ftp E-Mail Server Help Message

The first thing you will do is ask the ftp e-mail server to send a message telling you how to use the server. To do so, send an e-mail message with the word **help** in the message body by following these steps:

1. On the main CompuServe Information Manager screen, pull down the **M**ail menu and choose **C**reate Mail. The Create Mail window and Recipient List dialog box appear.

2. In the Recipient List dialog box, type **ftpmail** in the **N**ame text box.

3. In the Address text box, type **internet:ftpmail@decwrl.dec.com**.

Filling in the **N**ame and Address text boxes.

4. Choose **A**dd. The address you typed appears in the **R**ecipients list box.

5. Choose OK. The Recipient List dialog box disappears, and the address you typed appears in the Address box on the Create Mail window.

6. In the Subject text box, type **help**. The ftp e-mail server doesn't process the information in the Subject text, but it does put the subject information in the return message. This makes identifying the messages it returns to you much easier.

7. In the scroll box under the **R**eformattable radio button, type **help**.

The completed mail message, ready to send.

8. Choose **S**end Now to send the message.

CompuServe may take a few hours to process your mail and send it to the ftp e-mail server. Generally, the ftp server will respond quickly to your request.

Reading the ftp Help Message

After CompuServe tells you that you have new mail, you can read the ftp e-mail server help message. Follow these steps:

1. Pull down the **M**ail menu and choose **G**et New Mail.

   If you were not already connected to the CompuServe system, CIM calls CompuServe to connect and retrieve your mail.

   The Get New Mail window appears, listing all the new mail messages you have received.

The Get New Mail window, with the message from the ftp e-mail server highlighted.

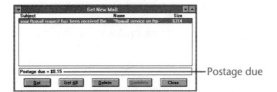

— Postage due

2. Double-click the line starting with *ftpmail service* as the Name (the person who sent the message).

   The mail message appears in a new window.

Reading the ftp
e-mail server help
message in the
message window.

3. If you don't want to keep the message, choose **D**elete. Otherwise, you can save the message to disk by choosing **I**n-Basket.

Sending a File Download Request

You will now use the e-mail ftp server to download a file. As an example, you will use the information retrieved by the archie search to download the file. As seen in the archie example, the file rfc822.txt is located on the site sunsite.unc.edu in the directory /pub/docs/rfc. With this information, you can set up the file download request.

To send the e-mail message to the ftp e-mail server, first perform steps 1 through 5 from the earlier section "Requesting the ftp E-Mail Server Help Message" to set up the CompuServe Create Mail window with the address of the ftp e-mail server. Then follow these steps:

1. In the Subject text box, type **get rfc822.txt**. (The ftp e-mail server ignores the subject of the message, but typing a subject will help identify the response you get back from the server.)

2. In the scroll box under the **R**eformattable radio button, type the following lines:

```
connect sunsite.unc.edu
chdir /pub/docs/rfc
get rfc822.txt
quit
```

The completed mail message, ready to send.

3. Choose **S**end Now to send the message.

CIM goes on-line with CompuServe and sends the message to the ftp e-mail server. CompuServe may take a few hours to process your message and deliver it to the ftp server. When the ftp server receives your message, it should send a response back within a few minutes.

Reading the File Request Results

The ftp e-mail server will acknowledge your file request with an e-mail message. This first message tells you that the server received your request and how many other requests are before yours. You can read this ftp e-mail server message by following these steps:

1. Pull down the **M**ail menu and choose **G**et New Mail.

If you weren't already connected to the CompuServe system, CIM calls CompuServe to connect and retrieve your mail.

The Get New Mail window appears, listing all the new mail messages you have received.

The Get New Mail window, with the new message from the ftp e-mail server highlighted.

Postage due——

2. Double-click the line starting with *ftpmail service* as the Name (the person who sent the message).

The mail message appears in a new window.

Reading the results of the ftp e-mail server file request message in the message window.

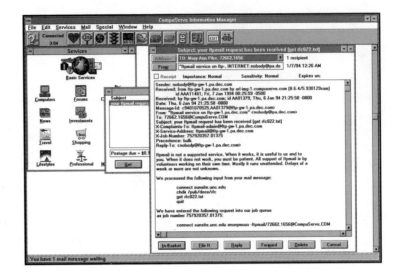

3. If you don't want to keep the message, choose **D**elete. Otherwise, you can save the message to disk by choosing **I**n-Basket.

After the ftp e-mail server processes your file request, it sends another message containing the actual file you requested. Depending on how many requests were queued before yours, it can take several days for the ftp server to send the file to you.

You can read this new message exactly the same way you read the first response from the server. If the file you requested is a standard text file, you can read it directly on-screen. If, however, you have requested a binary file (such as an executable program), the ftp server will translate the binary file into text so that it can be sent with Internet e-mail. In this case, you will have to save the mail message to your computer's disk and translate the file back to its original form.

uuencode

A program that lets you send binary data through e-mail.

uudecode

A program that lets you construct binary data that was uuencoded.

Note: *When the ftp server translates the binary file into text to send it, it usually uses a method called* uuencode *to do so. To translate the file back to binary, you will need a program called* uudecode, *which is available at many common ftp sites. The directory* /pub/msdos/starter *on the machine* *oak.oakland.edu, for example, has various uudecode programs that should work on most systems (including BASIC source programs).*

If you have problems...

One problem you may encounter when using the ftp e-mail server is that the file you are requesting may be too large to be sent to you in one mail message. If the file you are requesting is larger than a certain size (64,000 characters by default), the ftp server will split the file into more than one e-mail message. When you retrieve the messages, notice that they tell you the correct order to use to read them.

If you receive an error message from CompuServe that one of the messages from the ftp server is too large to be delivered to you, you can tell the ftp server to use a smaller message size by using the command chunksize.

4

Locating Information Using an E-Mail WAIS Server

WAIS
Wide Area Information Servers, a system for searching and retrieving documents from participating sites.

This chapter has already shown you how to use the e-mail archie server to locate files on ftp sites. *WAIS* is another information retrieval system that you can use via e-mail to locate information in document databases.

For the examples in this section, you will use the WAIS e-mail server on the machine quake.think.com. The e-mail address to use to send a message to the server is waismail@quake.think.com.

Requesting a Help Message from the WAIS E-Mail Server

The first thing you will do is send a request to the WAIS e-mail server for the help message (which describes the commands that the server recognizes). To do so, send an e-mail message with the word help in the message body. To send this message to the server, follow these steps:

1. On the main CIM screen, pull down the **M**ail menu and choose **C**reate Mail.

   The Create Mail window and Recipient List dialog box appear.

2. In the Recipient List dialog box, type **waismail** in the **N**ame text box.

3. In the Address text box, type `internet:waismail@quake.think.com`.

Filling the **N**ame
and Address text
boxes.

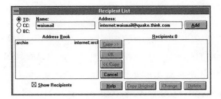

4. Choose **A**dd. The address you typed appears in the **R**ecipients list box.

5. Choose OK. The Recipient List dialog box closes, and the address you typed appears in the Address box on the Create Mail window.

6. In the Subject text box, type **help**. (The WAIS e-mail server doesn't process the information in the Subject text box, but it does put the subject information in the return message to make identifying the messages it returns to you much easier.)

7. In the scroll box under the **R**eformattable radio button, type **help**.

The completed mail
message, ready to
send.

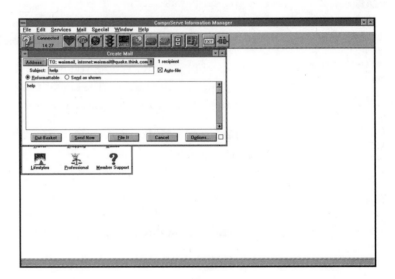

8. Choose **S**end Now to send the message.

CompuServe may take a few hours to process your mail and send it to the WAIS e-mail server. Generally, the WAIS server will respond quickly to your request.

Reading the WAIS E-Mail Server Help Message

After CompuServe sends your help message request to the WAIS e-mail server, the server will send the help message back to you. After Compu-Serve tells you that you have new mail, you can read the WAIS e-mail server help message. Follow these steps:

1. Pull down the **M**ail menu and choose **G**et New Mail.

If you weren't already connected to the CompuServe system, CIM calls CompuServe to connect and retrieve your mail.

The Get New Mail window appears, listing all the new mail messages you have received.

4

The Get New Mail window, with the new message from the WAIS e-mail server highlighted.

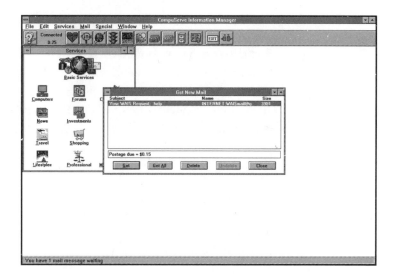

2. Double-click the line with *INTERNET:WAISmail* as the Name (the person who sent the message).

The mail message appears in a new window.

Reading the results
of the WAIS e-mail
server file request
message in the
message window.

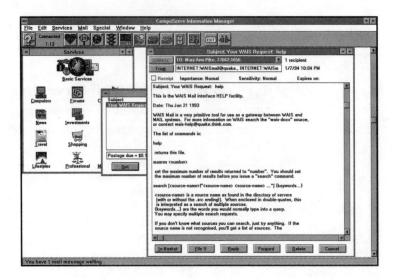

3. If you don't want to keep the message, choose **D**elete. Otherwise, you can save the message to disk by choosing **I**n-Basket.

Sending a Search Request to the WAIS E-Mail Server

Now that you have instructions on how to send commands to the WAIS e-mail server, you can use it to search the WAIS databases. As an example, you will search for speeches that President Clinton has made that mention the city of Atlanta.

First, you must search the WAIS directory of servers to see which databases contain speeches by President Clinton. To do so, you must send the WAIS e-mail server a message with the command search directory-of-servers clinton. The WAIS server will search through the master list of databases available for all those that have documents with the word *clinton* in them.

To send the e-mail message to the WAIS e-mail server, first perform steps 1 through 5 from the earlier section "Requesting a Help Message from the WAIS E-Mail Server" to set up the CompuServe Create Mail window with the address of the WAIS e-mail server. Then follow these steps:

1. In the Subject text box, type **search**. (The WAIS e-mail server ignores the subject of the message; the subject will help identify the response you get back from the server.)

2. In the scroll box under the **R**eformattable radio button, type `search directory-of-servers clinton`.

The completed mail message, ready to send.

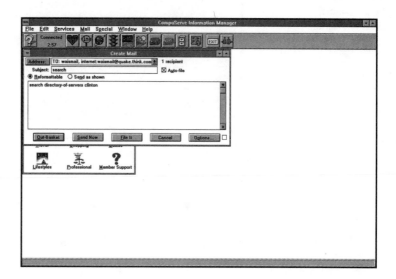

3. Choose **S**end Now to send the message. The message is sent to the WAIS e-mail server.

Normally, CompuServe may take a few hours to process your mail and deliver it to the WAIS e-mail server. The WAIS server usually responds quickly to your requests, however, so you should receive a response within a few hours.

Reading the Response from the WAIS Server

After CompuServe sends your search request to the WAIS e-mail server, the server sends results of the search back to you. Then, after Compu-Serve tells you that you have new mail, you can read the WAIS e-mail server message. Follow these steps:

1. Pull down the **M**ail menu and choose **G**et New Mail.

   If you weren't already connected to the CompuServe system, CIM calls CompuServe to connect and retrieve your mail.

   The Get New Mail window appears, listing all the new mail messages you have received.

4

The Get New Mail
window, with the
new message from
the WAIS e-mail
server highlighted.

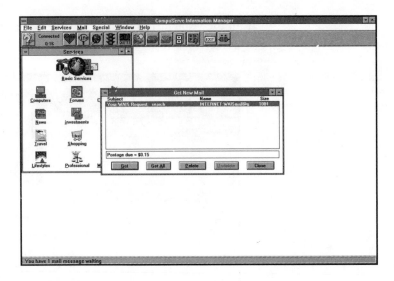

2. Double-click the line starting with *INTERNET:WAISmail* as the
Name (the person who sent the message).

The mail message appears in a new window.

Reading the results
of the WAIS e-mail
server search
request message in
the message
window.

Search results ———

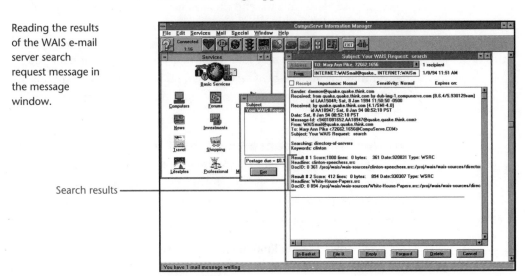

3. If you don't want to keep the message, choose **D**elete. Otherwise,
you can save the message to disk by choosing **In**-Basket.

From the results returned by the search, you can see that two databases have mentioned President Clinton: clinton-speeches and

White-House-Papers. You will use the second database (White-House-Papers) for the next search.

Searching the White-House-Papers Database

Now you will search the White-House-Papers database for those documents that mention Atlanta. To do so, send an e-mail message to the WAIS server with the command search White-House-Papers atlanta. The WAIS server will return a list of all the documents in the White-House-Papers database that have the word *atlanta* in them.

To send the e-mail message to the WAIS e-mail server, first perform steps 1 through 5 from the earlier section "Requesting a Help Message from the WAIS E-Mail Server" to set up the CompuServe Create Mail window with the address of the WAIS e-mail server. Then follow these steps:

1. In the Subject text box, type **search**. The WAIS e-mail server ignores the subject of the message, but this will help identify the response you get back from the server.

2. In the scroll box under the **R**eformattable radio button, type **search White-House-Papers atlanta**.

The completed mail message, ready to send.

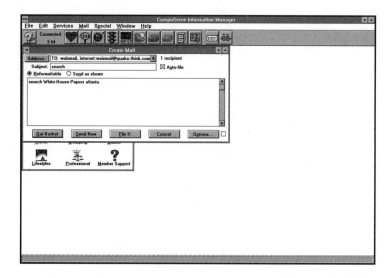

3. Choose **S**end Now to send the message. The message is sent to the WAIS e-mail server.

Reading the Search Response from the WAIS Server

After CompuServe sends your search request to the WAIS e-mail server, the server will send results of the search back to you. Then, when CompuServe informs you that you have new mail, you can read the WAIS e-mail server message. Follow these steps:

1. Pull down the **M**ail menu and choose Get New Mail.

   If you weren't already connected to the CompuServe system, CIM calls CompuServe to connect and retrieve your mail.

   The Get New Mail window appears, listing all the new mail messages you have received.

The Get New Mail window, with the new message from the WAIS e-mail server highlighted.

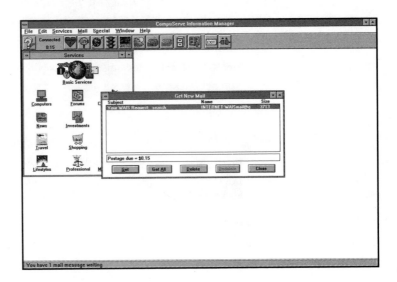

2. Double-click the line starting with *INTERNET:WAISmail* as the Name (the person who sent the message).

   The mail message appears in a new window.

Reading the results of the WAIS e-mail server search request message in the message window.

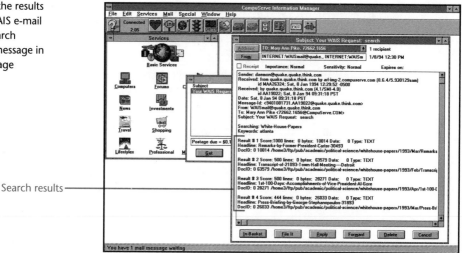

Search results ─

3. If you don't want to keep the message, choose **D**elete. Otherwise, you can save the message to disk by choosing **I**n-Basket.

You can see that quite a few documents contain the word *atlanta*. You can retrieve any of these documents by using the retrieve command to the WAIS server. The retrieve command uses the DocID (for Document ID) from the search results. So, to retrieve the second document on the list, you would send the WAIS e-mail server the command

```
retrieve 0 63579 /home3/ftp/pub/academic/political-science/
whitehouse-papers/1993/Feb/Transcript-of-21093-Town-Hall-
Meeting----Detroit:/home3/wais/White-House-
Papers@sunsite.unc.edu:210%TEXT
```

Note: *You must type the entire DocID for the retrieve command to work correctly. The easiest way is to use cut and paste to copy the line from the search results to the new message. You can split the line with carriage returns (as in the preceding example), but don't insert any spaces or other characters.*

Summary

As you can see, you can access a number of common Internet services from CompuServe, even though CompuServe's direct Internet access is currently limited to e-mail. You can make use of several important Internet services through CompuServe's Internet e-mail, including mailing lists, ftp, archie, and WAIS. Although the services aren't as easy to use through e-mail, you can use them to get information just as though you had direct access to them.

Part III of this book, "A Resource Guide to the Internet," provides information about some of the Internet resources you can access. Chapter 9 discusses a number of interesting ftp sites, whereas Chapter 11 discusses e-mail lists that pertain to some popular topics. These chapters should give you a good start for your exploration of the Internet.

Chapter 5

Using the Internet via Prodigy

Prodigy is one of the largest nationwide commercial on-line services. Since its beginning in 1988, Prodigy has offered many on-line services, including news and weather, sports, entertainment, and reference services. Prodigy also offers an e-mail connection to the Internet, which lets you access many Internet services.

This chapter explains how to:

- Send Internet e-mail

- Locate files using an e-mail archie server

- Download files using an e-mail ftp server

- Locate information using an e-mail WAIS server

This chapter assumes that you already know how to connect to Prodigy and have your Prodigy software running. This chapter also assumes that you have the Prodigy Mail Manager software. You can download the Mail Manager software from the Prodigy system.

Note: *The examples in this chapter were made using the Microsoft Windows version of the Prodigy Software and the DOS version of Mail Manager software for Prodigy. If you are running different versions of the software, your screens may look slightly different from what is shown.*

Sending and Receiving Internet E-Mail

Sending Internet e-mail on Prodigy is done using the Prodigy Mail Manager software. This software, separate from the program you use to connect to the Prodigy system, allows you to compose and read mail off-line (that is, while you aren't connected to the Prodigy system). This feature can be useful, because you can compose or read a large mail message without incurring connect time charges from the Prodigy system.

When you connect to the Prodigy system, you can upload your mail and it will be sent to the Internet addresses you specified. When you are connected to Prodigy, you also can download any mail you have received to your local disk, where you can use the Prodigy Mail Manager software to read it at your leisure.

Note: *Sending and receiving Internet e-mail on Prodigy may carry extra charges. You should review the Prodigy charge rates before using Internet e-mail.*

Sending Internet E-Mail

This section will show you how to use Prodigy to send Internet e-mail. To understand the process, you will send e-mail to an automatic mail server set up for this book. The address you will send the mail to is book@pittslug.sug.org.

To send Internet e-mail from Prodigy, follow these steps:

1. Start the DOS Prodigy Mail Manager software.

Prodigy Mail Manager's main screen.

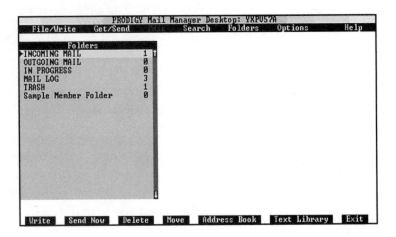

2. Click the Write button. The Delivery Method dialog box appears, asking you what type of message this will be.

Mail Manager asks for the delivery method for this message.

3. Select Internet E-Mail and then click OK. This tells Mail Manager that you will be sending a message to an Internet address.

4. Mail Manager now asks you to enter the recipients and subject for the message. In the top area (next to the TO: prompt), type **book@pittslug.sug.org**. Then move to the SUBJECT: area (click it or press Tab) and type **hello**.

Filling in the recipient and subject fields with the information you need to send a message to the book e-mail server.

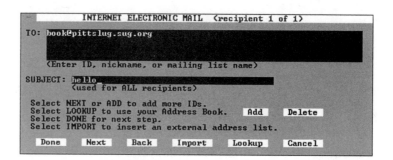

5. Choose Done.

6. You can now type the body of your message. This particular message doesn't require anything in the body, so you can type anything you like.

Typing the body of
the message to the
Internet book
server.

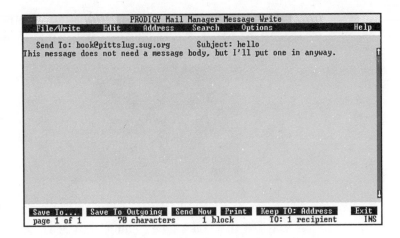

7. Click the Save to Outgoing button. This stores the message on your local disk, from which it will be sent the next time you use the Get/Send Mail feature when you are connected to Prodigy.

8. A message box appears. Click OK.

9. You can now exit the Mail Manager software by choosing Exit.

10. To actually deliver the message, start up Prodigy and jump to the **mail manager** keyword. The Mail Manager screen within Prodigy lets you upload your message and download any Internet messages you have received.

The Prodigy Mail
Manager screen is
used to send the
Internet message.

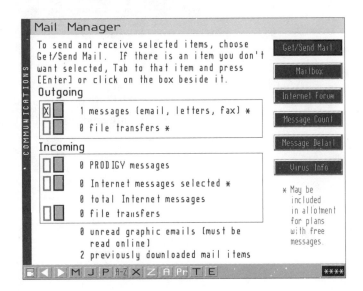

The Prodigy Mail Manager screen shows you what will be uploaded and downloaded. It tells you how many Internet (or Prodigy) mail messages will be transferred and whether you have any file transfers. When you start the transfer, the system tells you how much of the transfer has taken place.

11. Click the Get/Send Mail button. Prodigy uploads the mail from your local disk to the Prodigy main system and delivers it to the recipients you specified.

    Prodigy confirms that your message has been uploaded by removing the X from the outgoing message box.

Prodigy usually takes only a few minutes to process and send your mail to the Internet host you specified.

Reading Internet E-Mail

The process of reading mail you have received from an Internet address is similar to sending Internet mail. You use the Prodigy Mail Manager screen to download the Internet mail to your local disk, and then use the separate Mail Manager software to actually read the message.

Prodigy tells you when you have new mail waiting to be read (either from the Internet or Prodigy) by putting an envelope icon at the lower right corner of the screen. To read your Internet e-mail, follow these steps:

1. Jump to your mailbox by clicking the envelope at the bottom right of your screen or by jumping to **mail**. The information on your Internet message appears in your mailbox.

The Prodigy
mailbox, with the
message you have
received from the
Internet book
server.

Message from
the book server

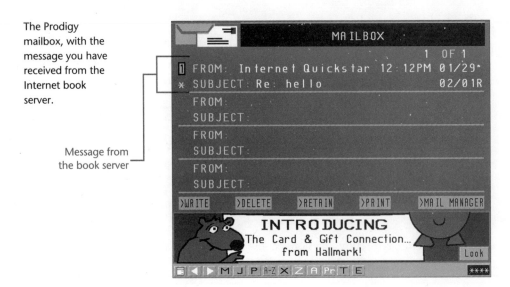

Note: *If you try to read an Internet mail message on the regular Prodigy
mail screen, Prodigy will tell you that you must download the mail using
the Prodigy Mail Manager software. You cannot read Internet mail messages on-line with the Prodigy software.*

2. Click the Mail Manager button to move to Prodigy's Mail Manager
screen. Prodigy asks you to confirm that you want to accept delivery of the Internet mail message, because of the extra charges that
may be involved.

The Prodigy Mail
Manager Internet/
COD Selection
dialog box lets you
select which type of
message you want
to download.

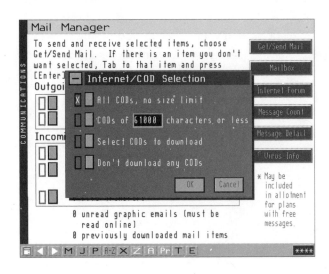

3. Click the All CODs button to tell Prodigy that you will accept all the messages (without a size limit). An X appears next to the selection. Then choose OK to allow downloading of the messages.

4. From the Prodigy Mail Manager screen, click the Get/Send Mail button to download the Internet message to your local disk, where you can read it with the off-line Mail Manager software. During the download, a Download in Progress box shows how much of the files have been downloaded.

5. After the download is complete, exit Prodigy.

6. Start the Mail Manager software. The Incoming Mail Messages screen shows that you have the new message from the Internet book server.

The Prodigy Mail Manager software showing the messages you have received.

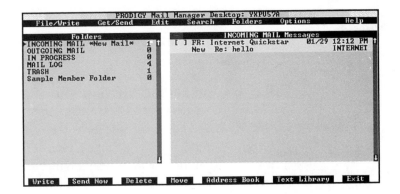

7. Double-click the line showing the message from the Internet Quickstart address to display the message you have received.

The Prodigy Mail Manager displays the message from the Internet Quickstart mail server.

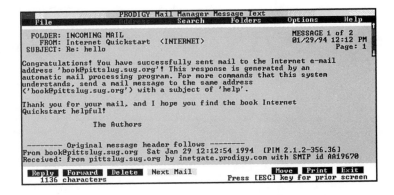

8. If you don't want to keep this message, click the Delete button to remove it from your disk. Alternatively, you can move the message to a different mail folder by clicking the Move button.

As you can see, sending and reading Internet e-mail through Prodigy is easy.

Locating Files with an E-Mail archie Server

archie
An application that lets you search easily for information at anonymous ftp sites on the Internet.

ftp
A program that lets you transfer data between different computers on a network.

telnet
A program that allows remote login to another computer.

archie (as described in Chapter 1, "Introducing the Internet") is a useful way to locate files on Internet *ftp* servers. Because Prodigy doesn't have direct access to an archie server (and doesn't let you use *telnet* to connect to a machine that does have an archie server), you will have to use Internet e-mail to send commands to an archie e-mail server.

For the examples in this section, you will use the archie e-mail server on the machine `archie.internic.net`.

Requesting the archie Help Message

The first thing you need to do is ask the archie server to send you a message telling you how to use the server. You do so by sending an e-mail message with the word `help` in the message body. (If you aren't familiar with the details of how to send an Internet mail message, see the earlier section "Sending Internet E-Mail.") To send this message to the archie server, follow these steps:

1. Start the off-line Mail Manager software and click the Write button to start sending a message.

2. Select Internet E-Mail from the list of mail types and then click OK.

3. For the address to send the message to, type `archie@archie.internic.net`. Click Done.

4. Type the word `help` in the message body.

The complete help message for the archie e-mail server includes help in the message body.

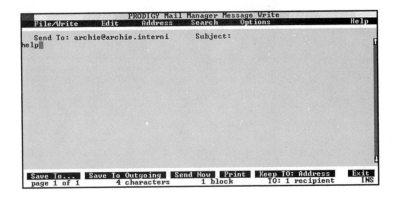

5. Click Save to Outgoing to save the message on your local disk for delivery when you log in to Prodigy.

6. Exit the Prodigy Mail Manager by choosing Exit.

You can now connect to Prodigy and upload the message, as described earlier in the section "Sending Internet E-Mail."

Prodigy may take a few minutes to process and send your mail to the archie server. Generally, the archie server will respond quickly to your request. Prodigy will let you know when you have received a response to your message by putting an envelope icon at the bottom of your screen.

Reading the archie Help Message

Reading the mail you have received from the archie server is the same as reading mail from any other Internet host. When you receive an Internet e-mail message on Prodigy, you must download the message to your local disk from Prodigy's Mail Manager screen. Follow the instructions in the earlier section "Reading Internet E-Mail" for instructions on how to do this.

After you download the message, start the off-line Mail Manager software. The Incoming Mail Message screen shows that you have a new message from the archie server. Double-click this line to read the message.

5

The Help message from the archie e-mail server explains how to use the server.

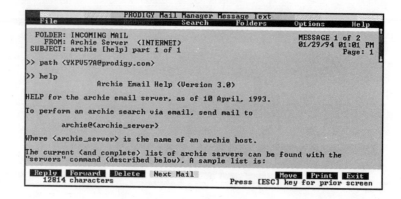

If you don't want to keep this message on your disk, you can remove it by clicking the Delete button. You can move the message to another folder by clicking the Move button.

Searching for a File

Request For Comments

RFC, a document submitted to the Internet governing board to propose Internet standards or to document information about the Internet.

You will now use the e-mail archie server to search for a file. As an example, you will search for the file rfc822.txt. This file is an Internet *Request For Comments* document that explains the format of an Internet e-mail message.

To send the e-mail message to the archie server, do the following:

1. Start the Mail Manager software and click the Write button to start sending a message.

2. Select Internet E-Mail from the list of mail types and then click OK.

3. For the address to send the message to, type **archie@archie.internic.net**. Click Done.

4. Type **find rfc822.txt** in the message body.

The complete message includes the find *filename* command

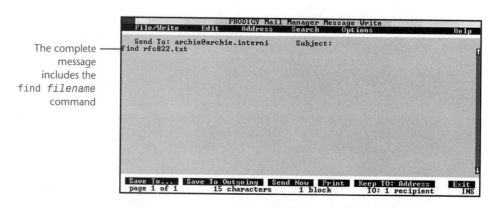

5. Click Save to Outgoing to save the message on your local disk for delivery when you log in to Prodigy.

6. Exit the Prodigy Mail Manager by clicking Exit.

You can now connect to Prodigy and upload the message, as described earlier in the section "Sending Internet E-Mail."

Prodigy may take a few minutes to process and send your mail to the archie server. Generally, the archie server will respond quickly to your request. Prodigy will let you know on-line when you receive a response to your message.

Reading the Results of the Search

After you are notified that you have received a mail message, you must download the message to your local disk from the Prodigy Mail Manager screen. Follow the instructions in the earlier section "Reading Internet E-Mail" for instructions on how to do this.

To read the message after you download it, start the off-line Mail Manager program. The Incoming Mail Message screen shows that you have a new message from the archie server. Double-click this line to read the message.

The results of the archie file search. The message has been scrolled down to show a complete file listing.

```
                    PRODIGY Mail Manager Message Text
   File                      Address    Search    Folders    Options       Help

    FOLDER: INCOMING MAIL                              MESSAGE 1 of 1
      FROM: Archie Server  <INTERNET>                  01/29/94 01:28 PM
   SUBJECT: archie [find rfc822.txt] part 1 of 1                Page: 3


Host sunsite.unc.edu    (152.2.22.81)
Last updated 08:05 22 Dec 1993

    Location: /pub/docs/rfc
        FILE   -r--r--r--  106299 bytes  23:00 19 Apr 1991  rfc822.txt


Host ugle.unit.no    (129.241.1.97)
Last updated 07:06  2 Dec 1993

    Location: /pub/rfc
        FILE   -rw-r--r--  106299 bytes  01:00 17 Mar 1988  rfc822.txt


  Reply  Forward  Delete                        Move  Print  Exit
    8733 characters                    Press [ESC] key for prior screen
```

If you don't want to keep this message on disk, you can remove it by clicking Delete. You can move the message to another folder by clicking Move.

As you can see from the results of the search, the file rfc822.txt is available at several different Internet ftp sites. You will use one of these sites to download the file in an example in the following section.

Downloading Files Using an E-Mail ftp Server

Since Prodigy doesn't have direct access to the ftp program, you will have to use an e-mail ftp server to download files from Internet ftp sites. To use an e-mail ftp server, you send a message containing commands that tell the server which ftp site to connect to, which directory the files are in, and which files to download. The e-mail ftp server processes your message and—if the commands are correct—returns the file you requested in an e-mail response.

In this example, you will use the ftp e-mail server located on host decwrl.dec.com. The e-mail address for the server is ftpmail@decwrl.dec.com.

Requesting the ftp E-Mail Server Help Message

The first thing you need to do is ask the ftp e-mail server to send you a message telling you how to use the server. You can do so by sending an e-mail message with the word **help** in the message body. To send this e-mail message to the server, follow these steps:

1. Start the off-line Mail Manager software and click the Write button.

2. Select Internet E-Mail from the list of mail types and then click OK.

3. For the address to send the message to, type **ftpmail@decwrl.dec.com**. Click Done.

4. Type **help** in the message body.

The complete help message for the ftp e-mail server includes the word help in the message body.

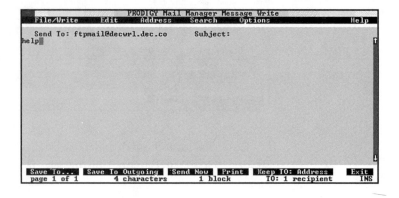

5. Click Save to Outgoing to save the message on your local disk for delivery when you log in to Prodigy.

6. Exit the Prodigy Mail Manager now by clicking Exit.

You can now connect to Prodigy and upload the message, as described earlier in the section "Sending Internet E-Mail."

Prodigy may take a few minutes to process and send your mail to the ftp e-mail server. Generally, the ftp server will respond quickly to your request. The Prodigy system will let you know on-line when you have received a response to your message.

Reading the ftp Help Message

After you are notified that you have received a mail message, you must download the message to your local disk from the Prodigy Mail Manager screen. Follow the instructions in the earlier section "Reading Internet E-Mail" for instructions on how to do this.

To read the ftp e-mail server's help message after you download it, start the off-line Mail Manager software. The Incoming Mail Message screen shows that you have a new message from the ftp e-mail server. Double-click this line to read the message.

The ftp e-mail server help message explains how to use the server. The message has been scrolled down to show some of the help message.

```
                         PRODIGY Mail Manager Message Text
    File                    Search         Folders        Options        Help
    FOLDER: INCOMING MAIL                                    MESSAGE 1 of 1
       FROM: ftpmail service on ftp-gw-1.pa.dec.com  <INTERNET  01/29/94 01:43 PM
    SUBJECT: your ftpmail request has been received                    Page: 1

>>> commands are:

        reply <MAILADDR>         set reply addr, since headers are usually wrong
        connect [HOST [USER [PASS [ACCT]]]]
                                 defaults to gatekeeper.dec.com, anonymous
        ascii                    files grabbed are printable ascii
        binary                   files grabbed are compressed or tar or both
        chdir PLACE              "get" and "ls" commands are relative to PLACE
                                 (only one CHDIR per ftpmail session,
                                 and it executes before any LS/DIR/GETs)
        compress                 compress binaries using Lempel-Ziv encoding
        compact                  compress binaries using Huffman encoding
        uuencode                 binary files will be mailed in uuencode format
        btoa                     binary files will be mailed in btoa format
        chunksize SIZE           split files into SIZE-byte chunks (def: 64000)

    Reply  Forward  Delete                        Move  Print  Exit
      6821 characters                        Press [ESC] key for prior screen
```

If you don't want to keep this message on disk, you can remove it by clicking Delete. You can move the message to another folder by clicking Move.

Sending a File Download Request

Now you will use the e-mail ftp server to download a file. As an example, you will use the information retrieved by the archie search to download the file. As seen in the archie example, the file rfc822.txt is located on the site sunsite.unc.edu in the directory /pub/docs/rfc. This information will let you set up the file download request.

To send this e-mail message to the server, follow these steps:

1. Start the Prodigy Mail Manager software and click the Write button.

2. Select Internet E-Mail from the list of mail types.

3. Type **ftpmail@decwrl.dec.com** as the address to send the message to.

4. In the Subject field, type **get rfc822.txt**. (The ftp e-mail server ignores the subject of the message, but typing one now will help identify the response you get back from the server.) Click Done.

5. In the message body, enter the following:

   ```
   connect sunsite.unc.edu
   chdir /pub/docs/rfc
   get rfc822.txt
   quit
   ```

The complete message includes commands to connect to the server,

change to the appropriate directory,

and retrieve the file.

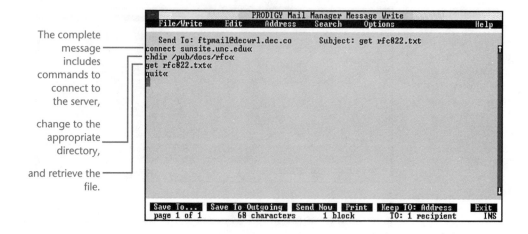

6. Click Save to Outgoing to save the message on your local disk for delivery when you log in to Prodigy.

You now can connect to Prodigy and upload the message, as described earlier in the section "Sending Internet E-Mail."

Prodigy may take a few minutes to process and send your mail to the ftp e-mail server. Generally, the ftp server will respond quickly to your request. The Prodigy system will let you know on-line when you have received a response.

Reading the File Request Results

The ftp e-mail server will acknowledge your file request with an e-mail message. This first message tells you that the server received your request and how many other requests are before yours.

After you are notified that you have received a mail message, you must download the message to your local disk from the Prodigy Mail Manager screen. Follow the instructions in the earlier section "Reading Internet E-Mail" for instructions on how to do this.

To read the response from the ftp e-mail server after you download it, start the off-line Mail Manager software. The Incoming Mail Message screen shows that you have a new message from the ftp e-mail server. Double-click this line to read the message.

An ftp e-mail server response message confirms that your message has been received.

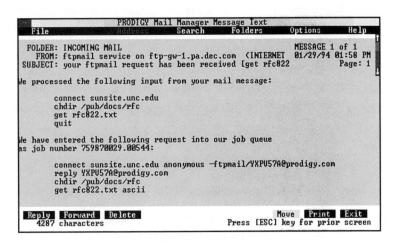

```
                       PRODIGY Mail Manager Message Text
      File          Address        Search       Folders      Options       Help

   FOLDER: INCOMING MAIL                                    MESSAGE 1 of 1
     FROM: ftpmail service on ftp-gw-1.pa.dec.com  <INTERNET  01/29/94 01:58 PM
   SUBJECT: your ftpmail request has been received [get rfc822    Page: 1

 We processed the following input from your mail message:

        connect sunsite.unc.edu
        chdir /pub/docs/rfc
        get rfc822.txt
        quit

 We have entered the following request into our job queue
 as job number 759870029.00544:

        connect sunsite.unc.edu anonymous -ftpmail/YXPU57A@prodigy.com
        reply YXPU57A@prodigy.com
        chdir /pub/docs/rfc
        get rfc822.txt ascii


   Reply  Forward  Delete                      Move  Print  Exit
      4287 characters                   Press [ESC] key for prior screen
```

If you don't want to keep this message on disk, you can remove it by clicking Delete. You can move the message to another folder by clicking Move.

The actual file you requested will come in a separate mail message. Because the decwrl ftp server is used by people throughout the Internet, many requests may be queued before yours, and it may take several days for your file to arrive. When it does arrive, it will come in a new mail message that you can download to your local disk.

Locating Information with an E-Mail WAIS Server

WAIS
Wide Area Information Servers, a system for searching and retrieving documents from participating sites.

This chapter has already discussed how to use the e-mail archie server to locate files on ftp sites. *WAIS* is another information retrieval system that you can use via e-mail to locate information in document databases.

For the examples in the following sections, you will use the WAIS e-mail server on the machine quake.think.com. The e-mail address to use to send a message to the server is waismail@quake.think.com.

Requesting a Help Message from the WAIS E-Mail Server

The first thing you will do is send a request to the WAIS e-mail server for the help message (which describes the commands that the server recognizes). To do so, send an e-mail message with the word help in the message body. To send this message to the server, follow these steps:

1. Start the off-line Mail Manager software and click the Write button.

2. Select Internet E-Mail from the list of mail types and then click OK.

3. Type **waismail@quake.think.com** as the address.

4. In the Subject field, type **help**. (The WAIS e-mail server ignores the subject of the message, but this will help identify the response you get back from the server.) Click Done.

5. In the message body, type **help**.

The complete
message for the
WAIS e-mail server
includes help in the
message body.

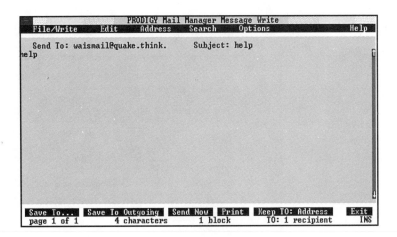

6. Click Save to Outgoing to save the message on your local disk for delivery when you log in to Prodigy.

7. Exit the Prodigy Mail Manager now by clicking Exit.

You can now connect to Prodigy and upload the message, as described earlier in the section "Sending Internet E-Mail."

Prodigy may take a few minutes to process and send your mail to the WAIS e-mail server. Generally, the WAIS server will respond quickly to your request. Prodigy will let you know on-line when you receive a response.

Reading the WAIS E-Mail Server Help Message

The WAIS e-mail server will send you its help message in an e-mail message. After you are notified that you have received a mail message, you must download the message to your local disk from the Prodigy Mail Manager screen. Follow the instructions in the earlier section "Reading Internet E-Mail" for instructions on how to do this.

To read the WAIS help message after you download it, start the off-line Mail Manager software. The Incoming Mail Message screen shows that you have a new message from the WAIS e-mail server. Double-click this line to read the message.

The WAIS e-mail server's help message explains how to use the WAIS server. The message has been scrolled down to show the beginning of the available commands.

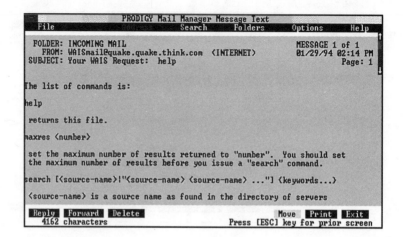

If you don't want to keep this message on your disk, you can remove it by clicking Delete. You can move the message to another folder by clicking Move.

Sending a Search Request to the WAIS E-Mail Server

Now that you know how to send commands to the WAIS e-mail server, you can use it to search the WAIS databases. For this example, you will search for speeches that President Clinton has made that have the word *atlanta* in them.

First, you must search the WAIS directory of servers to see which databases contain speeches by President Clinton. To do so, you must send the WAIS e-mail server a message with the command search directory-of-servers clinton. The WAIS server will search through the master list of databases available for all those that have documents with the word *clinton* in them.

To send this e-mail message to the server, start the off-line Mail Manager program and follow these steps:

1. Click the Write button.

2. Select Internet E-Mail from the list of mail types and then click OK.

3. Type waismail@quake.think.com as the address.

4. In the Subject field, type search. (The WAIS e-mail server ignores the subject of the message, but this will help identify the response you get back from the server.) Click Done.

5. In the message body, type **search directory-of-servers clinton**.

The complete message includes a search command to find the appropriate server —

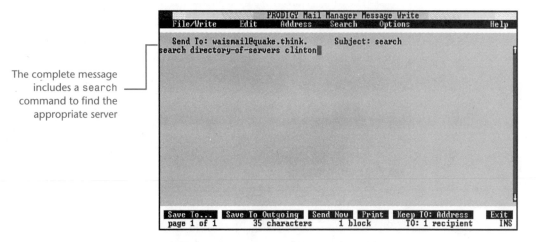

6. Click Save to Outgoing to save the message on your local disk for delivery when you log in to Prodigy.

7. Exit the Prodigy Mail Manager now by clicking Exit.

You can now connect to Prodigy and upload the message, as described earlier in the section "Sending Internet E-Mail."

Prodigy may take a few minutes to process and send your mail to the WAIS e-mail server. Generally, the WAIS server will respond quickly to your request. Prodigy will let you know on-line when you have received a response to your message.

Reading the Response from the WAIS Server

The WAIS e-mail server will send you the results of the search in an e-mail message. After you are notified that you have received a mail message, you must download the message to your local disk from the Prodigy Mail Manager screen. Follow the instructions in the earlier section "Reading Internet E-Mail" for instructions on how to do this.

To read the search results after you download the message, start the offline Mail Manager software. The Incoming Mail Message screen shows that you have a new message from the WAIS e-mail server. Double-click this line to read the message.

The results of the WAIS search.

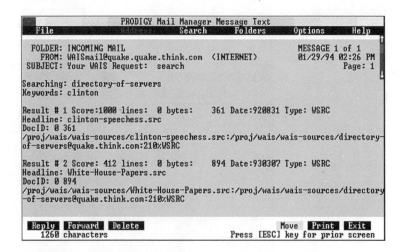

```
┌──────────────────────────────────────────────────────────────────────┐
│                    PRODIGY Mail Manager Message Text                   │
│    File      Address      Search      Folders      Options      Help   │
│                                                                      ↑ │
│   FOLDER: INCOMING MAIL                           MESSAGE 1 of 1       │
│     FROM: WAISmail@quake.think.com  (INTERNET)    01/29/94 02:26 PM    │
│   SUBJECT: Your WAIS Request:  search                       Page: 1    │
│                                                                      ↓ │
│  Searching: directory-of-servers                                       │
│  Keywords: clinton                                                     │
│                                                                        │
│  Result # 1 Score:1000 lines:  0 bytes:    361 Date:920831 Type: WSRC  │
│  Headline: clinton-speechess.src                                       │
│  DocID: 0 361                                                          │
│  /proj/wais/wais-sources/clinton-speechess.src:/proj/wais/wais-sources/directory│
│  -of-servers@quake.think.com:210%WSRC                                  │
│                                                                        │
│  Result # 2 Score: 412 lines:  0 bytes:    894 Date:930307 Type: WSRC  │
│  Headline: White-House-Papers.src                                      │
│  DocID: 0 894                                                          │
│  /proj/wais/wais-sources/White-House-Papers.src:/proj/wais/wais-sources/directory│
│  -of-servers@quake.think.com:210%WSRC                                  │
│                                                                        │
│                                                                        │
│  ▌Reply▐ ▌Forward▐ ▌Delete▐                      ▌Move▐ ▌Print▐ ▌Exit▐ │
│     1260 characters                     Press [ESC] key for prior screen│
└──────────────────────────────────────────────────────────────────────┘
```

If you don't want to keep this message on your disk, you can remove it by clicking Delete. You can move the message to another folder by clicking Move.

From the results returned by the search, you can see that two databases mention President Clinton: clinton-speeches and White-House-Papers. You will use the second database (White-House-Papers) for your next search.

Searching the White-House-Papers Database

Now you will search the White-House-Papers database for those documents that mention Atlanta. To do this, send an e-mail message to the WAIS server with the command search White-House-Papers atlanta. The WAIS server will return to you a list of all the documents in the White-House-Papers database that have the word *atlanta* in them.

To send this e-mail message to the server, start the off-line Mail Manager program and follow these steps:

1. Click the Write button to start sending a message.

2. Select Internet E-Mail from the list of mail types and then click OK.

3. Type **waismail@quake.think.com** as the address.

4. In the Subject field, type **search**. (The WAIS e-mail server ignores the subject of the message, but this will help identify the response you get back from the server.) Click Done.

5. In the message body, type search **White-House-Papers atlanta**.

Note: *Make sure that you type the command exactly as shown; the WAIS server is case-sensitive!*

The complete message for the WAIS e-mail server contains the search command to search the appropriate database for a supplied keyword.

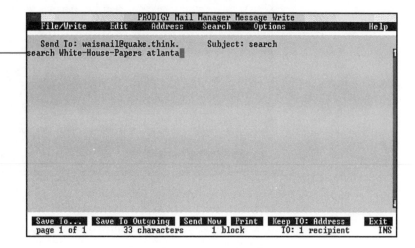

6. Click Save to Outgoing to save the message on your local disk for delivery when you log in to Prodigy.

7. Exit the Prodigy Mail Manager now by clicking Exit.

You can now connect to Prodigy and upload the message, as described earlier in the section "Sending Internet E-Mail."

Prodigy may take a few minutes to process and send your mail to the WAIS e-mail server. Generally, the WAIS server will respond quickly to your request. The Prodigy system will let you know when you have received a response to your message.

Reading the Search Response from the WAIS Server

The WAIS e-mail server will send you the results of the search in an e-mail message. After you are notified that you have received a mail message, you must download the message to your local disk from the Prodigy Mail Manager screen. Follow the instructions in the section "Reading Internet E-Mail" for instructions on how to do this.

To read the search results after you download the message, start the off-line Mail Manager software. The Incoming Mail Message screen shows that you have a new message from the WAIS e-mail server. Double-click this line to read the message.

The results of the WAIS search.

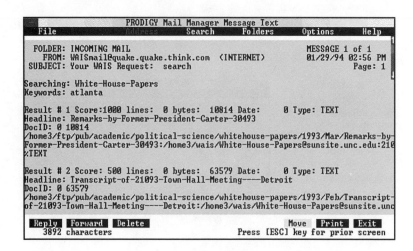

```
                       PRODIGY Mail Manager Message Text
     File        Address         Search      Folders      Options       Help

   FOLDER: INCOMING MAIL                            MESSAGE 1 of 1
     FROM: WAISmail@quake.quake.think.com  (INTERNET)    01/29/94 02:56 PM
  SUBJECT: Your WAIS Request:  search                         Page: 1

 Searching: White-House-Papers
 Keywords: atlanta

 Result # 1 Score:1000 lines:   0 bytes:  10814 Date:      0 Type: TEXT
 Headline: Remarks-by-Former-President-Carter-30493
 DocID: 0 10814
 /home3/ftp/pub/academic/political-science/whitehouse-papers/1993/Mar/Remarks-by-
 Former-President-Carter-30493:/home3/wais/White-House-Papers@sunsite.unc.edu:210
 %TEXT

 Result # 2 Score: 500 lines:   0 bytes:  63579 Date:      0 Type: TEXT
 Headline: Transcript-of-21093-Town-Hall-Meeting----Detroit
 DocID: 0 63579
 /home3/ftp/pub/academic/political-science/whitehouse-papers/1993/Feb/Transcript-
 of-21093-Town-Hall-Meeting----Detroit:/home3/wais/White-House-Papers@sunsite.unc

    Reply   Forward   Delete                         Move   Print   Exit
      3892 characters                    Press [ESC] key for prior screen
```

If you don't want to keep this message on your disk, you can remove it by clicking Delete. You can move the message to another folder by clicking Move.

You can see that quite a few documents have the word *atlanta* in them. You can retrieve any of these documents by sending the `retrieve` command to the WAIS server. The `retrieve` command uses the DocID (for Document ID) from the search results. So to retrieve the second document on the list, you would send the WAIS e-mail server the command

```
retrieve 0 63579 /home3/ftp/pub/academic/political-science/
whitehouse-papers/1993/Feb/Transcript-of-21093-Town-Hall-
Meeting----Detroit:/home3/wais/White-House-
Papers@sunsite.unc.edu:210%TEXT
```

If you have problems...

You must type the entire DocID for the `retrieve` command to work correctly. If you don't, the WAIS system won't be able to find the right document and will return an error message to you. You can split the line with carriage returns (as in the preceding example), but don't insert any spaces or other characters.

When you send a `retrieve` command to get a document, the WAIS e-mail server finds the correct document and returns it to you in a mail message. You should receive this message within a few minutes of sending your request.

Summary

As you can see, you can access a number of common Internet services from Prodigy, even though Prodigy's direct Internet access is limited to e-mail. You can make use of several important Internet services through Prodigy's Internet e-mail, including mailing lists, ftp, archie, and WAIS. Although the services aren't as easy to use through e-mail, you still can use them to get information just as though you had direct access to them.

5

Chapter 6

Using the Internet via America Online

Founded in 1985, America Online (AOL) is one of the fastest growing providers of on-line services in the United States. It offers many different on-line services, including software downloads, educational information, entertainment, and computer manufacturer support. The America Online system provides an easy-to-use graphical interface to its services.

In addition to the on-line services, America Online provides access to Internet e-mail and mailing lists, allowing you to send and receive e-mail from any Internet host and to subscribe to a large number of Internet mailing lists.

In the near future, AOL plans to offer direct connections to other Internet services, such as ftp file transfers, Gopher, WAIS, and telnet. These services weren't available at the time this book was being written. You should check with the AOL service personnel as to what is available now.

This chapter explains how to:

- ■ Send Internet e-mail
- ■ Locate files using an e-mail archie server
- ■ Download files using an e-mail ftp server
- ■ Locate information using an e-mail WAIS server

This chapter assumes that you already know how to connect to AOL, and have your America Online software set up and running.

Note: *The examples in this chapter were made using the Microsoft Windows version of the America Online software; if you are running a different version of the software, your screens may look slightly different than what is shown.*

Sending and Receiving Internet E-Mail

You can send Internet e-mail on America Online at any time while you are connected to America Online. You can use the mail system at any point in the AOL system, and your mail will be delivered immediately to Internet recipients when you send the mail.

Note: *Sending and receiving Internet e-mail on America Online carries extra charges. You should review AOL's charge rates before using Internet e-mail.*

Sending Internet E-Mail

This section will show you how to use the AOL system to send Internet e-mail. To understand the process, you will send e-mail to an automatic mail server set up for this book. The address you will send the mail to is book@pittslug.sug.org.

To send Internet e-mail from America Online, follow these steps:

1. Pull down the **M**ail menu and choose Compose Mail. The Compose Mail dialog box appears.

The Compose Mail dialog box, which lets you enter the information about the message you are sending.

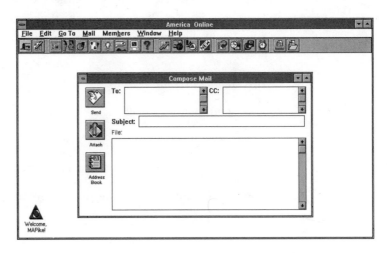

2. In the To field, enter the recipients for the message you are sending. For this example, type `book@pittslug.sug.org`.

3. In the Subject area, type `hello` for this example.

   Note: *For the mail server to understand your message, make sure that you type the information exactly as listed in the steps.*

4. In the message body area at the bottom of the dialog box, type anything you want, although this particular message doesn't require a message body.

5. Click the Send button to send the message to your recipient.

Enter the address,

subject,

and body of the message,

then click the Send button.

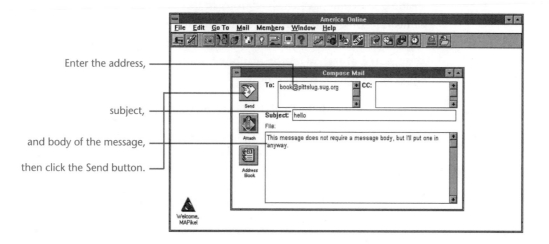

6. A message box appears, telling you that the message was sent. Click OK to dismiss this box.

America Online may take a few minutes to process your mail and send it to the Internet host you specified. The book mail server usually will respond immediately to your request.

If you have problems...

If you get an error message saying that the message couldn't be delivered and giving a short description of the problem, check to make sure that the address you typed is correct. If the host name was incorrect, you may get an error message such as host unknown; if you typed the name of the user you are trying to send to incorrectly, you may get an error message such as user unknown.

(continues)

You may also encounter other problems in sending mail from America Online to Internet machines. The machine you are sending mail to could be unavailable, for example, or a temporary problem may exist in the network between AOL and the destination machine.

In either situation, AOL will try several times to deliver your message but may eventually send you an error message. In this case, you can try to send the message again. If your mail continues to fail, you can send a message to the America Online staff asking for help in diagnosing the problem.

Reading Internet E-Mail

Reading mail you have received from an Internet address is exactly the same as reading mail from people internal to America Online. The AOL system informs you that you have mail waiting when you connect to the system, and also changes the mailbox button in the upper left corner of the screen to have letters in it.

To read your Internet e-mail, follow these steps:

1. Pull down the **M**ail menu and choose Read New Mail, or click the mailbox button on the upper left corner of the screen to open the mail reading window.

   The New Mail dialog box appears, listing the mail messages you have received.

The AOL New Mail dialog box shows mail messages you have received.

   Note: *America Online doesn't allow you to move a mail message to another folder, but you can use the Ignore button in the New Mail dialog box to delete a mail message without reading it.*

2. Double-click the line with the message from the book server. The message you have received appears in a new window.

AOL displays the message in a new dialog box, from which you can forward or reply to the message.

Reply buttons

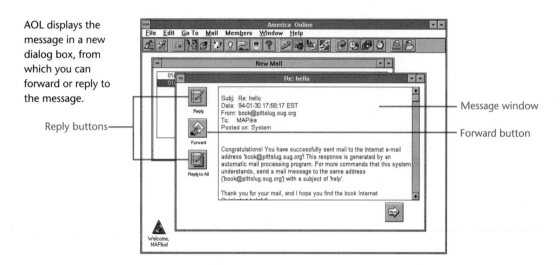

Message window

Forward button

As you can see, sending and reading Internet e-mail on America Online is easy. After you read a mail message, America Online gives you the option to reply to the message, forward it to another user, or reply to all people listed in the message. These options are the same as for regular AOL mail.

Accessing Internet Mailing Lists

America Online provides an on-line list of Internet mailing lists and helps you subscribe to these lists. You can search the on-line list of mailing lists for topics that are of interest to you, which makes finding a mailing list with useful information easy.

The Internet mailing list services are found in the America Online Internet Center. You can get to the Internet Center by pulling down the **G**o To menu, choosing Keyword, and typing **internet**.

The America Online Internet Center window.

6

When you are in the Internet Center, you can click the Mailing Lists button to bring up the Internet Mailing Lists dialog box. In this dialog box, you can search the on-line list of mailing lists for topics that interest you.

The America Online Internet Mailing Lists window, showing the text files available and the Search Mailing Lists button.

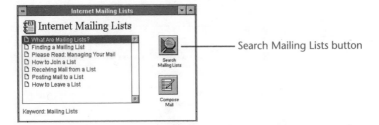

Search Mailing Lists button

Several text files that are available give you information about finding, joining, reading, and quitting Internet mailing lists on the America Online system. If you are interested in joining an Internet mailing list, these files are useful. Much of the information in these files is also available in Chapter 1, "Introducing the Internet."

Also available in this window is the Search Mailing Lists button, which lets you search through America Online's list of Internet mailing lists.

As an example of searching for a mailing list, suppose that you are interested in finding mailing lists that talk about musical instruments in the brass family. In the search window, type **brass and musical** and then choose List Articles to begin the search.

The America Online mailing list search function, after a search for "brass and musical" to find the brass mailing list.

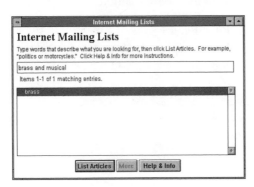

America Online searches through its on-line database and returns the single mailing list called "brass." For a brief description of this mailing list, click the brass line in the results box.

The description of the brass mailing list, giving the address to use to subscribe to the list.

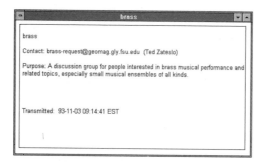

If you want to subscribe to this mailing list, click the Compose Mail button in the Internet Mailing Lists window to bring up the America Online compose mail window. You can use cut and paste to copy the subscription address from the description of the mailing list.

Reading an Internet mailing list is exactly the same as reading any other Internet mail; when you subscribe to a mailing list, you normally receive information telling you how to send messages to the list and how to send messages to the person who runs the list.

Locating Files with an E-Mail archie Server

archie
An application that allows you to search easily for information at anonymous ftp sites on the Internet.

archie (as described in Chapter 1, "Introducing the Internet") is a very useful way to locate files on Internet ftp servers. Because America Online doesn't currently have direct access to an archie server (and also doesn't currently let you use *telnet* to connect to a machine that does have an archie server), you will have to use Internet e-mail to send commands to an archie e-mail server.

For the examples in this section, you will use the archie e-mail server on the machine `archie.internic.net`.

telnet
A program that allows remote login to another computer.

Requesting the archie Help Message

The first thing you need to do is ask the archie server to send you a message telling you how to use the server. Do this by sending an e-mail message with the word `help` in the message body. To send this message to the archie server, follow these steps:

6

1. Pull down the **M**ail menu and choose Compose Mail to open the Compose Mail dialog box.

2. In the To field, type `archie@archie.internic.net` and then press Tab twice to move to the Subject area of the dialog box.

3. Type the word `help` for the subject. Press Tab to move to the message body area.

4. Type `quit` for the message body. This command is ignored by the archie server, but the America Online software requires you to have something in the message body.

The complete message for the archie e-mail server with the address and `help` subject.

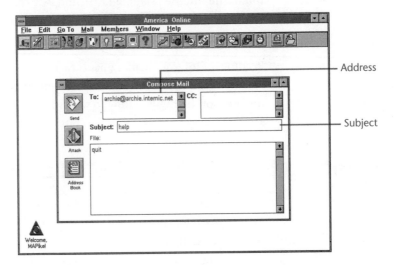

5. Click the Send button to send the message to the archie e-mail server.

6. A message box appears, telling you that the message was sent. Click OK to dismiss this box.

America Online may take a few minutes to process and send your mail to the archie server. Generally, the archie server will respond quickly to your request.

Reading the archie Help Message
The America Online system will tell you when you receive a response to your message by putting letters inside the mailbox button at the top

of the screen. Then you can read the archie help message by following these steps:

1. To display the list of mail messages you have received, click the mailbox button in the upper left corner of the screen, or pull down the **M**ail menu and choose Read New Mail.

2. On the list of mail messages, double-click the line from the archie e-mail server.

The help message from the archie e-mail server appears in a new window.

The help message from the archie e-mail server tells you more about how to use the archie server.

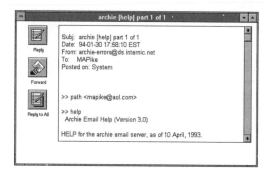

Searching for a File

Request For Comments

RFC, a document submitted to the Internet governing board to propose Internet standards or to document information about the Internet.

Now you will use the archie server to search for a file. For this example, you will search for the file rfc822.txt, which is an Internet *Request For Comments* document that explains the format of an Internet e-mail message.

To send the e-mail message to the archie server, do the following:

1. Open the Compose Mail dialog box by pulling down the **M**ail menu and choosing Compose Mail.

2. In the To field, type **archie@archie.internic.net**. Press Tab twice to move to the Subject area.

3. Type **find rfc822.txt** for the subject. Press Tab to move to the message body area.

4. Type **quit** for the message body. This command is ignored by the archie server, but the America Online software requires that you have something in the message body.

6

To tell the archie server to search for a file, use the `find` command with the file name as an argument. The `find` command is in the subject of the message.

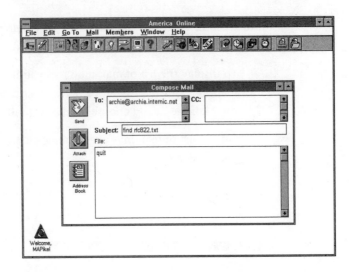

5. Click the Send button to send the message to the archie e-mail server.

6. A message box appears, telling you that the message was sent. Click OK to dismiss this box.

America Online may take a few minutes to process and send your mail to the archie server. Generally, the archie server will respond quickly to your request.

Reading the Results of the Search

The America Online system tells you when you have received a response to your message by putting mail inside the mailbox button at the top of the screen. You can read the results of the archie search by following these steps:

1. To display the list of mail messages you have received, click the mailbox button, or pull down the **M**ail menu and choose Read New Mail.

2. In the list of mail messages, double-click the line from the archie e-mail server.

The help message from the archie e-mail server appears in a new window.

The results of the archie file search. The message has been scrolled down to show a complete file location.

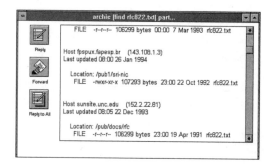

As you can see from the results of the search, the file `rfc822.txt` is available at several different Internet ftp sites. You will use one of these sites to download the file in an example in the next section.

Downloading Files Using an E-Mail ftp Server

ftp
A program that allows you to transfer data between different computers on a network.

Since America Online doesn't currently have direct access to *ftp*, you will have to use an e-mail ftp server to download files from Internet ftp sites.

To use an e-mail ftp server, you will send an e-mail message containing commands that tell the server which ftp site to connect to, which directory the files are in, and which files to download. The e-mail ftp server processes your message and (if the commands are correct) returns the file you requested in an e-mail response.

In the following sections, you will use the ftp e-mail server located on the host `decwrl.dec.com`. The e-mail address for the server is `ftpmail@decwrl.dec.com`.

Requesting the ftp E-Mail Server Help Message

The first thing you will do is ask the ftp e-mail server to send you a message telling you how to use the server. You do this by sending an e-mail message with the word `help` in the message body. To send this e-mail message to the server, follow these steps:

1. Open the Compose Mail dialog box by pulling down the **Mail** menu and choosing Compose Mail.

2. In the To field, type **ftpmail@decwrl.dec.com**. Press Tab twice to move to the Subject area of the dialog box.

3. Type the word **help** for the subject. The ftp e-mail server ignores the subject of the message, but this will help identify the response you get back from the server.

4. Press Tab to move to the message body area. Type **help** for the message body.

The complete message for the ftp e-mail server, requesting help.

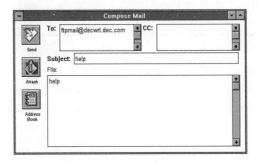

5. Click the Send button to send the message to the ftp e-mail server.

6. A message box appears, telling you that the message was sent. Click OK to dismiss this box.

America Online may take a few minutes to process and send your mail to the ftp e-mail server. Generally, the server will respond quickly to your request.

Reading the ftp Help Message

The America Online system tells you when you have received a response to your message by putting letters in the mailbox button at the top of the screen. You can read the ftp e-mail help message by following these steps:

1. To display the list of received messages, click the mailbox button, or pull down the **M**ail menu and choose Read New Mail.

2. On the list of mail messages, double-click the line from the ftp e-mail server.

The help message from the ftp e-mail server appears in a new window.

The ftp e-mail server help message. The message has been scrolled down to show some of the help message.

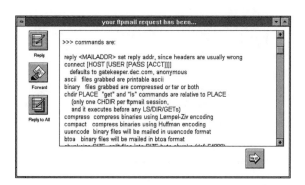

Sending a File Download Request

You now will use the e-mail ftp server to download a file. For this example, you will use the information retrieved by the archie search to download the file. As seen earlier in the archie example, the file rfc822.txt is located on the site sunsite.unc.edu in the directory /pub/docs/rfc. This information will let you set up the file download request.

To send this e-mail message to the server, follow these steps:

1. Open the Compose Mail dialog box by pulling down the **M**ail menu and choosing Compose Mail.

2. In the To field, type **ftpmail@decwrl.dec.com**. Press Tab twice to move to the subject area.

3. Type **get rfc822.txt**. The ftp e-mail server ignores the subject of the message, but this will help identify the response you get back from the server.

4. Type a tab to move to the message body area. In the message body, type the following:

    ```
    connect sunsite.unc.edu
    chdir /pub/docs/rfc
    get rfc822.txt
    quit
    ```

6

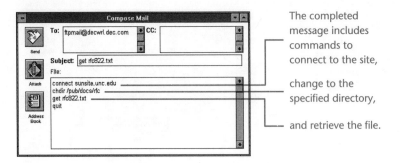

The completed message includes commands to connect to the site,

change to the specified directory,

and retrieve the file.

5. Click the Send button to send the message to the ftp e-mail server.

6. A message box appears, telling you that the message was sent. Click OK to dismiss this box.

America Online may take a few minutes to process and send your message to the ftp e-mail server. Generally, the ftp e-mail server will respond quickly to your request.

Reading the File Request Results

The ftp e-mail server will acknowledge your file request with an e-mail message. This first message tells you that the server received your request and how many other requests are before yours. The actual file you requested will come in a separate e-mail message when the ftp server reaches your request in its queue.

Note: *Because the* decwrl *ftp server is used by many people throughout the Internet, many requests may be queued before yours. It may take a few days before you receive the file you requested; you should be patient.*

When you receive the e-mail message from the ftp e-mail server with the file request acknowledgment, the mailbox button on the AOL screen changes to show letters in it. You can read this acknowledgment by following these steps:

1. To display the list of mail messages you have received, click the mailbox button in the upper left corner of the screen, or pull down the **M**ail menu and choose Read New Mail.

2. On the list of mail messages, double-click the line from the ftp e-mail server.

The file request acknowledgment from the ftp e-mail server appears in a new window.

An ftp e-mail server response message confirms your request.

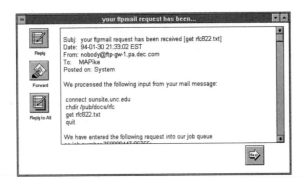

Locating Information with an E-Mail WAIS Server

WAIS
Wide Area Information Servers, a system for searching and retrieving documents from participating sites.

This chapter has already discussed how to use the e-mail archie server to locate files on ftp sites. *WAIS* is another information retrieval system that you can use via e-mail to locate information in document databases.

For the examples in the following sections, you will use the WAIS e-mail server on the machine `quake.think.com`. The e-mail address to use to send a message to the server is `waismail@quake.think.com`.

Requesting a Help Message from the WAIS E-Mail Server

The first thing you need to do is send a request to the WAIS e-mail server for the help message (which describes the commands that the server recognizes). To do this, send an e-mail message with the word `help` in the message body. To send this message to the server, follow these steps:

1. Open the Compose Mail dialog box by pulling down the **M**ail menu and choosing Compose Mail.

2. In the To field, type `waismail@quake.think.com`. Press Tab twice to move to the Subject area.

3. Type **help**. The WAIS e-mail server ignores the subject of the message, but this will help identify the response you get back from the server.

4. Press Tab to move to the message body area. In the message body, type **help**.

The complete help request message for the WAIS server specifies **help** in the body of the message.

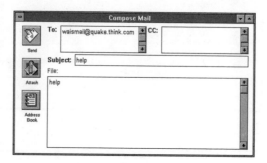

5. Click the Send button to send the message to the ftp e-mail server.

6. You will receive a message box telling you that the message was sent. Click OK to dismiss this box.

America Online may take a few minutes to process and send your mail to the WAIS e-mail server. Generally, the WAIS server will respond quickly to your request.

Reading the WAIS E-Mail Server Help Message

AOL will let you know when you receive a help message back from the WAIS e-mail server by putting letters inside the mailbox button at the top of the screen. You can read this help message by following these steps:

1. To display the list of mail messages you have received, click the mailbox button at the upper left corner of the screen, or pull down the **M**ail menu and choose Read New Mail.

2. On the list of mail messages, double-click the line from the WAIS e-mail server.

The help message from the WAIS e-mail server appears in a new window.

The WAIS e-mail server returns a message with information on how to use the server. The message has been scrolled down to show some of the help message text.

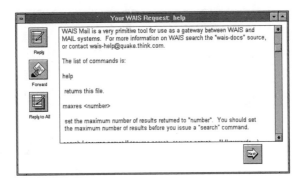

Sending a Search Request to the WAIS E-Mail Server

Now that you know how to send commands to the WAIS e-mail server, you can use it to search the WAIS databases. For the example in this section, you will search for speeches that President Clinton has made that mention the city of Atlanta.

First, you must search the WAIS directory of servers to see which databases contain speeches by President Clinton. To do this, you must send the WAIS e-mail server a message with the command `search directory-of-servers clinton`. The WAIS server will search through the master list of databases available for all those that have documents with the word *clinton* in them.

To send this e-mail message to the server, follow these steps:

1. Open the Compose Mail dialog box by pulling down the **M**ail menu and choosing Compose Mail.

2. In the To field, type `waismail@quake.think.com`. Press Tab twice to move to the Subject area of the dialog box.

3. Type `search`. The WAIS e-mail server ignores the subject of the message, but this will help identify the response you get back from the server.

4. Press Tab to move to the message body area. In the message body, type `search directory-of-servers clinton`.

6

The complete search request message for the WAIS server includes the search command in the message body.

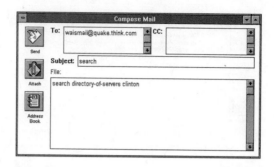

5. Click the Send button to send the message to the WAIS e-mail server.

6. You will receive a message box telling you that the message was sent. Click OK to dismiss this box.

America Online may take a few minutes to process and send your message to the WAIS e-mail server. Generally, the WAIS e-mail server will respond quickly to your request.

Reading the Response from the WAIS Server

When you receive the e-mail message with the search results from the WAIS e-mail server, America Online changes the mailbox button at the top of the screen to show letters in it. You can read the WAIS search results by following these steps:

1. To display the list of mail messages you have received, click the mailbox button, or pull down the **M**ail menu and choose Read New Mail.

2. On the list of mail messages, double-click the line from the WAIS e-mail server.

The help message from the WAIS server appears in a new window.

The WAIS e-mail server search results message. The message has been scrolled down to show the results better.

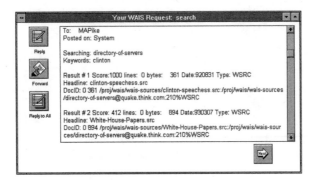

From the results returned by the search, you can see that two databases mention President Clinton: clinton-speeches and White-House-Papers. You will use the second database (White-House-Papers) for your next search.

Searching the White-House-Papers Database

Now, you will search the White-House-Papers database for those documents that mention Atlanta. To do this, send an e-mail message to the WAIS server with the command search White-House-Papers atlanta. The WAIS server will return a list of all the documents in the White-House-Papers database that have the word *atlanta* in them.

To send this e-mail message to the server, follow these steps:

1. Open the Compose Mail dialog box by pulling down the **M**ail menu and choosing Compose Mail.

2. In the To field, type **waismail@quake.think.com**. Press Tab twice to move to the Subject area of the dialog box.

3. Type **search**. The WAIS e-mail server ignores the subject of the message, but this will help identify the response you get back from the server.

4. Press Tab to move to the message body area. In the message body, type **search White-House-Papers atlanta**.

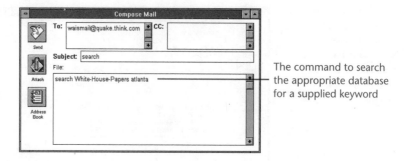

The command to search
the appropriate database
for a supplied keyword

5. Click the Send button to send the message to the WAIS e-mail server.

6. You will receive a message box telling you that the message was sent. Click OK to dismiss this box.

America Online may take a few minutes to process and send your mail to the WAIS e-mail server. Generally, the WAIS e-mail server will respond quickly to your request.

Reading the Search Response from the WAIS Server

The America Online system will tell you when you receive the search results from the WAIS e-mail server with the search results by putting letters inside the mailbox button at the top of the screen. You can read the search results by following these steps:

1. To display the list of mail messages you have received, click the mailbox button, or pull down the **M**ail menu and choose Read New Mail.

2. On the list of mail messages, double-click the line from the WAIS e-mail server.

The search response results from the WAIS e-mail server appears in a new window.

The WAIS e-mail server search results message. The message has been scrolled down to show the results better.

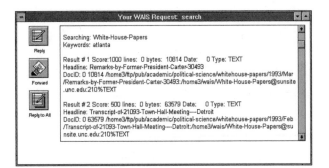

You can see that quite a few documents have the word *atlanta* in them. You can retrieve any of these documents by sending the `retrieve` command to the WAIS server. The `retrieve` command uses the DocID (for Document ID) from the search results. So to retrieve the second document on the list, you would send the WAIS e-mail server the command

```
retrieve 0 63579 /home3/ftp/pub/academic/political-
science/whitehouse-papers/1993/Feb/Transcript-of-21093-
Town-Hall-Meeting----Detroit:/home3/wais/White-House-
Papers@sunsite.unc.edu:210%TEXT
```

If you have problems...

You must type the entire DocID for the `retrieve` command to work correctly. If you don't, the WAIS system won't be able to find the right document and will return an error message to you. You can split the line with carriage returns (as in the preceding example), but don't insert any spaces or other characters. Using cut and paste to copy the document ID from the mail message that has the search results to the retrieve command often works correctly.

6

After your request is processed, you receive the document in a mail message.

Other Internet Services

Also under the Internet Center are other available Internet services. Several text files available describe the Internet in some detail. You also can use the Internet Center Message Board, which is a forum to discuss the Internet and provide help.

The America
Online Internet
Center window.
The different text
files and activities
are shown.

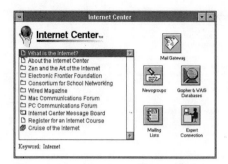

Summary

As you can see, you can access a number of common Internet services
from America Online, even though America Online's direct Internet
access is now limited to e-mail. You can make use of several important
Internet services through America Online's Internet e-mail, including
mailing lists, ftp, archie, and WAIS. Although the services aren't as easy
to use through e-mail, you can use them to get information just as
though you had direct access to them.

Chapter 7

Using the Internet via Delphi

Delphi was one of the first Internet access providers that gave full access to all Internet resources. As more and more resources have become available (such as information retrieval systems), Delphi has continued to provide access to them.

Note: *Although you aren't charged extra to use most Internet services on Delphi, you do have to register to use them. Read the Delphi documentation for more information about the Internet services and any extra charges that may apply for these services.*

This chapter explains how to:

■ Send Internet e-mail

■ Connect to Internet host resources

■ Download files using ftp

■ Find information

■ Read USENET news groups

This chapter assumes that you already know how to connect to the Delphi system and have set up your account and password. You should be somewhat familiar with how Delphi works and how to move around in the Delphi system. Now, connect to the Delphi system so that you are ready to begin using the Internet.

The Delphi main screen after you connect to the system.

```
us YOUR story.  Type GO USING PROFILE for more details.

Get your wish list into Santa early -- send it via Internet mail!  Visit the
Holiday Gopher and choose "Letters to Santa".  While you are there, access
holiday stories, songs, recipes and more!  Type GO ENT HOLIDAY.

Join the hosts of the national radio talk show, "On Computers" online today,
from 1:00 - 4:00 ET, as they broadcast live from the new Dell Computer Factory
Outlet store in Austin, Texas.  A Dell representative will also be online to
answer your PC questions!  Type GO REF RADIO.


MAIN Menu:

Business and Finance        News, Weather, and Sports
Computing Groups            Reference and Education
Conference                  Shopping
Entertainment and Games     Travel and Leisure
Groups and Clubs            Using DELPHI
Internet Services           Workspace
Mail                        HELP
Member Directory            EXIT

MAIN>What do you want to do?
```

Note: *When you connect to the Delphi system, you usually will be using a communications program running on your local computer. The figures in this chapter were created using the Crosstalk for Windows package from Digital Communications Associates, Inc.*

Accessing Delphi Internet Services

ftp
A program that allows you to transfer data between different computers on a network.

Everything you will do in this chapter—sending e-mail, using *ftp*, and so forth—are accessed from the Internet Services menu item under the main screen. To go to the Internet Services menu, start with the Delphi main menu (the one seen when you log in to the Delphi system). Then type any unique part of the words *Internet Services*, such as **inter**, **internet**, or **internet services**.

The Internet Services menu shows the Internet services available on Delphi: e-mail, ftp, Gopher, telnet, and USENET news.

```
About the Internet     Help
Conference             Exit
Databases (Files)
EMail                  FTP
Forum (Messages)       Gopher
Guides (Books)         IRC-Internet Relay Chat
Register/Cancel        Telnet
Who's Here             Utilities (finger, traceroute, ping)
Workspace              Usenet Newsgroups (NEW MENU)

Internet SIG>Enter your selection:
```

Note: *If you don't see the Internet Services menu, that means you must register for Internet access. Read the Delphi documentation for more information.*

Delphi has many other services available from the main screen; these services aren't Internet-related and won't be discussed in this book. You should read the Delphi documentation for other available services and the costs for using them.

Using Internet E-Mail

Only one mail program is available on Delphi; this character-oriented program presents your messages a page at a time on-screen. You can send and receive Internet mail (as well as mail to and from other Delphi users), reply to messages, forward mail, and organize mail into separate folders.

You can access Delphi's mail system from the Internet Services menu by entering **email** at the prompt. Information about sending Internet mail appears. You are now running the Delphi e-mail program.

Type **email** at the prompt

Delphi takes you to the mail system

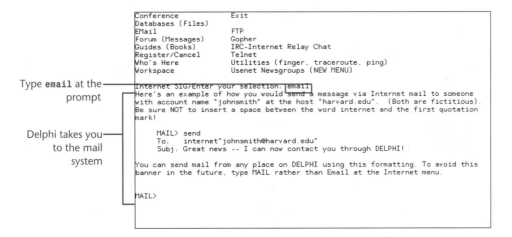

```
Conference           Exit
Databases (Files)
EMail                FTP
Forum (Messages)     Gopher
Guides (Books)       IRC-Internet Relay Chat
Register/Cancel      Telnet
Who's Here           Utilities (finger, traceroute, ping)
Workspace            Usenet Newsgroups (NEW MENU)

Internet SIG>Enter your selection: email
Here's an example of how you would send a message via Internet mail to someone
with account name "johnsmith" at the host "harvard.edu". (Both are fictitious).
Be sure NOT to insert a space between the word internet and the first quotation
mark!

    MAIL> send
    To:    internet"johnsmith@harvard.edu"
    Subj: Great news -- I can now contact you through DELPHI!

You can send mail from any place on DELPHI using this formatting. To avoid this
banner in the future, type MAIL rather than Email at the Internet menu.

MAIL>
```

7

Sending Internet E-Mail on Delphi

Now you will use the Delphi e-mail system to send a message. For this example, you want to receive a response, so you will use the Internet address book@pittslug.sug.org, which is set up specifically for this book. Follow these steps:

1. Enter **send** to begin sending an e-mail message.

2. At the To prompt, enter **internet"book@pittslug.sug.org"**. (The quotes are part of the address and must be entered as written.)

   Note: *When sending Internet mail on Delphi, you must put the word* **internet** *in front of the address you are sending to.*

3. At the Subj prompt, type **hello**.

4. The message Enter your message below. Press CTRL/Z when complete, or CTRL/C to quit appears. You can now begin typing your message. For this particular message, you don't need to type anything, but you can if you want.

5. To send the message, press Ctrl+Z (hold down the Ctrl key and press Z). If you don't want to send the message, you can abort it by pressing Ctrl+C.

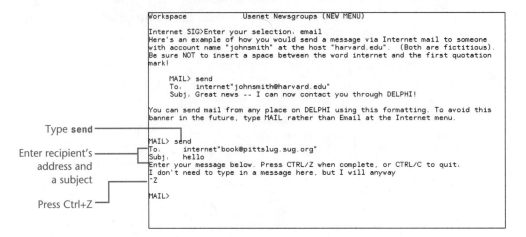

```
Workspace            Usenet Newsgroups (NEW MENU)

Internet SIG>Enter your selection: email
Here's an example of how you would send a message via Internet mail to someone
with account name "johnsmith" at the host "harvard.edu".  (Both are fictitious).
Be sure NOT to insert a space between the word internet and the first quotation
mark!

     MAIL> send
     To:   internet"johnsmith@harvard.edu"
     Subj: Great news -- I can now contact you through DELPHI!

You can send mail from any place on DELPHI using this formatting. To avoid this
banner in the future, type MAIL rather than Email at the Internet menu.

MAIL> send
To:      internet"book@pittslug.sug.org"
Subj:    hello
Enter your message below. Press CTRL/Z when complete, or CTRL/C to quit:
I don't need to type in a message here, but I will anyway
^Z

MAIL>
```

Type **send** ──────────

Enter recipient's ──────── address and a subject

Press Ctrl+Z ────────

After you send the message to the e-mail server set up for this book, you should receive a response back within a few minutes.

Delphi notifies you
of new e-mail.

```
Internet SIG>Enter your selection: email
Here's an example of how you would send a message via Internet mail to someone
with account name "johnsmith" at the host "harvard.edu".  (Both are fictitious).
Be sure NOT to insert a space between the word internet and the first quotation
mark!

      MAIL> send
      To,    internet"johnsmith@harvard.edu"
      Subj, Great news -- I can now contact you through DELPHI!

You can send mail from any place on DELPHI using this formatting. To avoid this
banner in the future, type MAIL rather than Email at the Internet menu.

MAIL> send
To,       internet"book@pittslug.sug.org"
Subj,     hello
Enter your message below. Press CTRL/Z when complete, or CTRL/C to quit,
I don't need to type in a message here, but I will anyway
^Z

MAIL>
New mail on node BOS1A from IN%"book@pittslug.sug.org"  "Internet Quickstart"
MAIL>
```

Notification line ——————

Occasionally, the connection between the Delphi system and the
Internet may be down, or the Delphi system may be very heavily used;
your mail may take longer at these times.

**If you have
problems...**

If a problem occurs in delivering your e-mail, you may receive an error message from the Delphi system telling you that your mail couldn't be delivered,
and giving a short description of the problem. If, for example, you get an
error message such as host unknown or user unknown, you should check to
make sure that the address you typed is correct.

You also may encounter other problems in sending mail from Delphi to
Internet machines. The machine you are sending mail to could be unavailable, for example, or there may be a temporary problem in the network
between Delphi and the destination machine.

In any case, the Delphi system will try several times to deliver your message,
but it may eventually send you an error message saying that it could not
deliver your mail. In this case, you can try to send the message again. If your
mail continues to fail, you can send a message to the Delphi staff asking for
help in diagnosing the problem.

7

Reading E-Mail on Delphi

When the Delphi system tells you that you have e-mail waiting to be
read, you can use the read command to read it. Make sure that you are in
the Delphi e-mail system (by using the email command from the Internet
Services menu), and then follow these steps:

1. Type the command **read** to read the message you have received.

The Delphi system displays the first page of the message you have received. This page contains the header information from the message, including information about who the message is from and the time it was sent.

The first screen of messages received from the e-mail server set up for this book.

```
    #1         19-DEC-1993 13.55.47.78                      NEWMAIL
From:   IN%"book@pittslug.sug.org"  "Internet Quickstart"
To:     IN%"PIKEDEMO@delphi.com"
CC:
Subj:   RE: hello

Return-path: <book@pittslug.sug.org>
Received: from pittslug.sug.org by delphi.com (PMDF V4.2-11 #4520) id
 <01H6NZRZN6UO94H6TI@delphi.com>; Sun, 19 Dec 1993 13.55.43 EDT
Received: by pittslug.sug.org (5.64/2.5) id AA16256; Sun,
 19 Dec 93 13.55.58 -0500
Date: Sun, 19 Dec 1993 13.55.58 -0500
From: Internet Quickstart <book@pittslug.sug.org>
Subject: RE: hello
In-reply-to: <01H6NZRC3R8I94H5SM@delphi.com>
To: PIKEDEMO@delphi.com
Message-id: <9312191855.AA16256@pittslug.sug.org>
Content-type: text/plain; charset=us-ascii
Content-transfer-encoding: 7BIT


Press RETURN for more...

MAIL>
```

If the message is more than one page long, you can show the next page by pressing Enter. (In this case, the second page will be the actual text of the message.)

Message number —————

Second screen of the message received from the e-mail server

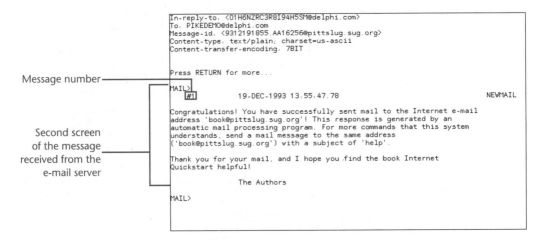

```
In-reply-to: <01H6NZRC3R8I94H5SM@delphi.com>
To: PIKEDEMO@delphi.com
Message-id: <9312191855.AA16256@pittslug.sug.org>
Content-type: text/plain; charset=us-ascii
Content-transfer-encoding: 7BIT


Press RETURN for more...

MAIL>
    #1         19-DEC-1993 13.55.47.78                      NEWMAIL

Congratulations! You have successfully sent mail to the Internet e-mail
address 'book@pittslug.sug.org'! This response is generated by an
automatic mail processing program. For more commands that this system
understands, send a mail message to the same address
('book@pittslug.sug.org') with a subject of 'help'.

Thank you for your mail, and I hope you find the book Internet
Quickstart helpful!

                The Authors

MAIL>
```

2. Type the command **delete** to remove this message if you don't want to keep it. The next section, "Using Other Delphi

E-Mail Commands," tells you about other commands you can use with your e-mail messages.

Note: *Most Delphi mail commands let you specify a message number. For example, to delete message number 1, you can type* **delete 1**.

3. Type **quit** to return to the Internet Services menu (**exit** will also work).

Examples of the **delete** and **quit** commands

```
('book@pittslug.sug.org') with a subject of 'help'.

Thank you for your mail, and I hope you find the book Internet
Quickstart helpful!

                    The Authors

MAIL> delete 1

MAIL> quit

Internet SIG Menu:

About the Internet     Help
Conference             Exit
Databases (Files)
EMail                  FTP
Forum (Messages)       Gopher
Guides (Books)         IRC-Internet Relay Chat
Register/Cancel        Telnet
Who's Here             Utilities (finger, traceroute, ping)
Workspace              Usenet Newsgroups (NEW MENU)

Internet SIG>Enter your selection:
```

Using Other Delphi E-Mail Commands

More commands are available in the Delphi e-mail program. Some of the most used Delphi e-mail commands are as follows:

Command	Description
BACK	Displays the message before the one you are now reading
COPY	Copies a message to another folder without removing it from the current folder
DIRECTORY	Displays a list of the messages in the current folder
FIRST	Displays the first message in the current folder
FORWARD	Sends a copy of the message you are reading to another user
LAST	Displays the last message in the current folder
MOVE	Moves the current message to another folder
NEXT	Displays the next message in the current folder
REPLY	Sends a reply to the message you are reading

7

Note: *Replying to a message is very similar to sending a new message. The* reply *command automatically fills in all the header information for you, and then lets you type your message. Just as when you are sending a message, when you are through typing your message, you can send the message by pressing Ctrl+Z. If you don't want to send the message, you can abort the message by pressing Ctrl+C.*

You can use help to get more information about any of these commands. After you type **help**, the system will ask you for a command you want more information on. You can type a command to get help on or press Enter to leave the help system. The command help * gives you help on all the available commands.

Using the Delphi e-mail help command.

```
        MAIL> HELP *

    To obtain information about individual  commands  or  topics,  enter
    HELP followed by the command or topic name.

     Format:

        HELP [topic]


   Additional information available:

   /EDIT      /PERSONAL_NAME    /SELF      /SUBJECT   ANSWER    ATTACH
   BACK       COMPRESS   COPY   CURRENT    DEFINE     DELETE    DIRECTORY
   EDIT       ERASE      EXIT   EXTRACT    FILE       FIRST     Folders
   FORWARD    GETTING_STARTED   HELP       KEYPAD     LAST      MAIL
   MARK       MOVE       NEXT   PRINT      PURGE      QUIT      READ
   REMOVE     REPLY      SEARCH SELECT     SEND       SET-SHOW  SPAWN
   V5_CHANGES

 Topic?

 MAIL> _
```

Connecting to Internet Resources with telnet

telnet
A program that lets you use a remote computer as though you were connected to it with a communications program or terminal.

You can use *telnet* to access information resources (called *host resources*) that aren't available on your local system. Using telnet to access remote resources is important because several Internet resources (such as *archie*, *WAIS*, and *WWW*) aren't available yet on the Delphi system. By using telnet, you can use one of the Internet sites that provides these services.

archie

A service that lets you look for anonymous ftp sites that have programs or files available for down-loading.

WAIS

Wide Area Informa-tion Servers, a system for search-ing and retrieving documents from participating sites.

WWW

World Wide Web, a system that lets you browse available Internet resources.

When using telnet, you must provide the host name of the machine you are going to connect to. Chapter 12, "Other Internet Resources," lists many systems that provide host resources and provides information about what you need to do to get access to the resource after you connect with telnet. After you read the examples in this section, you might want to look through Chapter 12 before experimenting with telnet to get an idea of the wide variety of resources available and how to use them.

This section uses the example of connecting to a host that provides an archie service. (For an overview of archie, read Chapter 1, "Introducing the Internet.") For the example in this section, you will look for an ftp site that has the document `fyi20.txt` (a file that gives an introduction to the Internet) available. Follow these steps:

1. From the Internet Services menu, type the command **telnet** to start the telnet program.

2. At the `Enter INTERNET` address prompt, type **archie.internic.net** as the name of the machine you want to connect to. This site provides archie service.

Enter the **telnet** command ⎯⎯⎯⎯⎯

Enter the host name ⎯⎯⎯⎯⎯

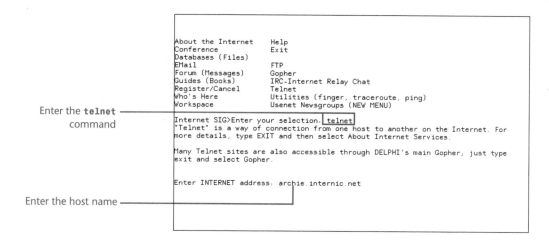

```
About the Internet      Help
Conference              Exit
Databases (Files)
EMail                   FTP
Forum (Messages)        Gopher
Guides (Books)          IRC-Internet Relay Chat
Register/Cancel         Telnet
Who's Here              Utilities (finger, traceroute, ping)
Workspace               Usenet Newsgroups (NEW MENU)

Internet SIG>Enter your selection: telnet
"Telnet" is a way of connection from one host to another on the Internet. For
more details, type EXIT and then select About Internet Services.

Many Telnet sites are also accessible through DELPHI's main Gopher; just type
exit and select Gopher.


Enter INTERNET address: archie.internic.net
```

7

If you have problems...

At this point, the system tries to connect to the remote machine. If this process fails, it generally means that the remote machine is unavailable (because the system is down or network problems are occurring between Delphi and the remote machine). You can pick another host that provides archie service from the following list:

```
archie.unl.edu
archie.ans.net
archie.rutgers.edu
archie.sura.net
```

After you are connected to an archie server, you can use the `servers` command to get a list of available servers.

Note: *If you use a different host, the example screens may not match what you see from the remote system.*

---

3. A welcoming message appears, and the remote computer asks for you to log in an account name. Type **archie** as the account name.

Note: *New Internet users can type **guest** as the account name to get information about the Internet and archie.*

Greeting message from the host archie.internic.net and login prompt.

```
Welcome to InterNIC Directory and Database Services provided by AT&T.
These services are partially supported through a cooperative agreement
with the National Science Foundation.

First time users may login as guest with no password to receive help.

Your comments and suggestions for improvement are welcome, and can be
mailed to admin@ds.internic.net.

AT&T MAKES NO WARRANTY OR GUARANTEE, OR PROMISE, EXPRESS OR IMPLIED,
CONCERNING THE  CONTENT OR  ACCURACY OF THE  DIRECTORY  ENTRIES AND
DATABASE  FILES  STORED  AND  MAINTAINED  BY  AT&T.   AT&T EXPRESSLY
DISCLAIMS AND EXCLUDES ALL EXPRESS WARANTIES AND IMPLIED WARRANTIES
OF MERCHANTABILITY AND FITNESS FOR A PARTICULAR PURPOSE.




SunOS UNIX (ds)

login: archie
```

Several informational messages appear, and then the archie program waits for you to type a command. The prompt from the archie program is `archie>`.

After you success-
fully log in, the
archie program
displays a welcome
message and a
prompt.

```
*********************************************************************************
                  Welcome to the InterNIC Directory and Database Server.
*********************************************************************************

# Message of the day from the localhost Prospero server.

         Welcome to Archie  server for the
         InterNIC Directory and Database Services.



# Bunyip Information Systems, 1993

# Terminal type set to `vt100 24 80'.
# `erase' character is `^?'.
# `search' (type string) has the value `sub'.
archie>
```

4. Now you must tell the archie program about the type of search you
   want to perform. The command **set search subcase** will tell the
   archie program to search for case-sensitive substrings.

5. To read what appears on-screen more easily, you need to tell the
   archie program to pause after every screen of information. To do so,
   enter the command **set pager**.

6. To search for the file you are interested in, enter **find fyi20.txt**.

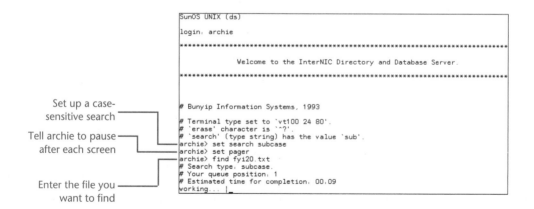

Set up a case-
sensitive search

Tell archie to pause
after each screen

Enter the file you
want to find

```
SunOS UNIX (ds)

login, archie

*********************************************************************************
                  Welcome to the InterNIC Directory and Database Server.
*********************************************************************************


# Bunyip Information Systems, 1993

# Terminal type set to `vt100 24 80'.
# `erase' character is `^?'.
# `search' (type string) has the value `sub'.
archie> set search subcase
archie> set pager
archie> find fyi20.txt
# Search type, subcase.
# Your queue position, 1
# Estimated time for completion, 00.09
working... |
```

After archie finishes searching its database for files that match what you
are looking for, it displays the results a page at a time. For each matching
file, archie displays several pieces of information that can help you
download the file:

7

■ The computer that the file is on (giving the host name and Internet address numbers for the host).

■ The last time that archie looked on the host system to update its database. This date can be important, because the file may have been deleted from the displayed computer system after archie updated its database. If the date displayed for the last update is more than a few weeks old, you may want to choose a different matching file.

■ The location of the matching file (generally a directory on the host machine) and information about the matching file, such as the full name, the size of the file, and when the file was created.

Results of archie search for fyi20.txt. The screen has been scrolled down to show the results for sunsite.unc.edu.

```
Host sunsite.unc.edu    (152.2.22.81)
Last updated 08.05 22 Dec 1993

    Location: /pub/docs/rfc
       FILE    -rwxrwxrwx    11 bytes  02.47 30 Jun 1993  fyi20.txt -> rfc1462.
txt

Host ugle.unit.no    (129.241.1.97)
Last updated 07.06  2 Dec 1993

    Location: /pub/rfc
       FILE    -rwxrwxrwx    11 bytes  00.00 29 May 1993  fyi20.txt -> rfc1462.
txt

Host ftp.technion.ac.il    (132.68.1.10)
Last updated 07.01 23 Nov 1993

    Location: /pub/unsupported/doc/RFC
       FILE    -rwxr-xr-x    11 bytes  13.34 31 Aug 1993  fyi20.txt -> rfc1462.
txt
```

The first matching file in the above figure looks promising. The machine the file is on is sunsite.unc.edu, which is a major ftp site that holds many software packages. The matching file is in directory /pub/docs/rfc, which indicates that the files in the directory are documentation (which is what you are looking for). And finally, the file name itself is fyi20.txt, which is exactly what you were looking for. You will use this information about the file to download the file using ftp in the next section.

While you're using the archie program, you can press the space bar to move to the next page of output. To get back to the main archie prompt, enter **q**.

You also can access help information on archie by typing **help**. From the help screen, you can read the information about the pager program (which is what archie uses to stop the output at the end of each page) by typing **pager**. To quit the help system and return to the archie program, press Ctrl+D.

The initial help screen, listing the commands you can use.

```
Host louie.udel.edu    (128.175.1.3)
archie> help
These are the commands you can use in help.

                .       go up one level in the hierarchy

                ?       display a list of valid subtopics at the current level

<newline>
done, ^D, ^C            quit from help entirely

        <string>       help on a topic or subtopic
Eg.

        "help show"

will give you the help screen for the "show" command

        "help set search"

Will give you the help information for the "search" variable.

The command "manpage" will give you a complete copy of the archie manual page.
help/english/= (END)
```

You can type a question mark to get a list of commands for archie.

```
#       help
#       list
#       mail
#       motd
#       nopager
#       pager
#       prog
#       quit
#       regex
#       servers
#       show
#       site
#       term
#       unset
#       version
#       whatis
#       whats_new
#       stty
#       compress
#       manpage
#       path
#       domains
help> ^D
archie>
```

You can read a general description of how the archie system works by typing **manpage** at the archie> prompt. You should read this information to get a better idea of how to use the archie system. This output is quite lengthy, so to leave the manpage output and return to the archie> prompt, type **q**.

7

Output of the archie manpage command.

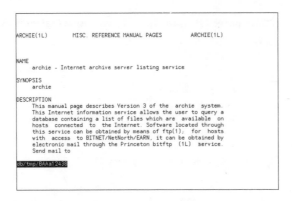

```
ARCHIE(1L)        MISC. REFERENCE MANUAL PAGES        ARCHIE(1L)


NAME
      archie - Internet archive server listing service
SYNOPSIS
      archie
DESCRIPTION
      This manual page describes Version 3 of the  archie  system.
      This Internet information service allows the user to query a
      database containing a list of files which are  available  on
      hosts  connected  to  the Internet. Software located through
      this service can be obtained by means of ftp(1);  for  hosts
      with  access  to BITNET/NetNorth/EARN, it can be obtained by
      electronic mail through the Princeton bitftp  (1L)  service.
      Send mail to
      db/tmp/BAAa12438
```

To leave the archie program and return to the Delphi system, type **quit** at the archie> prompt.

As you can see from the example in this section, you can use telnet to get access to programs that aren't available on Delphi. This way, you can take advantage of many Internet resources that aren't directly available (or may not be available yet). More examples of using telnet to use resources such as WAIS and WWW are given in the section "Finding Information" later in this chapter.

Transferring Files with ftp

The section "Connecting to Internet Resources with telnet" showed how to use archie to locate an Internet ftp site that had the file fyi20.txt on it. This section shows you how to use ftp to connect to the site you found with archie and download this file. With the Internet Services menu on-screen, follow these steps:

1. Type **ftp** to start the ftp program.

2. At the Enter destination INTERNET address prompt, type **sunsite.unc.edu** for this example.

3. At the Enter username (default: anonymous) prompt, enter the account name to use on the ftp server. For this example, because you will be using an anonymous ftp site, you can accept the default by pressing Enter.

The Delphi ftp program displays informational messages explaining how to use the ftp program.

The Delphi ftp program displays informational messages showing how to use the ftp program.

```
About the Internet     Help
Conference             Exit
Databases (Files)
EMail                  FTP
Forum (Messages)       Gopher
Guides (Books)         IRC-Internet Relay Chat
Register/Cancel        Telnet
Who's Here             Utilities (finger, traceroute, ping)
Workspace              Usenet Newsgroups

Internet SIG>Enter your selection: ftp
Enter destination INTERNET address: sunsite.unc.edu
Enter username (default: anonymous):

To get a binary file, type BINARY and then GET "remote filename" myfilename
To get a text file,   type ASCII  and then GET "remote filename" myfilename
  Upper and lower case ARE significant; use the "quotes" shown above.
To get a directory, use DIR.
To type a short text file, use TT for myfilename
To get out, type EXIT or Control-Z.

Enter password [PIKEDEMO@DELPHI.COM]:
```

4. At the Enter password prompt, enter the password to use when it connects to the remote machine. For this example, just press Enter to let the system provide your Delphi e-mail address.

After you provide the information that the Delphi ftp program needs, the system tries to connect to the machine you indicated. If you typed the information correctly, the program will connect and log you in automatically to the remote machine.

In the case of the machine sunsite.unc.edu, the ftp program displays a welcome message.

```
230-
230-   Or telnet to sunsite and login as swais to test out a simple wais client.
230-   Or telnet to sunsite and login as gopher to test out a sample gopher clien
t.
230-   If you email to info@sunsite.unc.edu you will be sent help information
230-   about how to use the differenct services sunsite provides.
230-
230-   We are experimenting with description based searches and downloads from
230-   this archive with WAIS. If you would like to try this, get and read the fi
le
230-   /pub/wais/ftp-wais.readme.
230-
230-   We use the Wuarchive experimental ftpd. if you "get" <directory>.tar.Z
230-   or <file>.Z it will compress and/or tar it on the fly. Using ".gz"  instea
d
230-   of ".Z" will use the GNU zip (/pub/gnu/gzip*) instead, a superior
230-   compression method.
230-
230-   Mail suggestions and questions to ftpkeeper@sunsite.unc.edu.
230-
230-
230-
230 Guest login ok, access restrictions apply.
FTP>
```

7

If you have problems...

If the remote machine is unavailable, or Delphi and the remote machine are experiencing network problems, you may not be able to connect. If this happens, you should check the information you provided to make sure that you spelled everything correctly. If you typed everything right and still can't connect, you should wait a while to see whether the remote machine becomes available, and then try again. You also can try one of the ftp sites listed in Chapter 9, "Software and Files (ftp and Gopher Sites)."

Another problem with some anonymous ftp sites is that they place a limit on the number of people who can use them at one time. If too many people are on the system when you try to log in, you will get a message telling you to try again later. The best time to use anonymous ftp is after normal working hours (after 6 p.m. or on weekends, for example).

5. From the earlier archie output, you know that the file `fyi20.txt` is located in the directory `pub/docs/rfc`. Now type **cd "/pub/docs/rfc"** at the ftp prompt to move to that directory. (The quotation marks are necessary and must be typed as shown.)

You've moved into the directory that holds the file you want. Now you can retrieve it.

```
230-  Or telnet to sunsite and login as gopher to test out a sample gopher clien
t.
230-  If you email to info@sunsite.unc.edu you will be sent help information
230-  about how to use the differenct services sunsite provides.
230-
230-  We are experimenting with description based searches and downloads from
230-  this archive with WAIS. If you would like to try this, get and read the fi
le
230-  /pub/wais/ftp-wais.readme.
230-
230-  We use the Wuarchive experimental ftpd. if you "get" <directory>.tar.Z
230-  or <file>.Z it will compress and/or tar it on the fly. Using ".gz"  instea
d
230-  of ".Z" will use the GNU zip (/pub/gnu/gzip*) instead, a superior
230-  compression method.
230-
230-  Mail suggestions and questions to ftpkeeper@sunsite.unc.edu.
230-
230-
230-
230 Guest login ok, access restrictions apply.
FTP> cd "/pub/docs/rfc"
250 CWD command successful.
FTP>
```

Note: *With some versions of the ftp software, when you move to a directory you may see a message that tells you about the software in this directory.*

6. Type the `dir fyi*` command to list the files available in this directory that start with the letters *fyi*. This limits the directory listing to only those files you are interested in.

Several files start with *fyi*, including the file `fyi20.txt` that you found with archie. These files are different documents that describe parts of the Internet.

The `fyi20.txt` file ——

```
lrwxrwxrwx   1 root       daemon        11 Jun 28  1993 fyi1.txt -> rfc1150.txt
lrwxrwxrwx   1 root       daemon        11 Jun 30  1993 fyi10.txt -> rfc1402.txt
lrwxrwxrwx   1 root       daemon        11 Jun 30  1993 fyi11.txt -> rfc1292.txt
lrwxrwxrwx   1 root       daemon        11 Jun 30  1993 fyi12.txt -> rfc1302.txt
lrwxrwxrwx   1 root       daemon        11 Jun 30  1993 fyi13.txt -> rfc1308.txt
lrwxrwxrwx   1 root       daemon        11 Jun 30  1993 fyi14.txt -> rfc1309.txt
lrwxrwxrwx   1 root       daemon        11 Jun 30  1993 fyi15.txt -> rfc1355.txt
lrwxrwxrwx   1 root       daemon        11 Jun 30  1993 fyi16.txt -> rfc1359.txt
lrwxrwxrwx   1 root       daemon        11 Oct  8 07.22 fyi17.txt -> rfc1539.txt
lrwxrwxrwx   1 root       daemon        11 Jun 30  1993 fyi18.txt -> rfc1392.txt
lrwxrwxrwx   1 root       daemon        11 Jun 30  1993 fyi19.txt -> rfc1463.txt
lrwxrwxrwx   1 root       daemon        10 Jun 28  1993 fyi2.ps -> rfc1147.ps
lrwxrwxrwx   1 root       daemon        11 Jun 30  1993 fyi2.txt -> rfc1470.txt
lrwxrwxrwx   1 root       daemon        11 Jun 30  1993 fyi20.txt -> rfc1462.txt
lrwxrwxrwx   1 root       daemon        11 Jul 23  1993 fyi21.txt -> rfc1491.txt
lrwxrwxrwx   1 root       daemon        11 Jun 28  1993 fyi3.txt -> rfc1175.txt
lrwxrwxrwx   1 root       daemon        11 Jun 30  1993 fyi4.txt -> rfc1325.txt
lrwxrwxrwx   1 root       daemon        11 Jun 28  1993 fyi5.txt -> rfc1178.txt
lrwxrwxrwx   1 root       daemon        11 Jun 28  1993 fyi6.txt -> rfc1198.txt
lrwxrwxrwx   1 root       daemon        11 Jun 28  1993 fyi7.txt -> rfc1207.txt
lrwxrwxrwx   1 root       daemon        11 Jun 28  1993 fyi8.txt -> rfc1244.txt
lrwxrwxrwx   1 root       daemon        11 Jun 30  1993 fyi9.txt -> rfc1251.txt
226 Transfer complete.
FTP>
```

7. You now can download the file `fyi20.txt` by entering the **get "fyi20.txt"** command.

   Note: *Including the quotation marks at all times is a good practice. The Delphi ftp program requires them if the file you are downloading has any uppercase characters in its name.*

The ftp program tells you when the `fyi20.txt` file is successfully downloaded. It's now on your account directory on the Delphi system.

```
lrwxrwxrwx   1 root       daemon        11 Jun 30  1993 fyi13.txt -> rfc1308.txt
lrwxrwxrwx   1 root       daemon        11 Jun 30  1993 fyi14.txt -> rfc1309.txt
lrwxrwxrwx   1 root       daemon        11 Jun 30  1993 fyi15.txt -> rfc1355.txt
lrwxrwxrwx   1 root       daemon        11 Jun 30  1993 fyi16.txt -> rfc1359.txt
lrwxrwxrwx   1 root       daemon        11 Oct  8 07.22 fyi17.txt -> rfc1539.txt
lrwxrwxrwx   1 root       daemon        11 Jun 30  1993 fyi18.txt -> rfc1392.txt
lrwxrwxrwx   1 root       daemon        11 Jun 30  1993 fyi19.txt -> rfc1463.txt
lrwxrwxrwx   1 root       daemon        10 Jun 28  1993 fyi2.ps -> rfc1147.ps
lrwxrwxrwx   1 root       daemon        11 Jun 30  1993 fyi2.txt -> rfc1470.txt
lrwxrwxrwx   1 root       daemon        11 Jun 30  1993 fyi20.txt -> rfc1462.txt
lrwxrwxrwx   1 root       daemon        11 Jul 23  1993 fyi21.txt -> rfc1491.txt
lrwxrwxrwx   1 root       daemon        11 Jun 28  1993 fyi3.txt -> rfc1175.txt
lrwxrwxrwx   1 root       daemon        11 Jun 30  1993 fyi4.txt -> rfc1325.txt
lrwxrwxrwx   1 root       daemon        11 Jun 28  1993 fyi5.txt -> rfc1178.txt
lrwxrwxrwx   1 root       daemon        11 Jun 28  1993 fyi6.txt -> rfc1198.txt
lrwxrwxrwx   1 root       daemon        11 Jun 28  1993 fyi7.txt -> rfc1207.txt
lrwxrwxrwx   1 root       daemon        11 Jun 28  1993 fyi8.txt -> rfc1244.txt
lrwxrwxrwx   1 root       daemon        11 Jun 30  1993 fyi9.txt -> rfc1251.txt
226 Transfer complete.
FTP> get "fyi20.txt"
200 PORT command successful.
150 Opening ASCII mode data connection for fyi20.txt (27811 bytes).
226 Transfer complete.
FTP>
```

7

After you complete the downloading, type **help** to see what ftp commands are available. If you want information about a particular ftp command, you can type the command now to get more information about it. For example, typing bye while in the help system gives you information about that command. You can leave the help system by pressing Enter.

Help on the bye
and exit com-
mands.

```
BYE

  BYE is a synonym for EXIT.  See the EXIT command.

Topic? exit
EXIT

  Use the EXIT command to exit FTP and return to DCL.
  If a connection is open, it is closed before exiting.
  You can use QUIT and BYE as synonyms for EXIT.
  Format:
        EXIT

Topic?
FTP>
```

You can leave the ftp program by typing **exit**.

If you followed the instructions in this section, you will have downloaded the file `fyi20.txt`, which is a fairly large file. You probably want
to delete this file if you don't want to pay to store it on your Delphi
account. You can use the `workspace` command from the Delphi main
menu to delete the file, or upload it to your computer's local disk.

Finding Information

As described in Chapter 1, "Introducing the Internet," several different
services on the Internet allow you to find information. The four main
ones are archie, Gopher, WAIS, and WWW. archie is used to locate files
available on anonymous ftp sites. Gopher allows you to locate and display files by selecting menu items; you also can move between Gopher
servers and different menus by selecting items. WAIS is a system that
allows you to search a database of documents for information that you
want. WWW lets you view documents that have links to other documents.

Delphi doesn't have direct access to many of these Internet services; only
a Gopher program is now available on Delphi. As shown earlier in the
section "Connecting to Internet Resources with telnet," though, you
can get access to archie, WAIS, and WWW programs on other Internet
machines through the telnet service.

Using Gopher on Delphi

From the Internet Services menu, you can start the Gopher program on Delphi by typing **gopher**. The main Gopher screen appears, listing menu items that help you get information about the Gopher program and move to other Gopher menus.

The top lines of the main Gopher screen show you what menu page you are on, and that you are now seeing the first (only) page of this menu.

```
Internet SIG Gopher
Page 1 of 1

1    PERSONAL FAVORITES                                           Menu
2    "ABOUT DELPHI'S GOPHER SERVICE"                              Text
3    ***  FAQ, FREQUENTLY ASKED QUESTIONS  *** (REVISED 12/15)   Menu
4    ALL THE GOPHER SERVERS IN THE WORLD                          Menu
5    ARTS, LITERATURE, AND RELIGION                               Menu
6    BUSINESS AND ECONOMICS                                       Menu
7    COMPUTERS                                                    Menu
8    FREE-NETS AND COMMUNITY ACCESS                               Menu
9    FTP: DOWNLOADABLE PROGRAMS, IMAGES, SOUNDS                    Menu
10   GAMES AND MUDS, MUSHES, MUSES, AND MOOS                       Menu
11   GOVERNMENT AND POLITICS                                      Menu
12   HEALTH AND MEDICINE                                          Menu
13   INTERNET SEARCH UTILITIES AND INFORMATION                    Menu
14   LAW                                                          Menu
15   LIBRARIES, GUIDES, AND RESEARCH                              Menu
16   MATHEMATICS, SCIENCE, AND TECHNOLOGY                         Menu
17   SCHOOLHOUSE (K-12)                                           Menu
18   SOCIAL SCIENCES, HISTORY, AND EDUCATION                      Menu
19   THE GRAB BAG (WITH 'NEW THIS WEEK 12/16)                      Menu

Enter Item Number, ?, or EXIT,
```

Note: *The Gopher screens can change as new items are added or old items are removed. The information you see may be slightly different from the examples presented here.*

In the middle of the screen are the Gopher menu items. The numbers on the left side are the numbers you would enter to select a menu item (for example, to select the menu item All The Gopher Servers In The World, type **4**).

Along the right side of the menu items are labels telling you what the menu item is. A menu item of type Text, for example, is a file that you can look at; selecting one of these menu items will display the file. Items that have a Menu label will take you to another menu screen. This new screen can have more items of type Menu, and so on. Other menu item types are available (such as Search, which indicates that the menu item allows you to search a database), but Text and Menu are the ones you see most often.

7

One of the main features of a Gopher system is that any of these menu items can move you to another Gopher server anywhere on the Internet. By using the Delphi Gopher program, you can find information on any Gopher server in the world!

Now you can use the Gopher system to explore some Internet Gopher servers. Follow these steps:

1. From the main Gopher menu, enter the number **4** to select the menu All The Gopher Servers In The World.

The Delphi Gopher program displays the menu All The Gopher Servers In The World, which lets you access Gopher servers all over the Internet.

```
ALL THE GOPHER SERVERS IN THE WORLD
Page 1 of 2

1   Connect to any gopher (Type a gopher address)          Search
2       ****SELECTED SPECIAL INTEREST GOPHERS****          Text
3   Carnegie Mellon U English Server                       Menu
4   Gopher Jewels                                          Menu
5   IBM ACIS Higher Education Information Server - IKE      Menu
6   Library of Congress MARVEL Gopher                      Menu
7   RiceInfo, Rice U                                       Menu
8   University of California - Santa Cruz, InfoSlug System  Menu
9   University of North Carolina (SunSite)                 Menu
10  U of Minnesota (the mother of all gophers)             Menu
11  Washington & Lee U                                     Menu
12  WHAT'S NEW?, New Gophers List (updated daily)          Menu
13      ****GOPHERS BY GEOGRAPHICAL LOCATION****           Text
14  USA Gophers                                            Menu
15  United Nations Gopher                                  Menu
16  International Organizations                            Menu
17  Africa                                                 Menu
18  Asia                                                   Menu
19  Europe                                                 Menu

Enter Item Number, MORE, ?, or BACK: more
```

This menu screen allows you to connect to Gopher servers around the world. The first menu item lets you connect to a Gopher server if you know its name. This item is convenient if you have seen a reference to a particular server and want to connect to it directly.

A group of menu items following the first item lists a few interesting or important Gopher servers. This group is followed by another set of menu items (numbered 14 and higher) that allow you to look through lists of Gopher servers in particular geographic locations, such as the United States or Europe.

Note: *Typing* **more** *moves you to the next page of the menu. The second page lists more menus that organize Gopher servers by geographic areas, an item that gives you a complete list of all Gopher servers in the world, and the menu Search titles in Gopherspace using veronica. (The veronica service, as described in Chapter 1, "Introducing the Internet," lets you search through a database of information on Gopher servers for a particular topic.) Type* **prev** *to return to the first page of the menu.*

2. As an example of an interesting Gopher server, you can select menu item 6, the United States Library of Congress Gopher server. Do so by entering **6**.

   The main screen of this server lists the information that's available about the Library of Congress, the Library of Congress on-line systems, the U.S. Congress, and even employee information.

The Library of
Congress Gopher
server's main
screen.

```
17  Africa                                                   Menu
18  Asia                                                     Menu
19  Europe                                                   Menu

Enter Item Number, MORE, ?, or BACK, 6

Library of Congress MARVEL Gopher
Page 1 of 1

1   About LC MARVEL (Please Read First)                      Menu
2   Library of Congress, Facilities, Activities, and Services Menu
3   Research and Reference                                   Menu
4   Library of Congress Online Systems                       Menu
5   The U.S. Congress                                        Menu
6   Federal Government Information                            Menu
7   Services to Libraries and Publishers                     Menu
8   Copyright                                                Menu
9   Employee Information                                     Menu
10  The Global Electronic Library (by Subject)               Menu
11  Internet Resources                                       Menu
12  What's New on LC MARVEL                                  Menu
13  Search LC MARVEL Menus                                   Menu

Enter Item Number, SAVE, ?, or BACK,
```

7

3. To see what other screens of this Gopher server look like, you can select menu item 1, which gives information about the Library of Congress Gopher server.

   This menu has several text items that tell you about the history and development of the Gopher server, how to use the Library of Congress Gopher server, and information about Gopher in general.

4. After you explore this menu, enter **top** to return to Delphi's main Gopher screen.

This screen shows some of the information available about the Library of Congress Gopher system.

```
5    The U.S. Congress                            Menu
6    Federal Government Information               Menu
7    Services to Libraries and Publishers         Menu
8    Copyright                                    Menu
9    Employee Information                         Menu
10   The Global Electronic Library (by Subject)   Menu
11   Internet Resources                           Menu
12   What's New on LC MARVEL                      Menu
13   Search LC MARVEL Menus                       Menu

Enter Item Number, SAVE, ?, or BACK: 1

About LC MARVEL (Please Read First)
Page 1 of 1

1    Welcome                              Text
2    History and Development              Text
3    Facts About Gopher                   Menu
4    How to Access LC MARVEL              Text
5    How to Participate in LC MARVEL      Menu
6    LC Marvel Usage Statistics           Menu
7    We Want Your Reactions!              Text

Enter Item Number, SAVE, ?, or BACK: top
```

5. To see what happens when you use Gopher to look at a file, enter **2** on Delphi's main Gopher screen. To stop reading this file, type **n** at the More? prompt. You are returned to the Library of Congress Gopher system.

Typing **2** displays a file that describes a little about how the Gopher system is set up on Delphi, and how to use it.

```
DELPHI's new Gopher service allows you to easily access select
Internet sites.  The primary list of sites is created by the manager
of this special interest group.  The listing will probably change on
a regular basis to feature different types of information and new
services.

When you find a Gopher site that has information that you find
especially valuable, you can type SAVE to add it as an option to your
"Personal Favorites" menu.  In this way you can build your own
customized list of Internet information.

When you save options as Personal Favorites, it creates a file called
"favorites.sav" in your workspace.  If you are familiar with gopher
formatting and DELPHI's file editor, you can also modify your personal
favorites list by editing this file. Each entry is on a single line,
although it may be longer than 80 characters and appear as if it is on
more than one line.

DELPHI's gopher also supports downloads direct to your own home computer.
When you select a file to download, the file is transferred to a holding
area on DELPHI (not your workspace). This may take a minute or so depending
on how large the file is. When it has transferred, it will tell you how large
More?n_
```

6. To leave the Gopher program, type **exit**.

   Note: *You can type* **exit** *at any time to leave the program; you don't need to be at the main menu.*

As you can see in the steps, when you are in the Delphi Gopher system, you can use a variety of commands. Commonly used Gopher commands include the following (they are shown in uppercase, but you can type them in lowercase also):

Command	Description
TOP	Moves you back to the Gopher main menu (the one you see when you first start up Gopher)
MORE	Displays the next page of the current menu (if there is one)
PREV	Displays the previous page of the current menu
BACK	Moves you back to the previous menu you were on

You can get a list of the available commands by typing **?**. Type **menu** to return to the main Gopher menu.

```
19   THE GRAB BAG (WITH 'NEW THIS WEEK 12/16)              Menu

Enter Item Number, ?, or EXIT: ?

Enter the number of the item you wish to select
               - or -
TOP        - go to top level menu
PREV       - display previous page of current menu
MORE       - display next page of current menu
PAGE 3     - display page 3 of current menu
PAGE LAST  - display last page of current menu
MENU       - redisplay current page of current menu
ROUTE      - show route you followed to reach current menu
SAVE       - save current menu as a Personal Favorite
SAVE 3     - save choice 3 from current menu as a Personal Favorite
INFO       - display Internet information about current menu
INFO 3     - display Internet information about choice 3 of current menu
BACK       - go back to previous menu
Control-Z  - same as BACK
Control-C  - interrupt slow or hung connection attempt
EXIT       - leave Gopher

Enter Item Number, ?, or EXIT:
```

The Delphi Gopher service makes exploring the information stored on Gopher servers around the world easy. When you find a Gopher menu that is interesting to you, you can use the SAVE command to put the menu into your Personal Favorites menu (which is the first item on the main Gopher menu). This way, you can personalize the Gopher system to your needs and easily return to interesting information you have found.

For example, when you were in the Library of Congress Gopher system, if you had typed **SAVE**, the Delphi system would have asked you to confirm that you wanted to add the screen to your Personal Favorites menu. If you confirmed this, your Personal Favorites menu (available under the Delphi main Gopher screen) would now have a menu item that takes you directly to the Library of Congress Gopher system.

7

Using WAIS on Delphi

Because Delphi doesn't have a WAIS program available (at the time this book was written), you will have to use the telnet service to connect to another computer system on the Internet that provides the WAIS service. Chapter 12, "Other Internet Resources," lists several different sites that provide WAIS services on the Internet. For the example in this section, you will use the computer `sunsite.unc.edu` to search for speeches that President Clinton has given in Atlanta, Georgia.

To access WAIS, follow these steps (starting at the Internet Services menu):

1. Start the telnet program by entering `telnet`.

   The Delphi system displays several informational messages about the telnet program.

2. At the `Enter INTERNET address` prompt, specify the name of the machine you want to connect to. For this example, enter **sunsite.unc.edu**.

Using the Delphi telnet command to connect to sunsite.unc.edu.

```
About the Internet    Help
Conference            Exit
Databases (Files)
EMail                 FTP
Forum (Messages)      Gopher
Guides (Books)        IRC-Internet Relay Chat
Register/Cancel       Telnet
Who's Here            Utilities (finger, traceroute, ping)
Workspace             Usenet Newsgroups (NEW MENU)

Internet SIG>Enter your selection: telnet
"Telnet" is a way of connection from one host to another on the Internet. For
more details, type EXIT and then select About Internet Services.

Many Telnet sites are also accessible through DELPHI's main Gopher; just type
eexit and select Gopher.


Enter INTERNET address: sunsite.unc.edu
```

The Delphi system should now connect to the computer
`sunsite.unc.edu`.

**If you have
problems...**   If the Delphi system can't connect to the remote system, it may be because
the remote computer is unavailable or the network between the two machines is broken. In this case, you will see an error message from the telnet
program. You can wait a while and try again, or you can try one of the other
WAIS sites listed in Chapter 12, "Other Internet Resources."

---

3. After the telnet program connects to the other computer, you see
several informational messages and then are asked to provide an
account to log in to. Type **swais** to log in and use a simple WAIS
client program, as explained on-screen.

Connecting to the
remote computer
system.

```
Many Telnet sites are also accessible through DELPHI's main Gopher; just type
eexit and select Gopher.

Enter INTERNET address: sunsite.unc.edu
Trying SUNSITE.UNC.EDU,telnet (152.2.22.81,23) ...
Escape (attention) character is "^\"
***************** Welcome to SunSITE.unc.edu *****************

SunSITE offers several public services via login. These include:

For a simple gopher client,                      login as gopher
For a simple WAIS client (over 500 databases),   login as swais
For WAIS search of political databases,          login as politics
For WAIS search of LINUX databases,              login as linux

For a FTP session, ftp to sunsite.unc.edu. Then login as anonymous

For more information about SunSITE, send mail to info@sunsite.unc.edu


SunOS UNIX (calypso)

login: swais
```

A simple WAIS program

7

4. More informational messages appear to tell you more about the
SunSITE computer system. Then the system prompts for the kind
of terminal you are using. Type **vt100** here.

Most computer systems and communications programs let you use the terminal type vt100. If you use a different terminal type, you can enter that type here instead.

```
We are aware with the new newsgroup problem with [t]rn; bear with us while
we try to figure it out.

thanks,
jem.

University of North Carolina Office For Information Technology
in cooperation with Sun Microsystems, Inc.

Materials available via this id are subject to the statements in
DISCLAIMER.readme found in the anonymous ftp area or on the main menu
of the SunSITE.unc.edu gopher

You could be running this code on your own machine.
You'll find it and other WAIS stuff available via anonymous ftp
from SunSITE.unc.edu in the pub/packages/infosystems/wais directory.

These databases are also available via gopher.
Just point your gopher client to sunsite.unc.edu 70
and enjoy using these databases from your gopher interface.

you're probably a vt100 or should be
TERM = (unknown) vt100
```

Now the remote computer system starts up the WAIS program. After a minute or so, you will see the main screen.

The WAIS main screen, showing the different databases of information that are available for you to search.

```
SWAIS                        Source Selection                Sources: 614
 #          Server                        Source                   Cost
001:  [           archie.au]  aarnet-resource-guide               Free
002:  [ndadsb.gsfc.nasa.gov]  AAS_jobs                            Free
003:  [ndadsb.gsfc.nasa.gov]  AAS_meeting                         Free
004:  [weeds.mgh.harvard.ed]  AAtDB                               Free
005:  [         munin.ub2.lu.se]  academic_email_conf             Free
006:  [wraith.cs.uow.edu.au]  acronyms                            Free
007:  [     archive.orst.edu]  aeronautics                        Free
008:  [ bloat.media.mit.edu]  Aesop-Fables                        Free
009:  [ bloat.media.mit.edu]  aesop                               Free
010:  [ ftp.cs.colorado.edu]  aftp-cs-colorado-edu                Free
011:  [nostromo.oes.orst.ed]  agricultural-market-news            Free
012:  [       sunsite.unc.edu]  alt-sys-sun                       Free
013:  [     archive.orst.edu]  alt.drugs                          Free
014:  [     wais.oit.unc.edu]  alt.gopher                         Free
015:  [sun-wais.oit.unc.edu]  alt.sys.sun                         Free
016:  [     wais.oit.unc.edu]  alt.wais                           Free
017:  [alfred.ccs.carleton.]  amiga-slip                          Free
018:  [       munin.ub2.lu.se]  amiga_fish_contents               Free

Keywords:

<space> selects, w for keywords, arrows move, <return> searches, q quits, or ?
```

Rather than look through all the databases available (614 at the time of this writing), you will use a directory of databases to find ones that would contain the speeches you want.

5. The WAIS program on the sunsite.unc.edu machine lets you look for a particular database by typing a slash (/) and then the name of the database. Because you want to find the directory-of-servers database, enter **/directory-of-servers**. (Other WAIS programs may use a different command.)

Note that the slash
doesn't show up,
but the program
prompts for the
source name.

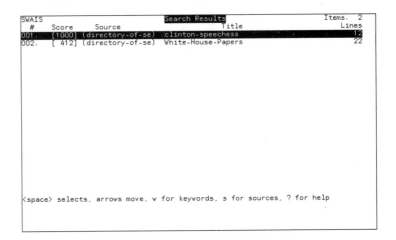

```
SWAIS                       Source Selection              Sources: 614
   #         Server                    Source                   Cost
001:  [          archie.au]  aarnet-resource-guide            Free
002:  [ndadsb.gsfc.nasa.gov]  AAS_jobs                         Free
003:  [ndadsb.gsfc.nasa.gov]  AAS_meeting                      Free
004:  [weeds.mgh.harvard.ed]  AAtDB                            Free
005:  [      munin.ub2.lu.se]  academic_email_conf             Free
006:  [wraith.cs.uow.edu.au]  acronyms                         Free
007:  [    archive.orst.edu]  aeronautics                      Free
008:  [ bloat.media.mit.edu]  Aesop-Fables                     Free
009:  [ bloat.media.mit.edu]  aesop                            Free
010:  [ ftp.cs.colorado.edu]  aftp-cs-colorado-edu             Free
011:  [nostromo.oes.orst.ed]  agricultural-market-news         Free
012:  [     sunsite.unc.edu]  alt-sys-sun                      Free
013:  [    archive.orst.edu]  alt.drugs                        Free
014:  [    wais.oit.unc.edu]  alt.gopher                       Free
015:  [sun-wais.oit.unc.edu]  alt.sys.sun                      Free
016:  [    wais.oit.unc.edu]  alt.wais                         Free
017:  [alfred.ccs.carleton.]  amiga-slip                       Free
018:  [      munin.ub2.lu.se]  amiga_fish_contents              Free

Source Name: directory-of-servers

<space> selects, w for keywords, arrows move, <return> searches, q quits, or ?
```

Searching for the
**directory-of-
servers** database

6. Press the space bar to tell the program that you want to use this database. An asterisk appears next to the line.

7. To do a keyword search (by using the w command) and look for the word *clinton*, enter **wclinton**.

   When you press Enter to start the search, the system goes through the directory of servers looking for all the databases that have information about Clinton. You see a list of any matches it finds on a new screen.

In this example, the
search finds two
databases:
clinton-
speeches and
White-House-
Papers.

```
SWAIS                        Search Results              Items:  2
   #   Score     Source              Title                   Lines
001:  [1000] (directory-of-se)  clinton-speechess            12
002:  [ 412] (directory-of-se)  White-House-Papers           22

<space> selects, arrows move, w for keywords, s for sources, ? for help
```

The White-House-Papers database looks a little more interesting, so you will use this database for more searches.

8. Go back to the list of databases by typing **s**.

9. Press the space bar to tell WAIS that you won't be searching through the directory of servers any more (the asterisk next to the entry disappears).

10. Just as before, you want to search for the `White-House-Papers` database; to do so, enter the command `/White`.

> **Note:** *You can use just a part of the database name when searching, if the part is unique.*

11. Press the space bar to tell WAIS to use this database for searching. An asterisk appears next to the `White-House-Papers` database listing.

12. You want to search the database for the words *clinton*, *atlanta*, and *georgia*, so type the command `wclinton atlanta georgia`.

The WAIS program will look through the database for documents with these words in them, and will assign a score to each one. The better the match with the search words, the higher the score will be. So if documents with all three words in them are available, they will have a high score and will appear near the top of the results list.

Searching the White-House-Papers database for *clinton, atlanta,* and *georgia*.

```
SWAIS                            Source Selection            Sources: 614
  #           Server                       Source                 Cost
595,    [     borg.lib.vt.edu]   vpiej-1                          Free
596,    [     quake.think.com]   wais-discussion-archives         Free
597,    [     quake.think.com]   wais-docs                        Free
598,    [     quake.think.com]   wais-talk-archives               Free
599,    [ cmns-moon.think.com]   wall-street-journal-sample       Free
600,    [hermes.ecn.purdue.ed]   water-quality                    Free
601,    [     quake.think.com]   weather                          Free
602,    [     sunsite.unc.edu]   Welsh                            Free
603,  * [     sunsite.unc.edu]   White-House-Papers               Free
604,    [     wais.nic.ddn.mil]  whois                            Free
605,    [            calypso]    windows-nt-knowledge-base        Free
606,    [     sunsite.unc.edu]   winsock                          Free
607,    [ cmns-moon.think.com]   world-factbook                   Free
608,    [        julian.uwo.ca]  world-factbook92                 Free
609,    [     quake.think.com]   world91a                         Free
610,    [        wais.cic.net]   vuarchive                        Free
611,    [        wais.cic.net]   x.500.working-group              Free
612,    [wais.unidata.ucar.ed]   xgks                             Free

Keywords: clinton atlanta georgia

Enter keywords with spaces between them; <return> to search; ^C to cancel
```

The system finds 40 documents that matched at least some of the words you gave, and the ones at the top of the list probably had all three words in them.

```
SWAIS                           Search Results                    Items: 40
  #      Score     Source                    Title                       Lines
001,    [1000]  (White-House-Pap)  The-First-100-Days-of-the-Administration  1185
002,    [ 929]  (White-House-Pap)  Press-Conference---Presidents-Clinton-an   569
003,    [ 905]  (White-House-Pap)  Clinton-Mitterrand-Press-Conference-3993   538
004,    [ 762]  (White-House-Pap)  White-House-Electronic-Publications,-FAQ   490
005,    [ 762]  (White-House-Pap)  White-House-Electronic-Publications,-FAQ   492
006,    [ 762]  (White-House-Pap)  Press-Availability-with-Pres-Ramos-Revis   478
007,    [ 738]  (White-House-Pap)  White-House-Electronic-Publications,-FAQ   387
008,    [ 715]  (White-House-Pap)  1st-100-Days,-Accomplishments-of-Vice-Pr   695
009,    [ 715]  (White-House-Pap)  Presidents-Remark-on-Larry-King-Live-7-2  1097
010,    [ 715]  (White-House-Pap)  Health-Care-Letters-Read-in-Rose-Garden-  1087
011,    [ 715]  (White-House-Pap)  White-House-Electronic-Publications,-FAQ   477
012,    [ 715]  (White-House-Pap)  Press-Availability-with-S-Korean-Pres-Ki   366
013,    [ 691]  (White-House-Pap)  Answers-to-Frequently-Asked-Questions-31   271
014,    [ 691]  (White-House-Pap)  Press-Conference-by-Presidents-Clinton-a   250
015,    [ 691]  (White-House-Pap)  White-House-Electronic-Publications-FAQs   386
016,    [ 691]  (White-House-Pap)  White-House-Electronic-Publications-and-   389
017,    [ 691]  (White-House-Pap)  White-House-Electronic-Publications,-FAQ   451
018,    [ 691]  (White-House-Pap)  White-House-Electronic-Publications,-FAQ   453


<space> selects, arrows move, w for keywords, s for sources, ? for help
```

13. To display a document, move to the document and press the space bar. Press the down-arrow key to move down one document in the list. Press the up-arrow key to move up one document in the list.

    For this example, move to the first document in the list and press the space bar. If you page down through the document, you will see that *clinton*, *atlanta*, and *georgia* are all mentioned.

The WAIS program displays the document, a copy of a speech given by President Clinton.

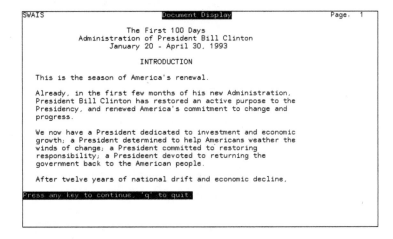

```
SWAIS                        Document Display                      Page:  1
                              The First 100 Days
                       Administration of President Bill Clinton
                           January 20 - April 30, 1993

                                  INTRODUCTION

        This is the season of America's renewal.

        Already, in the first few months of his new Administration,
        President Bill Clinton has restored an active purpose to the
        Presidency, and renewed America's commitment to change and
        progress.

        We now have a President dedicated to investment and economic
        growth; a President determined to help Americans weather the
        winds of change; a President committed to restoring
        responsibility; a Presideent devoted to returning the
        government back to the American people.

        After twelve years of national drift and economic decline,

Press any key to continue, 'q' to quit.
```

Note: *You can get more information about the WAIS commands by typing* **h** *or* **?** *in the WAIS program.*

You can quit the WAIS program and return to the Delphi system by typing **q**.

7

Using WWW on Delphi

Like Gopher and WAIS, WWW (which stands for World Wide Web) is a tool for locating and retrieving information on the Internet. WWW, though, is based on the idea of reading a document that contains links to other documents.

Using WWW on Delphi is very similar to using WAIS; because no WWW program is directly on Delphi, you have to use the telnet service to connect to another machine that provides a WWW program. The computer you will use for this example is ukanaix.cc.ukans.edu.

From the Internet Services menu, follow these steps:

1. Start the telnet program by typing `telnet`.

2. At the Enter INTERNET address prompt, type **ukanaix.cc.ukans.edu**.

Using telnet to connect to a WWW service provider.

```
Internet SIG Menu:

About the Internet      Help
Conference              Exit
Databases (Files)
EMail                   FTP
Forum (Messages)        Gopher
Guides (Books)          IRC-Internet Relay Chat
Register/Cancel         Telnet
Who's Here              Utilities (finger, traceroute, ping)
Workspace               Usenet Newsgroups (NEW MENU)

Internet SIG>Enter your selection: telnet
"Telnet" is a way of connection from one host to another on the Internet. For
more details, type EXIT and then select About Internet Services.

Many Telnet sites are also accessible through DELPHI's main Gopher; just type
exit and select Gopher.

Enter INTERNET address: ukanaix.cc.ukans.edu
```

After telnet connects to the ukanaix.cc.ukans.edu system, you see some informational messages and then a prompt asking you for an account to log in to.

3. To use the WWW service, enter the account name **www**. No password is needed for this account on this system.

Entering the account name to access WWW on the remote computer.

```
                        The University of Kansas
                IBM AIX Version 3 for RISC System/6000
                (C) Copyrights by IBM and by others 1982, 1990.

        For assistance call 864-0110 or to report network problems call 864-0200

        Login as 'kufacts' for  access to the Campus Wide Information System.
                 'history' for history network resources
                 'ex-ussr' for former Soviet Union info
login: www
```

The system runs the WWW program and displays the main screen. This WWW program, called Lynx, uses different-colored text to show where you can move to other documents.

The Lynx program's screen shown at startup. The screen gives some basic information about Lynx and lets you view information useful to beginners.

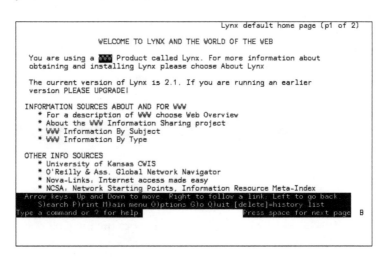

If you use the arrow keys on your keyboard to move to the words About Lynx and then press Enter, you will move to another document that gives you more information about the Lynx program. When you use the arrow keys to move around in a document, the links to other documents become *highlighted* (that is, they turn into white characters on a black background) to show which link you can move to.

For example, press the down-arrow key on your keyboard six times to highlight the link By Subject.

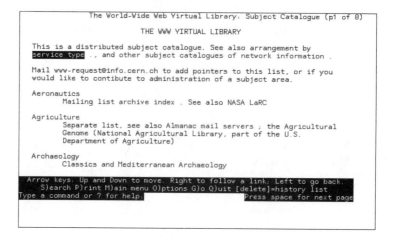

After you select By Subject and press Enter, the Lynx Subject Catalogue screen appears, showing some of the topics available.

Move back to the initial Lynx screen by pressing the left-arrow key (which always moves you back to the previous document you were reading).

Next, move to the By Type link by pressing the down-arrow key once and then pressing Enter. On this page, you can go to other documents that list all the available WWW, WAIS, Gopher, and archie servers available on the Internet. This page makes browsing around easy; you can spend hours simply looking at the various servers and seeing what is available!

The Lynx Resources
Classified by Type
of Service screen.

```
                    Data sources classified by access protocol (p1 of 3)

                    RESOURCES CLASSIFIED BY TYPE OF SERVICE

        See also categorization exist by subject . If you know what sort of a
        service you are looking for, look here.

        World-Wide Web servers
                List of W3 native "HTTP" servers. These are generally the most
                friendly. See also: about the WWW initiative .

        WAIS servers
                Find WAIS index servers using the directory of servers , or
                lists by name or domain . See also: about WAIS .

        Network News
                Available directly in all www browsers. See also this list of
                FAQs .

        Gopher
                Campus-wide information systems, etc, listed geographically.
        Arrow keys: Up and Down to move. Right to follow a link; Left to go back.
          S)earch P)rint M)ain menu O)ptions G)o Q)uit [delete]=history list
        Type a command or ? for help.                    Press space for next page
```

You can leave the Lynx program by typing the **q** command at any time.
The Lynx program asks you to confirm that you want to quit, and you
should type **y** to quit.

Reading USENET News Groups

USENET
A collection of
computer discus-
sion groups that
are read all over
the world.

Delphi has many discussion groups available only on the Delphi system,
but the *USENET* news groups are also available through the Internet Services menu. To access the USENET news groups, follow these steps:

1. At the Internet Services menu, type **usenet** to bring up the USENET
   menu.

The USENET menu
shows that Delphi
has two news
readers available:
the Delphi news
reader and the NN
news reader.

USENET menu——

```
Internet SIG Menu:

About the Internet    Help
Conference            Exit
Databases (Files)
EMail                 FTP
Forum (Messages)      Gopher
Guides (Books)        IRC-Internet Relay Chat
Register/Cancel       Telnet
Who's Here            Utilities (finger, traceroute, ping)
Workspace             Usenet Newsgroups (NEW MENU)

Internet SIG>Enter your selection: usenet


USENET Menu:

About Usenet Discussion Groups
Usenet (Delphi Newsreader)
NN Newsreader (Usenet)
Instructions for the NN Newsreader
Exit

USENET>Enter your selection: usenet
```

7

The Delphi news reading program is very easy to use and will be used for the examples in this section. It uses a format very similar to the Delphi Gopher program to present news groups. As you become more familiar with USENET and reading news groups, however, you may want to read the instructions for the NN news reading program and to try the NN news reader.

2. Start the Delphi news reader by typing the command **usenet**.

The middle part of the menu gives several different lists of the news groups and mailing lists available. The bottom part of the menu is the start of a list of selected news groups.

```
Usenet Discussion Groups
Page 1 of 3

1    PERSONAL FAVORITES                                       Menu
2    Access Any Newsgroup (by typing its name)               Usenet
3    DELPHI News Reader HELP files                           Text
4    New User Topics and FAQS (NEW USERS, START HERE!)       Menu
5    How to Create New Newsgroups (FAQs)                     Menu
6    Usenet FAQ Archive by hierarchy (rtfm.mit.edu)          Menu
7    Search Usenet for user's addresses                      Search
8                                                            Text
9    ==========NEWSGROUP LISTS (not always available)======= Text
10   Search newsgroups and mailing lists by topic            Search
11   List of Active Newsgroups, Part I   (comp, misc, news)  Text
12   List of Active Newsgroups, Part II  (rec, sci, soc, talk) Text
13   Alternative Newsgroup List, Part I  (alt thru bit)      Text
14   Alternative Newsgroup List, Part II (clarinet thru vmsnet) Text
15   Mailing Lists Available in Usenet                       Text
16                                                            Text
17   ==================SELECTED NEWSGROUPS==================  Text
18   Academic Freedom News (alt.comp.acad-freedom.news)      Usenet
19   Academic Freedom Talk (alt.comp.acad-freedom.talk)      Usenet

Enter Item Number, MORE, ?, or EXIT: 4
```

Notice at the top of the screen that this is the first page of three total pages on this menu. Just as in the Gopher system, you can use the more command to move to the next page of the menu.

The top part of this USENET Discussion Groups screen has several menu items with information for new users. You can read the Delphi news reader help files, and several menu items let you read the *FAQ* postings on many USENET news groups.

FAQs
Frequently Asked Questions documents, which contain a list of commonly asked questions on a USENET news group topic.

3. To read the New User Topics and FAQS menu items, enter **4**.

Delphi New User
Topics and FAQS
screen.

```
16                                                          Text
17   ==================SELECTED NEWSGROUPS===================  Text
18  Academic Freedom News (alt.comp.acad-freedom.news)       Usenet
19  Academic Freedom Talk (alt.comp.acad-freedom.talk)       Usenet

Enter Item Number, MORE, ?, or EXIT: 4

New User Topics and FAQS (NEW USERS, START HERE!)
Page 1 of 1

1    HELP File for the DELPHI newsreader                      Text
2    News Announce Newusers (news.announce.newusers)         Usenet
3    Newusers Questions (news.newusers.questions)            Usenet
4    ==================FAQ FILES FROM USENET==================  Text
5        NOTE, The items below are files from rtfm.mit.edu   Text
6    FAQ, What is Usenet?                                     Text
7    FAQ, Answers to Frequently Asked Questions about Usenet  Text
8    FAQ, A Primer on How to Work With the Usenet Community   Text
9    FAQ, Rules for posting to Usenet                         Text
10   FAQ, Emily Postnews Answers Your Questions on Netiquette Text
11   FAQ, Hints on writing style for Usenet                   Text
12   FAQ, Welcome to news.newusers.questions!                 Text

Enter Item Number, SAVE, ?, or BACK: 2
```

You probably will want to read through the items on this menu if you aren't familiar with USENET news groups. They provide valuable information that will make using USENET easier and less frustrating, including information on posting etiquette, writing style, and answers to frequently asked questions about USENET. You also can read the news groups news.announce.newusers and news.newusers.questions.

4. You should always read the information in news.announce.newusers first, to learn important details about USENET. Read this group now by entering **2**.

The Delphi news reader tells you how many messages have been posted recently to the group, and lets you pick the number of days of postings you want to read. You will be shown messages posted only during that time period.

5. Because news.announce.newusers doesn't have many posts, pick 14 days by entering **14**.

7

Accessing the
news group
news.announce.
newusers.

```
New User Topics and FAQS (NEW USERS, START HERE!)
Page 1 of 1

1    HELP File for the DELPHI newsreader                      Text
2    News Announce Newusers (news.announce.newusers)          Usenet
3    Newusers Questions (news.newusers.questions)             Usenet
4    =================FAQ FILES FROM USENET====================  Text
5       NOTE: The items below are files from rtfm.mit.edu     Text
6    FAQ: What is Usenet?                                     Text
7    FAQ: Answers to Frequently Asked Questions about Usenet  Text
8    FAQ: A Primer on How to Work With the Usenet Community   Text
9    FAQ: Rules for posting to Usenet                         Text
10   FAQ: Emily Postnews Answers Your Questions on Netiquette Text
11   FAQ: Hints on writing style for Usenet                   Text
12   FAQ: Welcome to news.newusers.questions!                 Text

Enter Item Number, SAVE, ?, or BACK: 2

News Announce Newusers (news.announce.newusers)

16 messages have been posted in the last 14 days.

Show messages posted in last ___ days: [5] 14
```

Threads
Groups of articles
that have the same
subject.

6. The news reader now lists the articles that you can read in
   news.announce.newusers. The articles are grouped into *threads*.
   You can read one of these threads by typing the number of the
   thread you want to read.

Articles available in
news.announce.
newusers.

```
News Announce Newusers
Page 1 of 1 [16 messages in 5 discussion threads]

1   How to become a USENET site
2   List of Periodic Informational Postings, Part 1/7 (7 msgs)
3   Changes to List of Periodic Informational Postings
4   Publicly Accessible Mailing Lists, Part 1/6 (6 msgs)
5   Introduction to the *.answers newsgroups

Enter Thread Number, ADD, ?, or EXIT:
```

7. To quit the Delphi news reader, enter **exit** twice, to return to the
   New User Topics menu and then to leave news reader.

8. The news reader asks you to confirm that you want to leave by
   typing **y** or pressing Enter. Press Enter.

At any time when reading articles in the Delphi news reader, you can post a new article to the news group, forward the current article to someone through electronic mail, reply to the author of an article through e-mail, or perform other news functions. A list of the commands you can use is available by typing **help**.

The Delphi news reader help screen.

```
[RETURN]   - Read next message.
ADD        - Start a new thread with a new subject.
ADD <filename> - Start a new thread with the message from a workspace file.
BACK       - Read message to which current message replies.
CURRENT    - re-read current message.
DIRECTORY  - Display a list of discussion threads.
EXIT or Control-Z - return to thread list (same as DIRECTORY).
FILE       - Copy this message to your workspace.
FORWARD    - Send a copy of this message via e-mail.
HEADER     - display the complete header for current message.
HELP       - show this screen.
LAST       - Re-read previous message.
MAIL REPLY - Send private reply via e-mail.
NEXT THREAD- Skip to next discussion thread (subject).
PREV       - Read first message in previous thread.
QUIT       - Return to list of discussion topics.
READ NEXT  - Read next message (same as [RETURN]).
REPLY      - Post a reply within the bulletin board.
SAVE       - save this discussion group in your Personal Favorites area
TOP        - Go back to first message in current thread.

Next thread [Return], Reply, or ?>
```

One important command is SAVE. This command saves the current news group you are reading to the Personal Favorites menu item on the main news reading screen. The Personal Favorites item lets you make up a menu that has all the news groups you read regularly and makes reading the groups you want simple.

The Delphi news reader makes moving around and reading USENET news groups easy. Replying to posts (using the REPLY command when you are reading an article) and posting new articles (using the ADD command when in a news group) are very similar to using the Delphi e-mail system. And because it's menu-based and lets you set up your own menu of personal groups, the Delphi news reader is perfect for people who are just starting to read USENET news.

Other Internet Services on Delphi

Delphi has a few other Internet-related services available under the Internet Services menu. For example, you can join a Delphi discussion group (called a *forum*) with messages about the Internet, access a Delphi

7

database of files about the Internet, and use a program called Internet Relay Chat, which lets you talk to other people on the Internet.

Delphi also has several Internet utilities available under the Utilities menu. One of these is the finger program, which lets you get information about users on the Internet. The netfind utility lets you look for a user's e-mail address through several databases on the Internet. Other utilities, such as ping and traceroute, are useful in diagnosing network problems. (These commands give brief descriptions of what they do when you run them.)

Summary

If you are looking for an on-line service that provides broad Internet access in addition to its own services, Delphi is a good choice. Delphi provides access to all available Internet services. Its menu-driven interface can be used from any terminal or terminal emulator (although people who are used to the Windows or Macintosh environment might find the interface cumbersome). In addition to its Internet services, Delphi provides access to many additional services such as news, weather, stock quotes, and its own forums.

When you're ready to experiment with using the different Internet services from Delphi, look over the chapters in Part III, "A Resource Guide to the Internet": Chapter 9 discusses a number of interesting ftp sites; Chapter 10 lists some of the USENET news groups that may interest you; Chapter 11 discusses mailing lists that pertain to some popular topics; and Chapter 12 talks about a number of other interesting Internet resources, including on-line newsletters, books, and library catalogs, and Internet BBS systems. These chapters should give you a good start for your exploration of the Internet.

Chapter 8

Using the Internet via a UNIX System

Throughout most of the Internet's history, most of the systems on the Internet have run on the UNIX operating system. Because so many UNIX systems are on the Internet, most of the software needed to get access to Internet resources is available on UNIX systems and easy to access from other UNIX systems.

Unless you are working from a UNIX console, you are limited mainly to using character-oriented programs that will work on a simple terminal or communications program. In fact, the examples in this chapter were made using a terminal communication program running under Microsoft Windows and communicating with a UNIX system.

Note: *You possibly may have a UNIX workstation that's running a graphical environment such as X Window. In this case, you may be able to take advantage of some of the graphical programs available for these Internet services. Check with your systems administrators to see what is available on your system.*

This chapter assumes that you are already familiar with UNIX and the commands necessary to connect and log in to your UNIX system.

This chapter will tell you how to

- Send Internet e-mail using the elm and MH programs
- Read USENET news groups using the rn news reader
- Find information on the Internet

- Upload and download files using ftp

- Connect to host resources using telnet

Be sure to read the general information about these topics in Chapter 1 before reading the following sections.

Sending Internet E-Mail

Several different programs are available to send electronic mail on UNIX systems. These programs fall into two main categories: command-line and screen-oriented. With command-line programs, you type a separate command for each mail function you want to do. For example, you may type a command to display a mail message, and then another command to reply to that message. Screen-oriented programs, on the other hand, usually allow you to type a single character to perform mail functions, and can display help information.

The following sections give examples of both types of programs. The screen-oriented program you will use is called *elm*, which is a commonly used mail program for UNIX systems. The command-line system is the MH (for Message Handling) mail system. Other commonly used screen-oriented mail programs for UNIX are *pine* and *mail* (the mail program commonly provided with UNIX). Another commonly used command-line mail program is MUSH (which stands for Mail User's SHell).

Although these sections show some of the most used features of these programs, they don't show you everything that they can do; if you have these programs on your system, you should look over the documentation for more information.

Using the elm E-Mail Program

elm is a very easy mail program to use, because it displays many of the commonly used commands on-screen, and has help messages for all its commands available through the help system.

On most UNIX systems, you start the elm program by typing `elm`. The elm program starts up and shows the main screen.

The top part of the main screen shows what messages can be read; the bottom part shows some of the commands available.

```
  Mailbox is '/usr/spool/mail/tpike' with 0 messages [ELM 2.4 PL23]




    You can use any of the following commands by pressing the first character;
  d)elete or u)ndelete mail,  m)ail a message,  r)eply or f)orward mail,  q)uit
    To read a message, press <return>.  j = move down, k = move up, ? = help
Command:
```

Sending Mail with elm. Now you will send an e-mail message to an Internet site. You want to get a reply back, so you'll use a special address set up just for this book. Follow these steps:

1. In the elm mailer, type the command m to start sending a message.

2. The program prompts (To:) for the address you are sending the message to. You can type any Internet e-mail address here, but for this example, enter **book@pittslug.sug.org**.

3. At the Subject of message: prompt, enter **hello**.

4. At the Copies to: prompt, enter any addresses to send copies of the message to. For this example, press Enter to leave this line blank.

elm's send message screen. The address and subject information is entered, and you're ready to enter the editor to compose the body of the message.

```
  Mailbox is '/usr/spool/mail/tpike' with 0 messages [ELM 2.4 PL23]




    You can use any of the following commands by pressing the first character;
  d)elete or u)ndelete mail,  m)ail a message,  r)eply or f)orward mail,  q)uit
    To read a message, press <return>.  j = move down, k = move up, ? = help
Command: Mail                            To: book@pittslug.sug.org
Subject of message: hello
Copies to:
```

8

5. elm starts a text editor so that you can type the body of the message. Because this example message isn't going to be read by a person, you don't need to put in a body, but you can if you want to.

   Note: *Because text editors vary from system to system, more detailed information can't be provided here. You should check with your system documentation for more information.*

6. After you leave the text editor, you can type **e** to edit the message again (if you made a mistake), **h** to edit the headers of the message (to change the addresses or the subject, for example), **s** to send the message, or **f** to abort the message (if you change your mind about it). For this example, type **s** to send the message.

elm immediately delivers your mail and returns to the elm main screen.

If you have problems...

Rather than receive a response back from the e-mail server, if you get an error message saying that the mail couldn't be delivered, see the "Troubleshooting" section near the end of this chapter for possible solutions.

Reading Mail with elm. After you send your mail message as instructed in the preceding section, you will get an automatic response back from the server set up for this book. Depending on how heavily loaded your system is, you should get a response back from the server within a few minutes.

When you start the elm program and have messages waiting to be read, at the top of the screen you will see the list of messages showing the message number, the author, and the subject. The first message is the most recent one you have received; any older messages (ones you have kept from the last time you ran elm) are listed after the new messages. New messages are marked with an N, messages that you haven't read but were kept after the last time you ran elm are marked with an O, and read messages aren't marked.

The first message is the most recent message received.

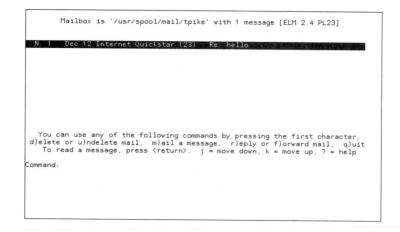

```
       Mailbox is '/usr/spool/mail/tpike' with 1 message [ELM 2.4 PL23]

   N  1   Dec 12 Internet Quickstar (23)    Re: hello




      You can use any of the following commands by pressing the first character;
   d)elete or u)ndelete mail,  m)ail a message,  r)eply or f)orward mail,  q)uit
      To read a message, press <return>.   j = move down, k = move up, ? = help
 Command:
```

You can move between the messages to be read by using the j command to move down one message and the k command to move up one message. To read a response, highlight the message you want to read (the current message will be highlighted in reverse characters—white character on a black background) and then press Enter. For this example, press Enter to read the only message available. You see the name of the person who sent the message, followed by the mail headers and the body of the message.

The elm screen, showing a mail message received from Book mail server.

```
Message 1/1  From Internet Quickstart          Dec 12, 93 03:27:38 pm -0500

Date: Sun, 12 Dec 93 15:27:38 -0500
To: tpike@pittslug.sug.org
Subject: Re: hello

Congratulations! You have successfully sent mail to the Internet e-mail
address 'book@pittslug.sug.org'! This response is generated by an
automatic mail processing program. For more commands that this system
understands, send a mail message to the same address
('book@pittslug.sug.org') with a subject of 'help'.

Thank you for your mail, and I hope you find the book Internet
Quickstart helpful!

                 The Authors




 Command ('i' to return to index):
```

You now can return to the main screen by typing the **i** command.

8

Replying to Mail Messages in elm. Rather than create a new mail message, you can send a reply to a message you have received. elm makes replying easy by filling in the address and subject of the message for you.

You should be in the main display window, either by starting elm from the UNIX system or by returning to the message index using the i command. Then follow these steps:

1. Move to the message you want to reply to by using the j command to move down one message in the list or the k command to move up one message. The current message will be highlighted in reverse video.

2. To reply to the current message, type the command **r**.

3. The elm program asks whether you want to include a copy of the current message in the message you are sending. At the Copy message? (y/n): prompt, type **y** to include a copy of the current message for this example.

4. At the Subject of message: line, elm includes the subject of the current message, with Re: in front of it. (If the current message has a subject of test, for example, elm displays Subject of message: Re: test.) If you want to keep the suggested subject, you can just press Enter, but you can edit the subject to something else, if you want.

5. At the Copies to: prompt, enter the e-mail address of people who should receive copies of this message. You can leave this blank by pressing Enter, or you can type an e-mail address here. For this example, press Enter to leave it blank.

The elm program now starts up a text editor to let you edit the message you want to send. The rest of the process is just like sending a normal mail message.

Deleting Mail Messages in elm. After you receive several e-mail messages, you probably will want to delete some that are no longer important.

You should be in the main display window, either by starting elm from the UNIX system, or by returning to the message index using the i command. Then follow these steps:

1. Move to the message you want to delete.

2. Delete the highlighted mail message by using the d command.

If you decide after the fact that you really wanted to keep the message, undelete it by using the u command. You can do this only before you leave elm, however; after you leave, the message is gone for good.

Using Other elm Commands. The following commands are useful to use from the elm main screen:

- The f command will forward the highlighted message to another user.

- You can get help on a command by typing ? followed by the letter for a command. For example, to get more information on the d command, type **?d.**

- The C command lets you move a mail message into a different mail folder.

Using the MH Mail System

Unlike the elm mailer, the MH mail system is made up of many individual commands that you can run from the UNIX command prompt (usually %) that you get when you log in to your system.

Mail messages in the MH system are kept in folders. New mail is put in your inbox folder. If you want to save your mail messages, you may want to keep related mail messages in their own folders to make them easier to find.

The most commonly used MH commands are as follows:

Command	Description
inc	Reads in any new mail messages you have received into your inbox, which is your default mail folder. Messages in your inbox are numbered, and MH keeps track of which message is the current one.
show	Displays your current message.
next	Moves to the next message in your folder and displays it.
prev	Moves to the previous message in your folder and displays it.

8

(continues)

Command	Description
comp	Allows you to compose a new mail message.
rmm	Removes the current mail message from your folder.
repl	Allows you to reply to the current message.
refile	Allows you to move a mail message into another folder.
scan	Displays an index of messages in the current folder.
folder	Allows you to change folders.

Other MH commands are available, but these are the ones you will use every day.

Sending Mail with MH. MH allows you to send mail to Internet users by using the comp command. For this example, you will send mail to an Internet address set up for this book. This address will automatically send a response to you.

To send an e-mail message using MH, follow these steps:

1. From your UNIX system prompt, type the command **comp**.

2. At the To: prompt, type the address you are sending the message to. For this example, enter **book@pittslug.sug.org**.

3. At the cc: prompt, type the addresses of the people who should receive carbon copies of the message. For this example, you can leave this line blank by pressing Enter.

4. At MH's Subject: prompt, enter the subject of the message. For this example, enter **hello**.

    Note: *When it's time for you to enter the body of your message, MH may—depending on how it's set up—start an editor to let you do so. If no special editor has been set up, MH will display a short line of dashes to separate the header from the message, and then let you type your message. Be sure to press Enter at the end of each line of your message.*

5. Type the body of your message. You can type anything you want for this particular message—a human won't be reading it.

6. Press Ctrl+D (hold down the Ctrl key and type **d**) to tell UNIX that you are finished typing a message.

7. At the What now? prompt, you can enter one of several commands: **edit** to enter a text editor (which allows you to change the body or the heading lines of the message), **quit** to abort the message, and **send** to send the message. For this example, type **send**. MH immediately tries to send the message to the destination.

Sending a mail message to the book server at the address book@pittslug. sug.org.

```
% comp
To, book@pittslug.sug.org
cc,
Subject, hello
--------
The server does not need a message body, but I typed
one in anyway.
--------
What now? send
%
```

If you have problems...

Rather than receive a response back from the e-mail server, if you get an error message saying that the mail couldn't be delivered, see the "Trouble-shooting" section near the end of this chapter for possible solutions.

Reading E-Mail with MH. After your mail system sends the message and the book server processes it, you will receive in your system mailbox a message back from the server. Normally, this message will appear within a few minutes. The UNIX system will normally tell you when you have new mail waiting to be read.

To read your mail messages, follow these steps:

1. Enter the **inc** command to read it into your inbox folder. When you use inc, the MH system makes the first new message your current message.

8

The `inc` command
gives some infor-
mation about the
message you have
received (the
sender, the subject,
etc.), as much as fits
on one line.

```
% comp
To: book@pittslug.sug.org
cc:
Subject: hello
--------
The server does not need a message body, but I typed
one in anyway.
--------
What now? send
% inc
Incorporating new mail into inbox...

   1+ 12/12 book@pittslug.sug  Re: hello <<Congratulations! You have successful
%
```

The inc command ┐
Message number ┐
Message date ┐

2. Type **show** to display the contents of the message.

The show com-
mand displays the
headers and
message body of
the e-mail message
you got back from
the Book server.

```
(Message inbox:1)
Return-Path: book
Received: by pittslug.sug.org (5.64/2.5)
        id AA07852; Sun, 12 Dec 93 16:41:04 -0500
Date: Sun, 12 Dec 93 16:41:04 -0500
From: Internet Quickstart <book@pittslug.sug.org>
Message-Id: <9312122141.AA07852@pittslug.sug.org>
To: tpike@pittslug.sug.org
Subject: Re: hello
In-Reply-To: <9312122140.AA07841@pittslug.sug.org>
Content-Type: text/plain; charset=us-ascii

Congratulations! You have successfully sent mail to the Internet e-mail
address 'book@pittslug.sug.org'! This response is generated by an
automatic mail processing program. For more commands that this system
understands, send a mail message to the same address
('book@pittslug.sug.org') with a subject of 'help'.

Thank you for your mail, and I hope you find the book Internet
Quickstart helpful!

                The Authors
%
```

After you read your message, you can display the next message by typing
next, or display the previous message by typing **prev**. If a message doesn't
exist before or after the current message, the system will tell you.

Type the **scan** command to see a list of all messages in your inbox.

To display a particular message, you can use a message number with show
(and many other MH commands). For example, you can type show 1 to
display the first message in your folder.

Replying to a Mail Message with MH. You can reply to a message using the `repl` command. This command fills in the header information automatically, requiring only that you enter the body of the message. The `To:` field contains the address of the person who sent the message to which you are replying. The `Subject:` field is the same as the original message, except with `Re:` preceding it. If the original message was carbon copied to other users, they are automatically included on the `cc:` list for the reply message.

To use the `repl` command, follow these steps:

1. To reply to the current message, simply type **repl**. To reply to any message in the folder, give the message number after the `repl` command. For example, to reply to message 4, type **repl 4**.

2. Enter the body of the reply message.

From here, proceed as instructed in steps 5 through 7 of the earlier section "Sending Mail with MH."

Deleting E-Mail with MH. The `rmm` command deletes mail messages. You can use the command alone to delete the current message (the last one you displayed), or specify a message number to delete that message:

■ To remove the first message in the current folder, type **rmm 1**.

■ To remove the message you have just read, type **rmm**.

Refiling E-Mail with MH. You can keep related messages in a single folder to allow you to find them more easily. To do so, move a message with the `refile` command to an appropriate folder, as follows:

1. To save the current message to a folder called `book`, for example, type the command `refile cur +book`. (Because the message you received was message number 1, you also can type **refile 1 +book**.)

8

Note: *The folder name must be preceded by a plus sign (+) when being used as an argument in an MH command.*

2. If the folder doesn't exist, the MH system will ask whether you want to create it. Type **y** to create the folder and move message 1 to it.

Changing Folders in MH. After you refile messages into other folders, you need to be able to go look at the messages in those folders. To do so, you need to change folders with the folder command. Follow these steps:

1. Type **folder +book** to make the book folder the one you are now working in. (If you want to change to a folder other than book, just substitute the name of that folder.)

Note: *If you use the inc command while you are in another folder, it automatically places you back in the inbox folder and makes the first new message the current message.*

2. Type **scan** to show a list of all the messages in the current folder (the book folder now). You may use any MH command on the messages in this folder (such as show, refile, and rmm).

Examples of various MH commands. The refile, folder, scan, and rmm commands are shown with their output.

```
Subject: Re: hello
In-Reply-To: <931212140.AA07841@pittslug.sug.org>
Content-Type: text/plain; charset=us-ascii


Congratulations! You have successfully sent mail to the Internet e-mail
address 'book@pittslug.sug.org'! This response is generated by an
automatic mail processing program. For more commands that this system
understands, send a mail message to the same address
('book@pittslug.sug.org') with a subject of 'help'.

Thank you for your mail, and I hope you find the book Internet
Quickstart helpful!

                The Authors
```

refile command —— `% refile cur +book`
folder command and result —— `% folder +book`
`                book+ has    1 message  (  1-  1); cur=  1.`
`% scan`
`    1+ 12/12 book@pittslug.sug  Re: hello <<Congratulations! You have successful`
`% rmm 1`
scan command and results —— `% scan`
`scan: no messages in book`
`%`

rmm command

Other MH Commands. A number of other MH commands are available. For example, a special MH command lets you search through a folder for messages that match a pattern (the `pick` command), another command allows you to delete folders, and another allows you to forward a message to another user. The documentation that you receive from your account manager should have information about other MH commands.

Reading USENET News Groups

USENET
A collection of computer discussion groups that are read all over the world.

When you read *USENET* news groups on a UNIX system, you probably will be using a program called rn, the most commonly used UNIX news reading program. It is a screen-oriented program that allows you to use single-character commands to perform most news functions.

Note: *Several other USENET news readers are available, such as trn, nn, and tin. All of these offer similar functions, but rn is the most common news reading program.*

rn has many features that you won't need when you first start using it. You should read the help screens and the system documentation for rn to learn what it can do for you.

Selecting News Groups within rn

Because several thousand USENET groups are available to be read, you probably will want to set up the rn program to list only the groups you are actually interested in reading. To select the groups you want to read, follow these steps:

Subscribe
Set up your USENET news reading software to show you when articles are available to be read in a particular news group.

1. You generally start rn by typing the command **rn** at the UNIX prompt.

   rn lists the news groups you are *subscribed* to. In most cases, this list is alphabetical and shows the number of articles you haven't read in each news group.

8

The rn news group selection screen, shown when the program is started.

```
% rn
Unread news in comp.admin.policy                    130 articles
Unread news in comp.ai.edu                           39 articles
Unread news in comp.ai.fuzzy                         119 articles
Unread news in comp.ai.genetic                       199 articles
Unread news in comp.ai.jair.announce                   1 article
etc.

******** 130 unread articles in comp.admin.policy--read now? [ynq]
```

Unsubscribe

Indicate to your USENET news reading software that you no longer want to read a particular news group (you don't want to see the group listed as having new articles).

Note: *On many systems, when you first start rn, you will be subscribed to all the news groups available on the system (possibly thousands of them!). You will need to spend some time* unsubscribing *the groups you definitely aren't interested in. You can subscribe to them again later on if you change your mind.*

At the bottom of the group list, the system asks you what you want to do with the first group in the list (comp.admin.policy, in the example shown).

2. You can get a list of options that are available at this point by typing **h**.

The rn news group selection help screen (first page), giving the main news group selection commands.

```
Newsgroup Selection commands:

y,SP     Do this newsgroup now.
.cmd     Do this newsgroup, executing cmd as first command.
=        Start this newsgroup, but list subjects before reading articles.
u        Unsubscribe from this newsgroup.
c        Catch up (mark this newsgroup all read).

n        Go to the next newsgroup with unread news.
N        Go to the next newsgroup.
p        Go to the previous newsgroup with unread news.
P        Go to the previous newsgroup.
-        Go to the previously displayed newsgroup.
1        Go to the first newsgroup.
^        Go to the first newsgroup with unread news.
$        Go to the last newsgroup.
g name   Go to the named newsgroup.  Subscribe to new newsgroups this way too.
/pat     Search forward for newsgroup matching pattern.
?pat     Search backward for newsgroup matching pattern.
         (Use * and ? style patterns.  Append r to include read newsgroups.)
l pat    List unsubscribed newsgroups containing pattern.
m name   Move named newsgroup elsewhere (no name moves current newsgroup).
o pat    Only display newsgroups matching pattern.  Omit pat to unrestrict.
[Type space to continue]
```

Note: *With most rn commands, you don't have to press Enter after typing a command—the system goes right ahead and executes the command.*

3. One important command at this point is the u command, which tells rn that you want to unsubscribe this group. If you type **u** now, you won't be presented with the news group `comp.admin.policy` the next time you enter rn.

4. To move to the next group in your list, type **n**. To move to the previous group in your list, type **p**. If you are at the top of your list, you automatically will be moved to the bottom of your list.

5. If you know the group you want to read, use the g command to go directly to that group. Type **g `news.announce.newusers`** now to go right to that group. If you weren't subscribed to that group before, the system asks you if you want to subscribe to it. Reply **y**.

Note: *Occasionally when you start rn, you see the name of a news group that has just been created and are asked whether you want to subscribe to it. News groups may be created several times a week, more or less, depending on when your news administrator creates new netnews groups.*

Reading News with rn

After you select a news group to read, you are now in the news reading part of rn, which has many commands that allow you (for example) to move between articles, skip articles you don't want to read, and search for articles.

The following figure shows an example article from the group `news.announce.newusers`, which explains how to create a new news group (of course, you may not see this exact article when you go to read the news group). You can see in this screen the headers of the news article, showing who posted it and what it is about, and the beginning of the article itself. At the bottom is the line --MORE--[5%], which indicates that the article is longer and that you've seen about 5 percent of the article so far.

8

The headers of the news article, showing who posted it and what it is about, and the beginning of the article.

```
Article 209 (7 more) in news.announce.newusers (moderated).
From: rdippold@happy.qualcomm.com (Ron Dippold)
Newsgroups: news.groups,news.announce.newusers,news.answers
Subject: Usenet Newsgroup Creation Companion
Followup-To: poster
Date: 20 Nov 1993 01:04:56 GMT
Organization: QUALCOMM, Incorporated; San Diego, CA, USA
Lines: 466
NNTP-Posting-Host: happy.qualcomm.com
Summary: Help with the process of newsgroup proposal, voting, and creation

Archive-name: creating-newsgroups/helper
Last-modified: 1993/11/15
Version: 1.06

The Usenet Newsgroup Creation Companion
------------------------------------------------------------------------
Posted once a month - Comments to rdippold@qualcomm.com welcome!

So you want to create a newsgroup...

Wallace Sayre said, "Academic politics is the most vicious and bitter
form of politics, because the stakes are so low."  He didn't know Usenet;
--MORE--(5%)
```

When you are reading a news article, the following commands are available:

- Press the space bar to move to the next page of this article (or go to the next article if you are at the end of the current article and another article follows).

- The n command takes you directly to the next article in the news group you are reading.

- The h command lists more commands that you can use now.

An rn news article help page, showing the first page of commands available.

```
Paging commands:
SP        Display the next page.
x         Display the next page decrypted (rot13).
d         Display half a page more.
CR        Display one more line.
^R,v,^X   Restart the current article (v=verbose header, ^X=rot13).
b         Back up one page.
^L,X      Refresh the screen.(X=rot13).
g pat     Go to (search forward within article for) pattern.
G         Search again for current pattern within article.
^G        Search for next line beginning with "Subject:".
TAB       Search for next line beginning with a different character.
q         Quit the pager, go to end of article.  Leave article read or unread.
j         Junk this article (mark it read).  Goes to end of article.
The following commands skip the rest of the current article, then behave
just as if typed to the 'What next?' prompt at the end of the article.

n         Scan forward for next unread article.
N         Go to next article.
^N        Scan forward for next unread article with same title.
p,P,^P    Same as n,N,^N, only going backwards.
[Type space to continue]
```

Junk
Stop reading and move to the end of the article.

■ Many useful commands are available when you have an article on-screen. You can type **j** to *junk* the article, for example.

■ Another useful command is the **c** command, which marks all articles in the group as read (this is called *catching up* in the group). Catching up is useful when, for example, you have returned after a vacation to find a very large number of articles to read in a group.

■ You also can use the **k** command to kill all articles in this group with the same subject as the one you are reading. This command is very useful in reducing the number of articles you must read—you can eliminate the ones with subjects that don't interest you.

Note: *After you read an article, rn won't show it to you again. The article eventually will be removed from the system (expired), but until it is, you can move back through the messages using the P command to find one you've already read. You also can save the article in a disk file by using the s command.*

Posting a News Article with rn

Although you will be reading many more articles than you will be posting (and you should read USENET news for a while before posting anything), you can post an article to a news group by posting a new article or by following up to an existing article.

If you want to post an entirely new article (which is what you want to do for the purposes of this example), follow these steps:

1. Leave the rn program by using the q command as many times as it takes to get back to your UNIX system prompt (one, two, or more times, depending on what you are doing when you want to quit).

2. Start up the Pnews (Post news) program, which comes with the rn system. Generally, you should do this at your UNIX system prompt by typing **Pnews** (note the capitalization!).

3. At the Newsgroup(s): prompt, enter the group you want to post the article to. For this example, type **misc.test**. This USENET group exists just for posting test messages.

8

Distributions

Geographic areas that you can limit an article to.

Pnews displays a list of *distributions*. Because you are just testing, you want to type **local** (pick the one closest to the top of the list, in your case).

4. At the `Title/Subject:` prompt, enter the subject of your article. For this example, you can type **testing** to indicate that you are simply testing the posting program.

5. After a warning message, the system asks whether you really want to post the message. Respond **y** to go ahead.

6. If you have your post prepared in a file that you have already edited, you can post that file immediately by typing the name of the file at the `Prepared file to include [none]:` prompt. If you haven't already set up such a file, press Enter to go into a text editor to create your message.

Using the Pnews program to post a news article. Everything up to when you enter the message body is shown here.

Select a distribution┘

Type a title┘

```
% Pnews

Newsgroup(s): misc.test

Your local distribution prefixes are:
    Local organization:    local
    Organization:          sug
    City:                  pgh
    State:                 pa
    Multi-State Area:
    Country:               usa
    Continent:             na
    Everywhere:            world

Distribution (world): local

Title/Subject: testing

This program posts news to machines throughout the local organization.
Are you absolutely sure that you want to do this? [ny] y

Prepared file to include [none]:
```

7. After you create your post in the editor, you can post the message, abort the post, edit the post again, or display the post for review. To post the message so you can read it in the news group `misc.test`, type **send** at the prompt `Send, abort, edit, or list?`

8. Start rn again. When rn asks what to do with the first news group, type **g misc.test** to go to the group `misc.test`. You should find your article in there, probably as the last article in the group. Use the # command to display the number of the last article in the group; then enter that number to go to that article.

A sample article posted to misc.test.

```
Article 14196 (300 more) in misc.test.
From: tpike@pittslug.sug.org (Tod Pike)
Subject: testing
Date: 13 Dec 1993 01:25:09 GMT
Organization: Pittsburgh Area Sun User Group
Lines: 2
Distribution: pgh
NNTP-Posting-Host: pittslug.sug.org

This is a test.
End of article 14196 (of 14196)--what next? [npq]
```

Posting a Follow-up Article with rn

Follow-up article
An article that is posted in response to another article.

While reading an article, you may want to post an article on the same subject to that news group. To do this, you should post a *follow-up article*.

Note: *To post a follow-up article, you must give the* f *command while you are reading the message that you want to follow up. If you go on to the next message, you will follow up to the wrong post.*

To create a follow-up article, follow these steps:

1. While reading the article you posted, you can use the f command to post a reply to the article. This command goes through the same process as posting a new article, but the program fills in the news group(s) to post the article to and the subject of the message for you. You need to enter only the body of the post.

   The F command (rather than f) also will post a follow-up article, but the system will automatically include a copy of the post you are replying to in your new post.

2. After you enter the body of the post and exit the editor, you are prompted with Send, abort, edit, or list? Type **send** to post the message, **abort** to forget it, **edit** to change the headers or body, and **list** to see it on-screen.

8

Replying to an Article with E-Mail in rn

While reading an article, you may want to send an e-mail message to the author of a post rather than post a follow-up article to the news group. Follow these steps to reply to an article:

1. Type the **r** command to reply to the current article, but through electronic mail to the author of the article. When you type **r**, rn will create a mail header with the author's address in the To: line and the subject of the post (preceded with Re:) in the Subject: line. Some other lines also will appear that you don't need to worry about.

   Similar to F, R includes a copy of the original post in your mail message.

2. If you have already composed the body of your reply in a separate file, enter the file name at the Prepared file to include [none]: prompt. The program immediately sends your response.

   If you don't have a reply already composed, just press Enter. The program starts a text editor to allow you to compose your reply.

3. After composing the body of your mail message and exiting the editor, you will get the prompt Send, abort, edit, or list?. Type **send** to mail the message, **abort** to forget it, **edit** to change the headers or body, and **list** to see it on-screen.

Finding Information Using archie, Gopher, WAIS, and WWW

Now that you are familiar with using e-mail and USENET, you now can try using information retrieval systems such as archie, Gopher, WAIS, and WWW from a UNIX system. For each of these different information retrieval systems you will be using a character-oriented program for the examples, because that is what most people use when they are connected to the Internet on a UNIX system.

archie
An application that lets you search easily for information at anonymous ftp sites.

Using archie on a UNIX System

archie, a very easy-to-use program, is valuable in finding a particular program or file on *ftp* sites. Although many different programs use the archie

ftp

A program that lets you transfer data between different computers.

servers to find information, the main archie program is the one available on most UNIX systems.

When you run the archie program without any options (generally by typing **archie** at the UNIX command prompt), the program will display a help message that tells you how to run the program.

archie help message, showing the options available.

```
% archie
Usage: archie [-acelorstvLV] [-m hits] [-N level] string
             -a : list matches as Alex filenames
             -c : case sensitive substring search
             -e : exact string match (default)
             -r : regular expression search
             -s : case insensitive substring search
             -l : list one match per line
             -t : sort inverted by date
        -m hits : specifies maximum number of hits to return (default 95)
     -o filename : specifies file to store results in
        -h host : specifies server host
             -L : list known servers and current default
       -N level : specifies query niceness level (0-35765)
%
```

When doing a search, you will most likely want to use the command options to help narrow the search. The most common options to archie are:

Substring

A part of the file name you are looking for.

■ -s, search without worrying about upper- and lowercase letters

■ -c, to search for *substrings*

■ -m, which specifies how many matches to return

The archie command options allow you easily to narrow down the files you find until you locate the one you are looking for. After you find a file or program that you are interested in, you can use another utility, such as ftp, to retrieve the file or program so that you can read it or run the program.

For this example, you will use archie to find an ftp site that has the Internet document fyi20.txt, which is an informational document called "What is the Internet." Type the command **archie fyi20.txt** at the UNIX prompt to return all files named fyi20.txt.

8

Results of an
archie search for
`fyi20.txt`
sources. The results
have been scrolled
down to show a
complete result.

```
    Location: /in-notes/fyi
         FILE lrwxrwxrwx        14  Dec  8 11:02  fyi20.txt
Host aramis.rutgers.edu

    Location: /rfc
         FILE lrwxrwxrwx        11  Jul  1 00:00  fyi20.txt
Host athos.rutgers.edu

    Location: /rfc
         FILE lrwxrwxrwx        11  Jul  1 00:00  fyi20.txt
Host sunsite.unc.edu

    Location: /pub/docs/rfc
         FILE lrwxrwxrwx        11  Jun 30 1993  fyi20.txt
Host mojo.ots.utexas.edu

    Location: /pub/netinfo/rfc
         FILE -rw-rw-r--     27811  Jun  9 1993  fyi20.txt
--More--
```

As you can see, file `fyi20.txt` is available at several sites. If you want to download this file (as you will do in the section on ftp), you can pick any of these sites, but for the purposes of the example, you will use the ftp site `sunsite.unc.edu`.

Using Gopher on a UNIX System

Gopher

An application that
lets you access
publicly available
information on
Internet hosts that
provide Gopher
service.

The *Gopher* system is set up so that you can start at one main site (the machine `gopher2.tc.umn.edu` at the time this book was written) and browse from there, so starting from that site is probably best when you begin to explore Gopher. Follow these steps to use Gopher:

1. To start the Gopher program, type the command **gopher** at the UNIX system prompt. The main Gopher screen appears.

   Note: *Some sites have their Gopher program set up so that it starts at a different site than the main Gopher machine, so you may have to start Gopher with the command* gopher gopher2.tc.umn.edu *to see screens similar to the examples.*

The top shows information about the server you are connected to; the middle shows menu items available; the bottom gives information about available commands and the menu page you are on.

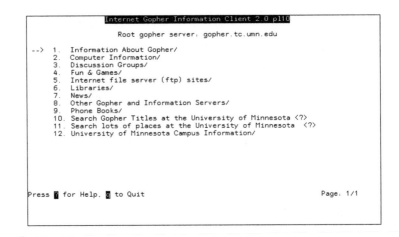

```
┌─────────────────────────────────────────────────────────────────┐
│                 Internet Gopher Information Client 2.0 p110       │
│                                                                   │
│                  Root gopher server: gopher.tc.umn.edu            │
│                                                                   │
│    --> 1.  Information About Gopher/                               │
│        2.  Computer Information/                                   │
│        3.  Discussion Groups/                                      │
│        4.  Fun & Games/                                            │
│        5.  Internet file server (ftp) sites/                      │
│        6.  Libraries/                                              │
│        7.  News/                                                   │
│        8.  Other Gopher and Information Servers/                  │
│        9.  Phone Books/                                            │
│       10.  Search Gopher Titles at the University of Minnesota <?>│
│       11.  Search lots of places at the University of Minnesota <?>│
│       12.  University of Minnesota Campus Information/             │
│                                                                   │
│                                                                   │
│                                                                   │
│                                                                   │
│  Press ? for Help, q to Quit                          Page: 1/1   │
│                                                                   │
└─────────────────────────────────────────────────────────────────┘
```

At the end of each menu choice is a special character (or group of characters) that tells you what the menu item will do. Menu items that end with a slash (/) will take you to another menu with more choices. Menu items that end with the characters <?> allow you to search through a database. Menu items that end with a period are files that will be downloaded and displayed when you select them. Other menu item types exist, but these are the main ones you will encounter.

On this screen, you can move down one menu item (the current menu item has --> pointing to it) by using the j command. If the current menu has more than one page, moving down past the last entry on this page will move you to the next page. You can move up one menu item by using the k command.

If you have moved to another menu, the u command moves you back to the previous menu you were on.

2. Select item 1, which gives more information about Gopher (press 1 and then Enter, or move to the item and press Enter). If you have just entered this menu, then item 1 should already be selected.

8

Items of interest are About Gopher, Gopher Software Distribution (which tells how to get Gopher software), Frequently Asked Questions about Gopher (which may answer questions about how Gopher works), and Reporting Problems or Feedback.

```
              Internet Gopher Information Client 2.0.p110
                        Information About Gopher

   -->  1.  About Gopher.
        2.  Search Gopher News <?>
        3.  Gopher News Archive/
        4.  comp.infosystems.gopher (USENET newsgroup)/
        5.  Gopher Software Distribution/
        6.  Commercial Gopher Software/
        7.  Gopher Protocol Information/
        8.  University of Minnesota Gopher software licensing policy.
        9.  Frequently Asked Questions about Gopher.
       10.  Gopher+ example server/
       11.  Gopher T shirt on MTV movie (big) <Movie>
       12.  Gopher T shirt on MTV movie (small) <Movie>
       13.  Gopher T-shirt on MTV #1 <Picture>
       14.  Gopher T-shirt on MTV #2 <Picture>
       15.  How to get your information into Gopher.
       16.  Reporting Problems or Feedback.



Press ? for Help, q to Quit, u to go up a menu          Page: 1/1
```

3. Move back to the main menu by using the u command.

4. Select item 8, Other Gopher and Information Servers, to see another interesting screen.

This screen allows you to connect to all Gopher servers that have been set up around the world, and to use the veronica service to search for information on Gopher servers.

```
              Internet Gopher Information Client 2.0.p110
                   Other Gopher and Information Servers

   -->  1.  All the Gopher Servers in the World/
        2.  Search titles in Gopherspace using veronica/
        3.  Africa/
        4.  Asia/
        5.  Europe/
        6.  International Organizations/
        7.  Middle East/
        8.  North America/
        9.  Pacific/
       10.  South America/
       11.  Terminal Based Information/
       12.  WAIS Based Information/




Press ? for Help, q to Quit, u to go up a menu          Page: 1/1
```

5. On this menu, select item 1 (All the Gopher Servers in the World). This menu alphabetically lists all Gopher servers set up around the world. Naturally, this list grows every day—at the time this chapter was written, well over 1,100 Gopher servers were available on this list.

The All the Gopher Servers in the World screen is valuable if you want to see who has set up a Gopher server or to browse around for information available on the Internet.

```
┌─────────────────────────────────────────────────────────────────┐
│              Internet Gopher Information Client 2.0 p110          │
│                                                                   │
│                  All the Gopher Servers in the World              │
│                                                                   │
│   --> 1.  Search Gopherspace using Veronica/                      │
│        2.  ACADEME THIS WEEK (Chronicle of Higher Education)/     │
│        3.  ACM SIGDA/                                             │
│        4.  ACM SIGGRAPH/                                          │
│        5.  ACTLab (UT Austin, RTF Dept)/                          │
│        6.  AMI -- A Friendly Public Interface/                    │
│        7.  AREA Science Park, Trieste, (IT)/                      │
│        8.  Academic Position Network/                             │
│        9.  Academy of Sciences, Bratislava (Slovakia)/            │
│       10.  Acadia University Gopher/                              │
│       11.  AgResearch Wallaceville, Upper Hutt, New Zealand/      │
│       12.  Agricultural Genome Gopher/                            │
│       13.  Alamo Community College District/                      │
│       14.  Albert Einstein College of Medicine/                  │
│       15.  Alpha Phi Omega/                                       │
│       16.  American Chemical Society/                             │
│       17.  American Demographics/                                 │
│       18.  American Mathematical Society /                        │
│                                                                   │
│  Press ▓ for Help, ▓ to Quit, ▓ to go up a menu    Page: 1/62    │
│                                                                   │
└─────────────────────────────────────────────────────────────────┘
```

6. Return to the Other Gopher and Information Servers screen by typing u.

Many other menu items on this menu allow you to view the list of available Gopher servers grouped by geographical location. For example, one menu item will take you to a list of Gopher servers available in Europe, or the servers in North America (including the United States). These lists can be valuable when you are searching for a Gopher site at a particular university or college, or run by a particular company.

7. Selecting item 2 on this menu brings up the Search titles in Gopherspace using veronica menu.

This menu gives you more information about the veronica service and lets you search several Gopher databases for information.

```
┌─────────────────────────────────────────────────────────────────┐
│              Internet Gopher Information Client 2.0 p110          │
│                                                                   │
│               Search titles in Gopherspace using veronica         │
│                                                                   │
│   --> 1.                                                          │
│        2.  FAQ: Frequently-Asked Questions about veronica (1993/08/23).│
│        3.  How to compose  veronica queries (NEW June 24) READ ME!!.│
│        4.  Search Gopher Directory Titles at PSINet <?>           │
│        5.  Search Gopher Directory Titles at U. of Manitoba <?>   │
│        6.  Search Gopher Directory Titles at University of Cologne <?>│
│        7.  Search Gopher Directory Titles at University of Pisa <?>│
│        8.  Search gopherspace at PSINet <?>                       │
│        9.  Search gopherspace at U. of Manitoba <?>               │
│       10.  Search gopherspace at University of Cologne <?>        │
│       11.  Search gopherspace at University of Pisa <?>           │
│                                                                   │
│                                                                   │
│                                                                   │
│                                                                   │
│  Press ▓ for Help, ▓ to Quit, ▓ to go up a menu    Page: 1/1     │
│                                                                   │
└─────────────────────────────────────────────────────────────────┘
```

8

8. As an example search, you should select item 6, Search Gopher Directory Titles at U. of Manitoba.

9. When the system asks what you want to search for, type **clinton**. Press Enter to begin the search.

Searching for the string reference *clinton* using the Veronica server at the University of Manitoba.

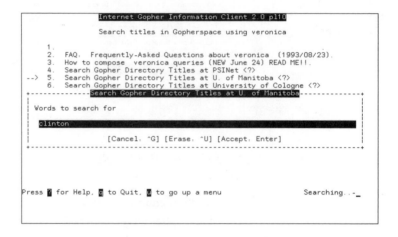

```
           Internet Gopher Information Client 2.0 p110

                Search titles in Gopherspace using veronica

         1.
         2.   FAQ.  Frequently-Asked Questions about veronica  (1993/08/23).
         3.   How to compose  veronica queries (NEW June 24) READ ME!!.
         4.   Search Gopher Directory Titles at PSINet <?>
    --> 5.    Search Gopher Directory Titles at U. of Manitoba <?>
         6.   Search Gopher Directory Titles at University of Cologne <?>
     +-------------Search Gopher Directory Titles at U. of Manitoba-------------+
     |                                                                          |
     | Words to search for                                                      |
     |                                                                          |
     | clinton                                                                  |
     |                                                                          |
     |              [Cancel, ^G] [Erase, ^U] [Accept, Enter]                    |
     +--------------------------------------------------------------------------+



 Press ? for Help, q to Quit, u to go up a menu           Searching..-
```

Veronica

A tool that searches through a database of Gopher menu items for items that contain a particular string.

The result is a menu made up of all the menu items that matched your search string. You can use similar techniques to look for Gopher menu titles for almost any topic. There are menu items giving more information about *Veronica* on the Search titles in Gopherspace using Veronica screen—you should review the information given there for more information about using Veronica effectively.

Search results from veronica. The menu shown lists all the items that have the word *clinton* in them.

```
           Internet Gopher Information Client 2.0 p110

         Search Gopher Directory Titles at U. of Manitoba: clinton

    --> 1.    Clinton Inauguration/
         2.   Clinton Administration Information/
         3.   Clinton Healthcare Plan/
         4.   Clinton Health Care Plan (Full Text)/
         5.   Information from the White House (Clinton)/
         6.   Campaign Speeches of Bill Clinton/
         7.   Clinton/
         8.   Presbyterian College (Clinton, SC)/
         9.   clinton.mail/
        10.   Clinton Hlth Plan/
        11.   480  alt.politics.clinton/
        12.   227  alt.president.clinton/
        13.   Clinton and Unions/
        14.   Clinton/
        15.   Clinton-Transition/
        16.   Clinton Positions/
        17.   Clinton-Transition/
        18.   Clinton Positions/

 Press ? for Help, q to Quit, u to go up a menu           Page: 1/7
```

Gopher is a very valuable tool for finding information on the Internet, and equally valuable for simply browsing to see what is available. Using Veronica to search through a database of all Gopher menu items makes locating Gopher items of interest easy. You easily can spend hours moving around the different Gopher sites looking to see what's in the next menu item.

Using WAIS on a UNIX System

WAIS

Wide Area Information Servers, a system for searching and retrieving documents from participating sites.

WAIS is meant to be a way to search many different databases for a particular subject, and as such it's basically a searching tool. Several different WAIS programs are available for UNIX systems, but the examples in this section are from the swais program, a simple, character-based WAIS program.

Note: *When using the swais program, all commands are single-character commands (no need to press Enter after typing them) unless otherwise noted.*

To use WAIS, follow these steps:

1. Start WAIS by typing the command **swais** at the UNIX command prompt. The swais program loads a list of all databases that it knows about.

   Note: *Because each site configures its server with a slightly different list, your server will probably appear a little different than the one used in the examples here.*

   The swais main screen lists available databases, showing the Internet host that provides the database and the name of the database.

The screen also shows the cost for accessing the database. All the generally available databases are free, but some commercial databases require you to set up an account to access them.

```
SWAIS                           Source Selection              Sources: 505
 #              Server                        Source                  Cost
001:   [          archie.au]  aarnet-resource-guide                   Free
002:   [ndadsb.gsfc.nasa.gov] AAS_jobs                                Free
003:   [ndadsb.gsfc.nasa.gov] AAS_meeting                             Free
004:   [     munin.ub2.lu.se] academic_email_conf                     Free
005:   [wraith.cs.uow.edu.au] acronyms                                Free
006:   [    archive.orst.edu] aeronautics                             Free
007:   [ ftp.cs.colorado.edu] aftp-cs-colorado-edu                    Free
008:   [nostromo.oes.orst.ed] agricultural-market-news                Free
009:   [    archive.orst.edu] alt.drugs                               Free
010:   [    wais.oit.unc.edu] alt.gopher                              Free
011:   [sun-wais.oit.unc.edu] alt.sys.sun                             Free
012:   [    wais.oit.unc.edu] alt.wais                                Free
013:   [alfred.ccs.carleton.] amiga-slip                              Free
014:   [     munin.ub2.lu.se] amiga_fish_contents                     Free
015:   [       150.203.76.2] ANU-Aboriginal-EconPolicies      $0.00/minute
016:   [   coombs.anu.edu.au] ANU-Aboriginal-Studies           $0.00/minute
017:   [       150.203.76.2] ANU-Ancient-DNA-L                 $0.00/minute
018:   [       150.203.76.2] ANU-Ancient-DNA-Studies           $0.00/minute

Keywords:

<space> selects, w for keywords, arrows move, <return> searches, q quits, or ?
```

8

At the bottom of the swais screen are instructions on what commands are available. Use the ? command to get information about the available commands.

The swais command help screen lists the commands you can use in WAIS.

```
SWAIS                          Source Selection Help              Page:  1
j, down arrow, ^N        Move Down one source
k, up arrow, ^P          Move Up one source
J, ^V, ^D                Move Down one screen
K, <esc> v, ^U           Move Up one screen
###                      Position to source number ##
/sss                     Search for source sss
<space>, <period>        Select current source
=                        Deselect all sources
v, <comma>               View current source info
<ret>                    Perform search
s                        Select new sources (refresh sources list)
w                        Select new keywords
X, -                     Remove current source permanently
o                        Set and show swais options
h, ?                     Show this help display
H                        Display program history
q                        Leave this program



Press any key to continue
```

Use the down-arrow key to move down one line in the list of databases. The up-arrow key moves up one line in the list of databases.

2. The slash (/) command followed by a database name lets you search for a particular database. As an example, you want to search for speeches that President Clinton has made that talk about Atlanta, Georgia. You want to use the directory-of-servers database, so type the command **/directory-of-servers** to move to that database.

3. Press the space bar to select this database.

4. Enter **wclinton** to search this database for entries with the word *clinton* in them. Notice that the w (which is the command) doesn't show on-screen.

An asterisk appears before directory-of-servers, indicating that you will be searching this database.

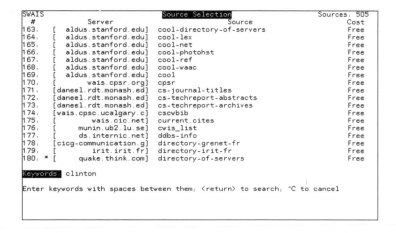

WAIS finds two databases with information about President Clinton: clinton-speechess and White-House-Papers.

The clinton-speechess database looks like it would be useful in finding speeches that were made in Atlanta, Georgia.

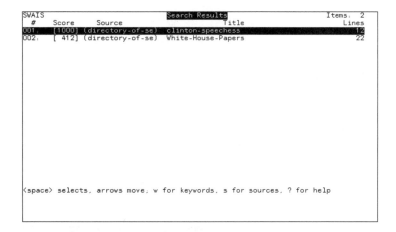

5. Type the command **s** to return to the database selection screen.

6. Press the space bar to deselect the directory-of-servers database, because you won't be using that database any more.

7. Type the command **/clinton-speechess** to move to the clinton-speechess database.

8. Use the space bar again to select this database as the next one to search.

9. Entering **watlanta** starts the search for documents in the clinton-speechess database that mention the word *atlanta*.

This screen shows the first 18 documents found, with the number under the title Score showing how well the document matched the search.

The first document, a speech given in Atlanta, matches perfectly (the score is 1000).

```
SWAIS                              Search Results                    Items: 19
 #      Score      Source                     Title                      Lines
001.   [1000] (clinton-speeche)     VARIOUS TOPICS. Interview - Atl       830
002.   [ 895] (clinton-speeche)     VARIOUS TOPICS. Speech - Atlant       601
003.   [ 368] (clinton-speeche)     FOREIGN POLICY. Speech by Al Go       575
004.   [ 368] (clinton-speeche)     L A  RIOTS. Speech - Birmingham       324
005.   [ 316] (clinton-speeche)     IRAQ/IRAN. Press Release - 10/1        78
006.   [ 316] (clinton-speeche)     IRAQ/IRAN . Speech - Oshkosh,WI       198
007.   [ 263] (clinton-speeche)     CAMPAIGN OFFICES. Addresses           405
008.   [ 263] (clinton-speeche)     ECONOMIC STRATEGY. 6/21/92            877
009.   [ 263] (clinton-speeche)     DEBATES. Press Release - 10/3/9        50
010.   [ 263] (clinton-speeche)     VARIOUS TOPICS. Analysis of Deb       273
011.   [ 263] (clinton-speeche)     URBAN PROBLEMS. Speech - Housto       397
012.   [ 263] (clinton-speeche)     VP DEBATE ANALYSIS. Encyclopedi       697
013.   [ 263] (clinton-speeche)     ECONOMIC PLAN. Press Release -         95
014.   [ 263] (clinton-speeche)     VARIOUS TOPICS. Analysis of Deb       183
015.   [ 263] (clinton-speeche)     DEBATE 2. Further Analysis - 10       272
016.   [ 263] (clinton-speeche)     STATEGATE. Press Release - 10/1       157
017.   [ 263] (clinton-speeche)     CRIME. Speech - New Orleans, LA       538
018.   [ 263] (clinton-speeche)     VARIOUS TOPICS. Speech - New Or       479


<space> selects, arrows move, w for keywords, s for sources, ? for help
```

10. To display one of these documents, move to the document you want to see and press the space bar to select the document.

The text of the speech given in Atlanta, Georgia.

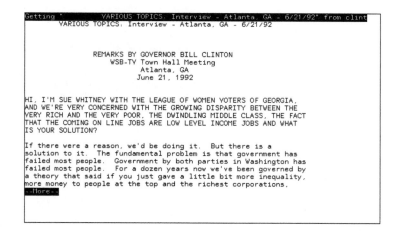

```
Getting "        VARIOUS TOPICS. Interview - Atlanta, GA - 6/21/92" from clint
            VARIOUS TOPICS. Interview - Atlanta, GA - 6/21/92


                    REMARKS BY GOVERNOR BILL CLINTON
                          WSB-TV Town Hall Meeting
                               Atlanta, GA
                              June 21, 1992


HI, I'M SUE WHITNEY WITH THE LEAGUE OF WOMEN VOTERS OF GEORGIA,
AND WE'RE VERY CONCERNED WITH THE GROWING DISPARITY BETWEEN THE
VERY RICH AND THE VERY POOR, THE DWINDLING MIDDLE CLASS, THE FACT
THAT THE COMING ON LINE JOBS ARE LOW LEVEL INCOME JOBS AND WHAT
IS YOUR SOLUTION?

If there were a reason, we'd be doing it.  But there is a
solution to it.  The fundamental problem is that government has
failed most people.  Government by both parties in Washington has
failed most people.  For a dozen years now we've been governed by
a theory that said if you just gave a little bit more inequality,
more money to people at the top and the richest corporations,
--More--
```

This process shows how WAIS can be used to search for many items of information on the Internet. WAIS doesn't allow you to browse through what documents are available, but it does allow you to look quickly for information in documents throughout the Internet.

Using WWW on a UNIX System

World Wide Web

A hypertext-based system that allows browsing of available Internet resources.

Another information retrieval system in use on the Internet is the *World Wide Web* (WWW). This system displays documents that have links to other documents. This type of system allows you to browse easily through documents that have information of interest to you.

The WWW program used in the examples for this section is called *Lynx*. Because the WWW system is based on showing a document that contains links to other documents, when the Lynx program displays the WWW documents, it displays the links to other documents in a different color from the background text. Several WWW browser programs are available for UNIX, such as Mosaic (which runs with the X Window system) and a line mode browser that can be used on any type of terminal.

Lynx

A character-oriented interface to WWW.

Follow these steps to use WWW:

1. Type **lynx** to start WWW. When you enter the WWW system, you are generally placed at the default *home* or starting page.

Lynx screen shown at startup.

```
                                           Lynx default home page
              WELCOME TO LYNX AND THE WORLD OF THE WEB

     You are using a WWW Product called Lynx. For more information about
     obtaining and installing Lynx please choose About Lynx

     The current version of Lynx is 2.0.12. If you are running an earlier
     version PLEASE UPGRADE! Lynx ver. 2.1 is now in Beta test stage.

     INFORMATION SOURCES ABOUT AND FOR WWW
        * For a description of WWW choose Web Overview
        * About the WWW Information Sharing project
        * WWW Information By Subject
        * WWW Information By Type

     OTHER INFO SOURCES
        * University of Kansas CWIS
        * O'Reilly & Ass. Global Network Navigator
        * Nova-Links, Internet access made easy
        * NCSA, Network Starting Points, Information Resource Meta-Index
        * Hytelnet database, Telnet information resources
        * All the Gopher servers in the world
     Commands: Use arrow keys to move, '?' for help, 'q' to quit, '<-' to go back
```

8

The links to other pages are highlighted, shown in blue text in this case. Many links to other documents exist. Some of these documents give information about the World Wide Web system itself, and others allow you to access WWW information by subject or by document type.

To maneuver around the screen, press the down-arrow key to move to the next keyword on the current screen, and the up-arrow key to move to the previous keyword. On the example lynx page, pressing the down arrow moves the selected keyword from WWW to About Lynx on the first screen; then pressing the up arrow moves you back to the WWW keyword.

2. For this example, press the down-arrow key enough times to move the selected keyword to WWW Information By Subject (the actual link is By Subject).

3. Press Enter to display this new document.

The start of the list of topics. You can see information about aeronautics, agriculture, archaeology, astronomy, and astrophysics.

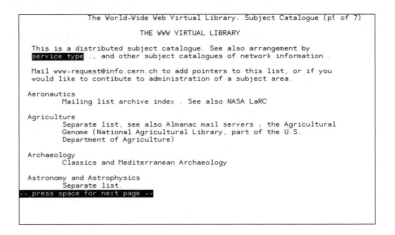

```
                    The World-Wide Web Virtual Library: Subject Catalogue (p1 of 7)

                                    THE WWW VIRTUAL LIBRARY

              This is a distributed subject catalogue. See also arrangement by
              service type  ., and other subject catalogues of network information .

              Mail www-request@info.cern.ch to add pointers to this list, or if you
              would like to contibute to administration of a subject area.

              Aeronautics
                      Mailing list archive index . See also NASA LaRC

              Agriculture
                      Separate list, see also Almanac mail servers ; the Agricultural
                      Genome (National Agricultural Library, part of the U.S.
                      Department of Agriculture)

              Archaeology
                      Classics and Mediterranean Archaeology

              Astronomy and Astrophysics
                      Separate list.
              -- press space for next page --
```

4. Press the down-arrow key enough times to move the selected keyword to Classics and Mediterranean Archaeology.

5. Press Enter to display this document.

The WWW Classics and Mediterranean Archaeology page.

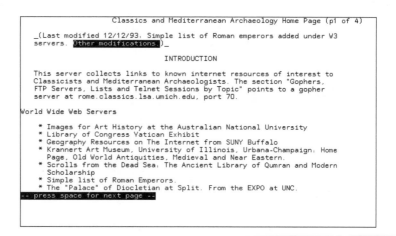

```
                     Classics and Mediterranean Archaeology Home Page (p1 of 4)

    _(Last modified 12/12/93. Simple list of Roman emperors added under W3
    servers. Other modifications.)_

                                   INTRODUCTION

    This server collects links to known internet resources of interest to
    Classicists and Mediterranean Archaeologists. The section "Gophers,
    FTP Servers, Lists and Telnet Sessions by Topic" points to a gopher
    server at rome.classics.lsa.umich.edu, port 70.

World Wide Web Servers

      * Images for Art History at the Australian National University
      * Library of Congress Vatican Exhibit
      * Geography Resources on The Internet from SUNY Buffalo
      * Krannert Art Museum, University of Illinois, Urbana-Champaign; Home
        Page, Old World Antiquities, Medieval and Near Eastern.
      * Scrolls from the Dead Sea; The Ancient Library of Qumran and Modern
        Scholarship
      * Simple list of Roman Emperors.
      * The "Palace" of Diocletian at Split. From the EXPO at UNC.
    -- press space for next page --
```

6. Use the left-arrow key to return to the previous page in the system. Use this key enough times to move back to the main (first) screen.

Note: *One important feature of the WWW system is that it lets you use other information retrieval system servers through your WWW software. On the main WWW page, for example, you will see an item All the Gopher servers in the world, which allows you to use any Gopher server available, just as though you were using a Gopher program.*

7. Use the arrow keys to move the selected keyword to WWW Information By Type. Press Enter to display the new document.

This page gives you access to WAIS, Gopher, and archie servers, as well as many other resources on the Internet.

```
                        Data sources classified by access protocol (p1 of 3)
                       RESOURCES CLASSIFIED BY TYPE OF SERVICE

    See also categorization exist by subject . If you know what sort of a
    service you are looking for, look here.

World-Wide Web servers
            List of W3 native "HTTP" servers. These are generally the most
            friendly. See also; about the WWW initiative .

WAIS servers
            Find WAIS index servers using the directory of servers , or
            lists by name or domain . See also; about WAIS .

Network News
            Available directly in all www browsers. See also this list of
            FAQs .

Gopher   Campus-wide information systems, etc, listed geographically.
            See also; about Gopher .

Telnet access
    -- press space for next page --
```

8

Many people find that they can use a WWW program to do all their Internet resource location, without needing any other piece of software.

Transferring Files Using ftp

Although several different programs often allow you to access other resources on the Internet (such as e-mail and netnews), UNIX systems have only one program—ftp—that lets you download and upload files. This program comes with almost every UNIX system and is used in the examples in this section.

ftp is a very simple program to use, but it provides an essential service on the Internet—it allows you to get files from remote parts of the Internet quickly and easily.

Note: *When using the ftp program, all commands must be followed by pressing Enter.*

As shown in the earlier section "Using archie on a UNIX System," a copy of the file fyi20.txt is on the machine sunsite.unc.edu. You will now use ftp to download this file to your local machine.

Note: *Be aware that the file used in this example is fairly large. If your Internet provider charges you based on the amount of files you download or keep on disk, you should download a smaller file than the one shown in the examples.*

Also, the machine sunsite.unc.edu is used just as an example in this chapter. If many people connect to it to download files, it will overload the machine so that legitimate users can't use it. You should try to find another machine if you want to try out ftp.

To use ftp to download the fyi20.txt file, follow these steps:

1. Start the ftp program on your local UNIX machine by typing the command **ftp sunsite.unc.edu** at the UNIX system prompt.

2. At the Name: prompt, type **anonymous** as the account name to log in using anonymous ftp.

3. At the Password: prompt, type anything you want (it's customary to use your Internet e-mail address for your anonymous ftp password). You can't see the password typed.

You are now logged into the remote machine and can find the file you want.

```
% ftp sunsite.unc.edu
Connected to calypso-2.oit.unc.edu.
220 SunSITE is from UNC & Sun. Read DISCLAIMER.readme for our legal disclaimer
Name (sunsite.unc.edu:tgp): anonymous
331 Guest login ok, send your complete e-mail address as password.
Password:
230-              WELCOME to UNC and SUN's anonymous ftp server
230-                       University of North Carolina
230-                     Office FOR Information Technology
230-                          SunSITE.unc.edu
230-
230-   An OpenLook FTPtool can be found in
230-      /pub/X11/Openlook/Ftptool4.3.unc.1.tar.Z
230-   For information on submitting software to this archive, retrieve
230-      /how.to.submit.
230-
230-   We archive most of the SUN related USENET news groups here as well as
230-   distributing SUN related announcements. Pub/wais contains a Sparc binary
230-   for a  simple wais client that you can run in your terminal window.
230-   We suggest that you download it and follow the installation instructions
230-   (they're simple) so that you may begin to use WAIS for your searching
230-   and retrieval.
230-
230-   Or telnet to sunsite and login as swais to test out a simple wais client.
```

4. Type the command **dir** to list the files available on the server at this point.

Notice that many items are actually directories (the item listing starts with a d), which can hold more files.

```
230-
230 Guest login ok, access restrictions apply.
ftp> dir
200 PORT command successful.
150 Opening ASCII mode data connection for /bin/ls.
total 7691
-rw-r--r--   1 root     wheel        2001 Aug 12  1993 DISCLAIMER.readme
-rwxr--r--   1 ftp      wheel     7836445 Feb 12 07:26 IAFA-LISTINGS
-rw-r--r--   1 root     wheel        1116 Aug 20  1992 IAFA-SITEINFO
-rw-r--r--   1 root     wheel         263 Feb  4 20:52 README
-rw-r--r--   1 root     daemon        534 Aug 18 02:57 US-Legal-Regs-ITAR-NOTICE
-rw-r--r--   1 root     wheel        1559 Nov 19 21:47 WELCOME
drwxr-xr-x   2 root     daemon        512 Feb  3 21:26 bin
drwxr-xr-x   2 root     wheel         512 Aug 13  1992 dev
drwxr-xr-x   3 root     daemon        512 Aug 20 19:45 etc
-rw-r--r--   1 root     daemon       8868 Sep  5  1992 how.to.submit
lrwxrwxrwx   1 root     daemon         13 Oct 15 20:59 ls-1R -> IAFA-LISTINGS
drwxr-xr-x  19 root     wheel        1024 Feb  9 19:23 pub
drwxr-xr-x   4 root     daemon        512 Jun  4  1993 unc
drwxrwx-wx   8 root     ftp-admi     2560 Feb 11 18:44 uploads
drwxr-xr-x   3 root     wheel         512 Mar 11  1992 usr
226 Transfer complete.
1008 bytes received in 0.093 seconds (11 Kbytes/s)
ftp>
```

5. If you remember from the archie output, the fyi20.txt file is in a directory called /pub/docs/rfc. Type the command **cd /pub/docs/rfc** to move to that directory.

6. Typing the **dir** command here lists the files available in this directory.

8

The files in the
/pub/docs/rfc
directory are all
Internet-related
documents. Quite a
few start with fyi,
and one of them is
the file fyi20.txt,
which is the one
you want.

```
ftp> cd /pub/docs/rfc
250 CWD command successful.
ftp> dir fyi*
200 PORT command successful.
150 Opening ASCII mode data connection for /bin/ls.
-r--r--r--   1 root     ftp-admi      933 Oct 14 17.08 fyi-by-author.txt
-r--r--r--   1 root     ftp-admi     2415 Oct 14 16.54 fyi-by-title.txt
-r--r--r--   1 root     ftp-admi     7299 Oct 14 17.43 fyi-index.txt
lrwxrwxrwx   1 root     daemon         11 Jun 28  1993 fyi1.txt -> rfc1150.txt
lrwxrwxrwx   1 root     daemon         11 Jun 30  1993 fyi10.txt -> rfc1402.txt
lrwxrwxrwx   1 root     daemon         11 Jun 30  1993 fyi11.txt -> rfc1292.txt
lrwxrwxrwx   1 root     daemon         11 Jun 30  1993 fyi12.txt -> rfc1302.txt
lrwxrwxrwx   1 root     daemon         11 Jun 30  1993 fyi13.txt -> rfc1308.txt
lrwxrwxrwx   1 root     daemon         11 Jun 30  1993 fyi14.txt -> rfc1309.txt
lrwxrwxrwx   1 root     daemon         11 Jun 30  1993 fyi15.txt -> rfc1355.txt
lrwxrwxrwx   1 root     daemon         11 Jun 30  1993 fyi16.txt -> rfc1359.txt
lrwxrwxrwx   1 root     daemon         11 Oct  8 07.22 fyi17.txt -> rfc1539.txt
lrwxrwxrwx   1 root     daemon         11 Jun 30  1993 fyi18.txt -> rfc1392.txt
lrwxrwxrwx   1 root     daemon         11 Jun 30  1993 fyi19.txt -> rfc1463.txt
lrwxrwxrwx   1 root     daemon         10 Jun 28  1993 fyi2.ps -> rfc1147.ps
lrwxrwxrwx   1 root     daemon         11 Jun 30  1993 fyi2.txt -> rfc1470.txt
lrwxrwxrwx   1 root     daemon         11 Jun 30  1993 fyi20.txt -> rfc1462.txt
lrwxrwxrwx   1 root     daemon         11 Jul 23  1993 fyi21.txt -> rfc1491.txt
lrwxrwxrwx   1 root     daemon         11 Jun 28  1993 fyi3.txt -> rfc1175.txt
```

Note: *If the file you are going to transfer is a compiled program or some other non-text file, you must use the* binary *command before doing the transfer. See Chapter 1, "Introducing the Internet," for more details.*

7. Type the command **get fyi20.txt** to download the file. (Make sure that you type the command exactly as written—case is important!)

The ftp program
opens a connection
between the two
machines to
download the file
and transfers the
data to your UNIX
machine.

```
lrwxrwxrwx   1 root     daemon         11 Oct  8 07.22 fyi17.txt -> rfc1539.txt
lrwxrwxrwx   1 root     daemon         11 Jun 30  1993 fyi18.txt -> rfc1392.txt
lrwxrwxrwx   1 root     daemon         11 Jun 30  1993 fyi19.txt -> rfc1463.txt
lrwxrwxrwx   1 root     daemon         10 Jun 28  1993 fyi2.ps -> rfc1147.ps
lrwxrwxrwx   1 root     daemon         11 Jun 30  1993 fyi2.txt -> rfc1470.txt
lrwxrwxrwx   1 root     daemon         11 Jun 30  1993 fyi20.txt -> rfc1462.txt
lrwxrwxrwx   1 root     daemon         11 Jul 23  1993 fyi21.txt -> rfc1491.txt
lrwxrwxrwx   1 root     daemon         11 Jun 28  1993 fyi3.txt -> rfc1175.txt
lrwxrwxrwx   1 root     daemon         11 Jun 30  1993 fyi4.txt -> rfc1325.txt
lrwxrwxrwx   1 root     daemon         11 Jun 28  1993 fyi5.txt -> rfc1178.txt
lrwxrwxrwx   1 root     daemon         11 Jun 28  1993 fyi6.txt -> rfc1198.txt
lrwxrwxrwx   1 root     daemon         11 Jun 28  1993 fyi7.txt -> rfc1207.txt
lrwxrwxrwx   1 root     daemon         11 Jun 28  1993 fyi8.txt -> rfc1244.txt
lrwxrwxrwx   1 root     daemon         11 Jun 30  1993 fyi9.txt -> rfc1251.txt
226 Transfer complete.
remote. fyi*
1987 bytes received in 0.47 seconds (4.1 Kbytes/s)
ftp> get fyi20.txt
200 PORT command successful.
150 Opening ASCII mode data connection for fyi20.txt (27811 bytes).
226 Transfer complete.
local. fyi20.txt remote. fyi20.txt
28429 bytes received in 0.74 seconds (38 Kbytes/s)
ftp>
```

At any time (at the ftp program prompt), you can access the ftp help program to get more information about ftp. You can type **help** to get a list of all commands, and **help** followed by another command to get information on that command. Typing **help binary**, for example, presents more information about the binary command.

Examples of the ftp
help commands.

```
remote: fyi*
1987 bytes received in 0.47 seconds (4.1 Kbytes/s)
ftp> get fyi20.txt
200 PORT command successful.
150 Opening ASCII mode data connection for fyi20.txt (27811 bytes).
226 Transfer complete.
local: fyi20.txt remote: fyi20.txt
28429 bytes received in 0.74 seconds (38 Kbytes/s)
ftp> help
Commands may be abbreviated.  Commands are:

!           cr          macdef      proxy       send
$           delete      mdelete     sendport    status
account     debug       mdir        put         struct
append      dir         mget        pwd         sunique
ascii       disconnect  mkdir       quit        tenex
bell        form        mls         quote       trace
binary      get         mode        recv        type
bye         glob        mput        remotehelp  user
case        hash        nmap        rename      verbose
cd          help        ntrans      reset       ?
cdup        lcd         open        rmdir
close       ls          prompt      runique
ftp>
```

Using telnet to Connect to Host Resources

telnet
A program that
allows remote login
to another com-
puter.

This chapter so far has discussed programs that you can run on your local UNIX system to use the Internet. When you use *telnet*, however, you are actually connecting to another machine on the Internet and running programs there. These programs, called host resources, are provided by people on the Internet as sources of information.

Many host resources are similar to bulletin board systems, where you log in to the resource to gain access to the information there. Most of these systems tell you how to use the accounts when you connect to the machine, or provide a "guest" account that doesn't need a password. Also, many resources don't require you to provide an account and password, but simply provide information to anyone who connects. You will use examples of both types of host resources in this section.

Note: *These host resources are provided as a service to the Internet community and shouldn't be abused. Every time you connect to a remote machine to use a resource there, you are slowing that machine down and making use of someone else's computer equipment. You shouldn't use a remote Gopher service, for example, unless you have no other way of getting access to Gopher; even then, you should limit yourself to using it infrequently.*

Suppose that you want to use the Gopher service to look for information, but your local UNIX system doesn't have a Gopher program available. You discover by looking in Chapter 12, "Other Internet Resources," that a host resource at the machine **gopher.msu.edu** provides Gopher service. Follow these steps to access that host machine:

8

1. To start telnet and connect to an Internet Gopher server, type the command **telnet gopher.msu.edu**.

   You receive the message that you are connected to the remote machine, and the remote machine displays several informational messages.

2. At the login: prompt, type **gopher**.

Connecting to gopher.msu.edu to use the Gopher host resource there.

```
% telnet gopher.msu.edu
Trying 35.8.2.61 ...
Connected to gopher.cl.msu.edu.
Escape character is '^]'.

AIX telnet (burrow.cl.msu.edu)

Type   gopher   to log in

To report problems with this system send mail to    gopher@gopher.msu.edu

login: gopher
```

The Gopher program works just as though you were running the program on your local machine, and you can use it just like a local Gopher program. So now you can make use of Gopher—even if you don't have a local Gopher program—by using an Internet host resource.

Output of Gopher program running on gopher.msu.edu.

```
                   Internet Gopher Information Client v1.11

                      Root gopher server: gopher.msu.edu

   --> 1.  Gopher at Michigan State University.
       2.  More About Gopher (Documentation & Other Gophers)/
       3.  Keyword Search of Titles in MSU's Gopher <?>
       4.  About Michigan State University/
       5.  MSU Campus Events/
       6.  News & Weather/
       7.  Phone Books & Other Directories/
       8.  Information for the MSU Community/
       9.  Computing & Technology Services/
       10. Libraries/
       11. MSU Services & Facilities/
       12. Outreach / Extension / Community Affairs/
       13. Network & Database Resources/




   Press ? for Help, q to Quit, u to go up a menu          Page: 1/1
```

3. After you finish with the Gopher program, type **q** to quit and to exit the telnet program.

For another example, you can get information about the U.S. Library of Congress by using the host resource on the machine `locis.loc.gov`. To gain access to the resource, follow these steps:

1. Enter the command **telnet locis.loc.gov**.

This resource doesn't ask for an account or password, so as soon as you connect, you will see the main screen.

```
        L O C I S :  LIBRARY OF CONGRESS INFORMATION SYSTEM
            To make a choice: type a number, then press ENTER

    1   Library of Congress Catalog       4   Braille and Audio

    2   Federal Legislation               5   Organizations

    3   Copyright Information             6   Foreign Law

*     *    *    *    *    *    *    *    *    *    *    *

    7   Searching Hours and Basics
    8   Documentation and Classes
    9   Library of Congress General Information

    12  Comments and Logoff


        Choice:
```

2. When you are connected to LOCIS, you select the items you want by typing the number next to the item. For this example, enter **9**.

The Library of Congress general information screen, which gives you telephone numbers to call for the various Library of Congress offices and functions.

```
            LIBRARY OF CONGRESS GENERAL INFORMATION
LC is a research library serving Congress, the federal government, the
library community world-wide, the US creative community, and any researchers
beyond high school level or age.  On-site researchers request materials by
filling out request slips in LC's reading rooms; requesters must present a
photo i.d.  Staff are available for assistance in all public reading rooms.

----------------------------------------------------------------------------
The following phone numbers offer information about hours and other services:

General Research Info:     202-707-6500    Reading Room Hours:    202-707-6400
Exhibits/Tours/Gift Shop:  202-707-8000    Location/Parking:      202-707-4700
Copyright Information:     202-707-3000    Cataloging Products:   202-707-6100
Copyright Forms:           202-707-9100         "        "  fax:  202-707-1334
----------------------------------------------------------------------------
NEXT PAGE for information on Interlibrary Loan & the LC Online News Service.

NEXT PAGE: press ENTER
 12  Return to LOCIS MENU screen.

Choice:
```

8

3. Enter **12** to leave this screen.

4. You now can quit the LOCIS system by entering **12** two more times, to return to your UNIX system.

Troubleshooting

You can run into several problems when using the Internet services described in this chapter. Some of these problems are temporary—that is, the problem will probably go away at some time in the future—whereas others are more or less permanent.

Problems Connecting to Machines

If you can't connect to another machine on the Internet, often you'll get an error message such as `connection refused`, `host unknown`, or `connection timed out`. You see these error messages most frequently when using services such as ftp and Gopher (which try to contact another machine while you wait), but you also can have the problem when sending e-mail.

The first thing to try is to check the spelling of the name of the machine you are trying to connect to. Be especially careful when typing the letter O and the number 0, and with the letter l and the number 1. Check the source of the host name to make sure that you copied it correctly.

If connections to the same machine worked in the past, the problem possibly is only temporary. The remote machine may be down, or the network between your machine and the remote machine may be broken. You should try the connection again in a few hours to see whether the problem has been fixed. If the problem doesn't go away in a day or so, you should try to find another machine with the same resource (another ftp site with the same file, for example), or ask the administrator of your local machine to try to find out why the remote machine isn't available.

Problems with Returned E-Mail

One common problem with using e-mail is that after you send a message to a person, your e-mail message is returned to you with an error saying that it couldn't be sent.

First, read the error message to get an idea of what the problem was. If the error was `user unknown` or `host unknown`, the mail processing programs didn't recognize the user or host computer you were trying to send a message to.

You should check the spelling of the user name and/or computer system to make sure that you have spelled them correctly. If this is the first time you have tried to send mail to this person, check your source for the mail address to make sure that you have copied it correctly. If the address you have seems correct, you may want to have your local administrator try to determine why the address is failing.

If the mail address you have has worked in the past, the problem may be temporary. You should try to send the message again in a few hours to see whether the problem has been fixed.

If the error message you received indicates a computer system error, such as `protection violation`, `disk limit exceeded`, or `connection refused`, you should probably have your local system administrator try to work out the problem with the remote systems' administrators.

Other Common Problems

Because the Internet is always changing, it's very possible that a mail address or computer system that worked or was available a week ago may not work today. The computer system may have been replaced with a new one with a different name, or the system may be unavailable because of a hardware problem. If you use a computer system frequently, you should read the messages displayed when you first connect to the system—these messages let you know whether the system is scheduled to be unavailable.

Also, the Internet itself (the network that connects our computers together) changes and can break. It's possible that your local site may be cut off from the rest of the Internet, or the site you are trying to reach may be cut off. These conditions are often temporary, but they can be frustrating.

When dealing with problems with computers on the Internet, your two best strategies are *patience* and *persistence*. Many problems are temporary, so if you wait a few hours and try again, the problem may have been fixed.

8

Summary

UNIX machines are the most common type of machines on the Internet today, and as such most Internet services are available on them. Many Internet services, such as ftp and e-mail, are built into most UNIX systems, and software for the other services is readily available.

Although UNIX can be more difficult to use than the interfaces provided by the commercial on-line services discussed elsewhere in this book, the wide variety of Internet services that you can take advantage of makes UNIX a good system to use if you expect to make heavy use of the Internet. A number of commercial Internet service providers offer access to UNIX accounts as one of their service options.

Part III
A Resource Guide to the Internet

## Chapter 9

Software and Files
(ftp and Gopher Sites)

This chapter lists some of the most interesting and important sites on the Internet that provide anonymous ftp services, with information on what files can be found there. You often can locate specific information and files on the Internet by browsing the large anonymous ftp sites.

Along with ftp sites, some major sites providing Gopher services are also listed, giving descriptions about what information is available at each site.

File Resource Category	Description	Starting Page
Major Internet ftp Sites	ftp sites that have large collections of files	219
Internet Gopher Sites	Gopher sites with a wide variety of information	235
ftp and Gopher Sites	Locations where information be found	239

Major Internet ftp Sites

In the following sections, the file locations for directories and files are given from the top of the anonymous ftp area for each site. The directories are shown in a UNIX format (*/directory*), and subdirectories are indented under the upper-level directories. When you log in via anonymous ftp, you can use the `cd` command to move to the directory listed. From there you can use the `ls` or `dir` commands to get listings of the individual files in each area.

ftp.uu.net

Site name: `ftp.uu.net` (192.48.96.9)

Contact: `archive@uunet.uu.net` or `tale@uunet.uu.net`

Description: UUNet, an Internet services provider, is also one of the central distribution sites for all netnews traffic across the Internet. The ftp archive at `ftp.uu.net` is one of the largest and most complete on the Internet—almost everything can be found here! It has a very broad collection of programs and informational files. It's essential that you get the index files and search them for the information you want.

Location	Description
`/index`	Lists of what files are available
`/systems`	Software for various types of systems
`/amiga`	Software for Amiga computers
`/next`	Software for NeXT computers
`/apple2`	Software for Apple II computers
`/gnu`	Free Software Foundation software
`/pyramid`	Fixes for Pyramid system software
`/sun`	Software and documentation for Sun systems
`/vms`	Software for VMS systems
`/iris`	Software for SGI Iris systems
`/mac`	Info-mac mailing list archives, mainly
`/msdos`	Lots of software for MS-DOS machines
`/unix`	Software for UNIX systems (LINUX, etc.)
`/simtel20`	Copy of the Simtel20 PC software archive
`/mach`	Software for systems running MACH
`/apollo`	Software for Apollo computers

Location	Description
/vendor	Information from many computer vendors
/info	Information about UUNet and the ftp area
/index	Index files for this ftp site
/news	Software for netnews transport and reading
/published	Information from publishers
/mail	Software for mail reading and transport
/pub	Miscellaneous software and information
/ai	AI (artificial intelligence) journals and information
/archiving	Compression and archiving software
/database	Information on different databases
/economics	Information on economics
/games	Game software for various computers
/linguistics	Linguistic information
/physics	Software for physicists
/security	Security software packages (COPS, etc.)
/shells	Shell software for UNIX systems
/text-processing	Editors and text-processing systems
/window-sys	Window system software (X Window, etc.)
/inet	Information on the Internet
/aups	Acceptable use policies from sites
/ddn-news	DDN management bulletin archives
/doc	General network documentation
/ien	Internet Engineering Notes
/iesg	Internet Engineering Steering Group documents

9

(continued)

Location	Description
/ietf	Internet Engineering Task Force documents
/internet-drafts	IETF draft documents
/isoc	Internet Society documents
/maps	Maps of the Internet and subnets
/netinfo	General network information
/nren	*NREN* documents and information
/protocols	Information about different network protocols
/resource-guide	The Internet Resource Guide
/rfc	All Internet Request For Comments documents
/networking	Different network software packages
/doc	Documents of general interest
/dictionaries	Various language dictionaries
/libraries	Lists of libraries on the Internet
/music	Musical scores for various instruments
/patents	Patent documents
/political	Political documents (U.S. Constitution, for example)
/security	Computer security related documents
/standards	Standards documents (IEEE, ISO, etc.)
/style	Written style documents
/supreme-court	U.S. Supreme Court decisions
/graphics	Graphics software and documentation
/languages	Computer language software

NREN

National Research and Education Network, a proposed nationwide high-speed data network.

wuarchive.wustl.edu

Site name: wuarchive.wustl.edu (128.252.135.4)

Contact: postmaster@wuarchive.wustl.edu

Mirror

Hold copies of software from other sites.

Description: This site, at Washington University at St. Louis, is one of the biggest ftp sites on the Internet. It *mirrors* software archived at many different Internet sites. It holds very large collections of IBM PC and Apple Macintosh software, as well as software and documents covering almost every topic.

Location	Description
/decus	DEC Users' Society tapes
/systems	Software for different computer systems
/aix	IBM AIX software (large collection)
/amiga	Amiga computer software
/apple2	Software for Apple II computers
/atari	Software for Atari computers
/aux	Apple AUX software (large collection)
/cpm	Software for CPM machines
/gnu	All Free Software Foundation software
/hp	Software for Hewlett-Packard machines and calculators
/ibmpc	Huge amount of IBM PC software
/linux	Software for machines running LINUX
/mac	Huge amount of Macintosh software
/minix	Software for systems running Minix
/misc	Miscellaneous software for various systems
/next	Software for NeXT machines
/novell	Software specifically for Novell NetWare
/os9	Information and software for OS/9 systems
/penpoint	Software and information on PenPoint
/sinclair	Software for Sinclair systems

(continued)

9

Location	Description
/sun	Software from Sun Exchange
/svr4-pc	UNIX System V.R4 for PC systems
/unix	Software for UNIX systems
/vax-vms	Software for people running VAX VMS
/xenix	Software for Xenix systems
/mirrors	Copies of information on different sites across the Internet
/info	Information about this site
/languages	Information about the Ada language
/packages	Different software packages
/TeX	The TeX document formatting system
/X11R5	The X11R5 windowing system
/benchmarks	Different computer benchmark software
/compression	Compression and archiving software
/dialslip	Serial Line IP dialup software
/dist	Software distribution software
/gopher	Gopher client and server software
/mail	Mail-reading software
/news	Netnews software
/wuarchive-ftpd	The special ftp server software written here
/www	The World Wide Web software system
/graphics	Different computer graphics packages
/usenet	Archives of some USENET groups
/doc	General documents
/EFF	Electronic Frontier Foundation information
/bible	The Bible in electronic form
/graphics-formats	Different graphics formats

Location	Description
/ietf	Internet Engineering Task Force documents
/nsfnet	NSFNET network-related documents
/nsfnet-stats	Network statistics collected by NSF
/rfc	Network Request For Comments documents
/techreports	Reports from various universities
/edu	Software and information for educational sites
/multimedia	Multimedia data files
/audio	Internet Talk Radio files
/images	Pictures in different formats

sunsite.unc.edu

Site name: sunsite.unc.edu (198.86.40.81)

Contact: ftpkeeper@sunsite.unc.edu

Description: Sunsite is run by the University of North Carolina as a major site for academic information. It contains collections of software and information for many academic areas, and also is a central site for information about computers manufactured by Sun Microsystems, Inc.

Note: *All directories listed for this site are under the* /pub *directory. You should issue a* cd /pub *command after logging in.*

Location	Description
/Linux	Software for sites running LINUX
/X11	Distribution and information about X11
/academic	Software for academic use, arranged by area of knowledge
/agriculture	
/astronomy	
/athletics	

9

(continued)

Location	Description
/biology	
/business	
/chemistry	
/computer–science	
/data_analysis	
/economics	
/education	
/engineering	
/environment	
/fine–arts	
/geography	
/geology	
/history	
/languages	
/library	
/mathematics	
/medicine	
/physics	
/political–science	
/psychology	
/religious_studies	
/russian–studies	
/archives	Archives of mailing lists, USENET news groups, and publications
/docs	Written materials, Internet documents, computers, literature, politics
/gnu	All Free Software Foundation software
/languages	Compilers and interpreters of computer languages

Location	Description
/micro	Software for microcomputers
/mac-stuff	Archives of Mac software
/mips-pc	Archives of MIPS PC software
/pc-stuff	Archives of IBM PC software
/multimedia	Software and information about computer-based video and sound
/packages	Large source distributions for UNIX
/TeX	The TeX document production system (sources)
/bbs	Bulletin board systems
/cygnus	Software from Cygnus Corporation
/gopher	Gopher client and server software
/infosystems	Different information retrieval systems
/Mosaic	Mosaic clients
/WWW	World Wide Web system
/Z39.50	Software implementation of Z39.50
/archie	archie clients for different machines
/ftp-archive	Software to run an ftp archive
/gopher	Gopher client and server software
/wais	WAIS client and server software
/mail	Different mail packages
/news	Different news software
/pctelnet	telnet protocol for PC systems
/terminal-emulators	Terminal emulation software
/sun-info	Information about Sun computer systems
/catalyst	Copies of Sun's Catalyst catalog
/development-tools	Tools for software development
/sun-dist	Sun-distributed patches for its software

9

(continued)

Location	Description
/sun-fixes	Security fixes from Sun
/sun-managers	Archives of Sun-Managers mailing list
/sunenergy	Archives of SunEnergy bulletins
/sunflash	Archives of SunFlash newsletters
/sunspots	Archives of SunSpots mailings
/white-papers	Copies of different Sun white papers
/talk-radio	Audio files from Internet Talk Radio

oak.oakland.edu

Site name: oak.oakland.edu (141.210.10.117)

Description: oak.oakland.edu is a major mirror site. Because Oak is very well connected to the Internet, retrieving the software is easier.

Location	Description
/pub	
/ada	Simtel20 Ada language archives
/misc	Simtel20 miscellaneous software (lots!)
/msdos	Very large archive of MS-DOS software
/pc-blue	PC-BLUE archive of PD and user-contributed PC software
/pub2	
/cpm	Software for CPM machines (lots!)
/cpmug	CPM User's Group software
/macintosh	Very large Macintosh software archive
/unix-c	Very large archive of UNIX software

rtfm.mit.edu

Site name: rtfm.mit.edu (18.70.0.209)

Description: This important site holds the archives of all Frequently Asked Questions (FAQ) informational postings made to various netnews groups. If you have a question about a topic covered by a netnews group, check here to see whether it's covered by one of the FAQ postings.

Note: *All directories listed for this site are under the /pub directory. You should issue a cd /pub command after logging in.*

Location	Description
/pcm	A PC emulator package
/popmail	A Post Office Protocol mail package
/usenet-by-group	FAQ postings organized by news group
/usenet-by-hierarchy	FAQ postings organized by news hierarchy
/usenet-addressed	Database and information on the USENET address server

ftp.cica.indiana.edu

Site name: ftp.cica.indiana.edu (129.79.20.27)

Description: This archive, a central site for Microsoft Windows applications, is run by the Center for Innovative Computer Applications at Indiana University. If you are looking for a Windows application, check here first.

Note: *All directories listed for this site are under the /pub directory. You should issue a cd /pub command after logging in.*

Location	Description
/laser	Information on Laser Sailboating
/next	Software and information on NeXT machines
/pc	IBM PC software
/borland	Software and information from Borland International
/misc	Miscellaneous PC software and information
/starter	Important first software (UNZIP, uudecode, etc.)

9

(continued)

Location	Description
/win3	Microsoft Windows applications
/unix	Miscellaneous UNIX software
/wx	Weather files (GIF images, etc.)

ds.internic.net

Site name: ds.internic.net (198.49.45.10)

Description: The InterNIC sites (ds, is, and rs) collectively form the InterNIC services. They provide different types of information, but ds is the most useful for new users. This site has collections of all Internet documents and information; it is a good site to look for answers to questions about the Internet.

Location	Description
/dirofdirs	Pointers to information at different sites, organized by category
/fyi	Internet FYI (informational) documents
/iesg	Internet Engineering Steering Group documents
/ietf	Internet Engineering Task Force documents
/internet-drafts	Drafts of common Internet documents
/internic.info	Information about the InterNIC
/isoc	Internet Society documents
/nsf	National Science Foundation documents
/policies-procedures	Network policies and procedures from sites
/pub	Other information
/conf.announce	Conference announcements
/current-ietf-docs	Documents under IETF review
/internet-doc	General Internet documents (zen, EARN)

Location	Description
`/netpolicies`	NSFNET acceptable use policy
`/the-scientist`	On-line issues of *The Scientist*
`/z39.50`	Databases available using the Z39.50 protocol
`/resource-guide`	The Internet Resource Guide
`/rfc`	Internet Request For Comments standards
`/std`	Internet Activities Board standards

ftp.eff.org

Site name: `ftp.eff.org` (192.77.172.4)

Description: This site is maintained by the Electronic Frontier Foundation, an organization interested in exploring the legal aspects of computers and networks.

Note: *All directories listed for this site are under the* `/pub` *directory. You should issue a* `cd` `/pub` *command after logging in.*

Location	Description
`/EFF`	Electronic Frontier Foundation information
`/SJG`	Notes on the Steve Jackson Games case, in which a bulletin board system was impounded because of alleged illegal material on the system (the EFF represented Games in the case)
`/academic`	Information from academic sites
`/cpsr`	Notes from the Boston chapter of Computer Professionals for Social Responsibility
`/cud`	Archives of the Computer Underground Digest
`/internet-info`	Copies of Internet documents
`/journals`	Various journals on-line

9

ftp.cso.uiuc.edu

Site name: ftp.cso.uiuc.edu (128.174.5.61)

Description: This large, general-purpose site, run by the University of Illinois at Champaign-Urbana, holds a good variety of programs and information, but an especially large collection of software for Amiga, IBM PC, and Macintosh computers.

Location	Description
/ACM	UIUC's student Association for Computing Machinery information
/pgsi	Power glove serial interface project documentation and software
/amiga	
/amoner	On-line *Amoner* magazine
/cucug	Champaign-Urbana Commodore User Group
/fish	Fred Fish collection—500 disks' worth!
/virus	Virus scanners for Amiga systems
/bbs	Information on local bulletin board systems
/doc	General computing-related documentation
/pcnet	Lists of compression and network software
/mac	
/MUG	Champaign-Urbana Macintosh User Group collection of software
/eudora	E-mail package for Macintosh computers
/virus	Antivirus software for Macintosh
/mail	sendmail and smail packages
/math	PD math software and source code
/mrc	Index to materials available at the CSO resource center

Location	Description
/pc	IBM personal computer software and files
/adf	IBM Adapter Description Files and other PS/2-related items
/exec-pc	Index and sample files from Exec-PC BBS
/local	Collection of local files and software
/pbs	Disks from Public Brand Software
/pcmag	*PC Magazine* files from Exec-PC or PC-Magnet
/pcsig	Files from the largest PC-SIG (Special Interest Group) CD-ROM
/scripts	Kermit and other login scripts
/virus	UIUC collection of antivirus files
/tandy	Tandy Model 100/102 laptop files
/uiuc	MOTIF and X11R4 for various systems
/unix/virus	UNIX information and patches, Internet worm information, Sun sendmail and ftp

wiretap.spies.com

Site name: wiretap.spies.com (130.43.43.43)

Contact: archive@wiretap.spies.com

Description: This site collects interesting information that flows over the Internet. It has a large and eclectic collection of documents ranging from jokes to White House press releases. If you are looking for an official document (such as a government charter or report), this is the place to look.

Location	Description
/Clinton	White House press releases
/Economic_Plan	Clinton's economic plan
/GAO_Reports	General Accounting Office reports

(continued)

9

Location	Description
/Gov	Government and civics archives from around the world
/Aussie	Australian law documents
/Canada	Canadian documents
/Copyright	Copyright laws
/Economic	Clinton's economic plan
/Forfeit	Civil Forfeiture of Assets laws
/GAO-Report	GAO miscellaneous reports
/GAO-Risk	GAO high-risk reports
/GAO-Tech	GAO technical reports
/GAO-Trans	GAO transition reports
/Maast	Maastricht Treaty of European Union
/NAFTA	North American Free Trade Agreement document
/NATO	NATO press releases
/NATO-HB	NATO handbook
/Other	Miscellaneous world documents
/Patent	Patent office reform panel final report
/Platform	Political platforms of the United States
/Treaties	Treaties and international covenants
/UCMJ	Uniform code of military justice
/UN	United Nations resolutions (selected)
/US-Docs	U.S. miscellaneous documents
/US-Gov	U.S. government today
/US-History	U.S. historical documents
/US-Speech	U.S. speeches and addresses
/US-State	Various U.S. state laws
/World	World constitutions

Location	Description
/Library	Wiretap on-line library of articles
/Articles	Various articles
/Classics	Classic literature
/Cyber	Cyberspace documents
/Document	Miscellaneous documents
/Fringe	Fringes of reason
/Humor	Funny material of all types
/Media	Mass media
/Misc	Miscellaneous unclassified documents
/Music	Music scores and lyrics
/Religion	Religious articles and documents
/Techdoc	Technical information of all sorts
/Untech	Non-technical information
/Zines	Magazines

Internet Gopher Sites

Because Gopher is based in a hierarchical structure, you easily can browse among many sites. The following sections list a few of the major Gopher sites to get you started.

In addition to the sites that provide access using a Gopher client program (listed in the following sections), here are the sites that allow telnet access to Gopher. These sites let you access the Gopher system without you having any client software on your end, just the telnet program.

Host Name	Address	Login	Area
consultant.micro.umn.edu	134.84.132.4	gopher	U.S.
ux1.cso.uiuc.edu	128.174.5.59	gopher	U.S.
panda.uiowa.edu	128.255.200.2	panda	U.S.

(continued)

Host Name	Address	Login	Area
gopher.msu.edu	35.8.2.61	gopher	U.S.
gopher.ebone.net	192.36.125.10	gopher	Europe
info.anu.edu.au	150.203.84.20	info	Australia
gopher.chalmers.se	129.16.221.40	gopher	Sweden
tolten.puc.cl	146.155.1.16	gopher	Chile
ecnet.ec	157.100.45.2	gopher	Ecuador
gan.ncc.go.jp	160.190.10.1	gopher	Japan

gopher.micro.umn.edu

Site name: gopher.micro.umn.edu (128.101.62.12)

Description: This is the Gopher home site, where the Gopher software was developed. As such, it has the complete list of all available Gopher sites around the world and keeps the most recent information about Gopher on-line.

Menu Items

```
Information About Gopher
Computer Information
Discussion Groups
Fun & Games
Internet file server (ftp) sites
Libraries
News
Other Gopher and Information Servers
Phone Books
Search Gopher Titles at the University of Minnesota
Search lots of places at the University of Minnesota
University of Minnesota Campus Information/Information about
  Gopher
```

boombox.micro.umn.edu

Site name: boombox.micro.umn.edu (134.84.132.2)

Description: This site, also run by the University of Minnesota, holds the source code for most of the Gopher servers and clients. If you don't already have Gopher client code running, you can anonymous ftp to this machine to retrieve the current versions.

wiretap.spies.com

Site name: wiretap.spies.com (130.43.43.43)

Description: Also described under the earlier anonymous ftp section, wiretap contains many interesting documents that have moved over the Internet. All the following headings have more categories under them—there are too many interesting files to list.

Menu Items

```
About the Internet Wiretap
Clinton Press Releases
Electronic Books at Wiretap
GAO Transition Reports
Government Documents (US & World)
North American Free Trade Agreement
Usenet alt.etext Archives
Usenet ba.internet Archives
Various ETEXT Resources on the Internet
Video Game Archive
Waffle BBS Software
Wiretap On-Line Library
Worldwide Gopher and WAIS Servers
```

gopher.internic.net

Site name: gopher.internic.net (198.49.45.10)

Description: The InterNIC site is the central Network Information Center for the Internet. The site allows you to find information easily about the Internet and many of its resources.

Menu Items

```
Information about the InterNIC
InterNIC Information Services
    Welcome to the InfoSource
    Infosource Update <As of 11/9/93>
    InfoSource Table of Contents.
    Getting Connected to the Internet
    InterNIC Store
    About the InterNIC Information Services
    Getting Started on the Internet
    Internet Information for Everybody
    Just for NICs
    NSFNET, NREN, National Information Infrastructure
      Information
    Beyond InterNIC: Virtual Treasures of the Internet
    Searching the InfoSource by Keyword
InterNIC Registration Services
    InterNIC Registration Archives
    Whois Searches for InterNIC Registries
    Whois Searches for Non-MILNET Individuals
```

9

```
InterNIC Directory and Database Services
    About InterNIC Directory and Database Services
    InterNIC Directory of Directories
    InterNIC Directory Services ("White Pages")
    InterNIC Database Services (Public Databases)
    Additional Internet Resource Information
    Internet Documentation (RFCs, FYIs, etc.)
    National Science Foundation Information
```

gopher.nsf.gov

Site name: gopher.nsf.gov (128.150.195.40)

Description: This server—the main Gopher server run by the National Science Foundation—is a central clearinghouse for many scientific reports and documents. This server also provides pointers to many other government Gopher servers; if you are looking for information from a government office or department, look here.

Menu Items

```
About this Gopher
About STIS
Index to NSF Award Abstracts
Index to NSF Publications
NSF Phone Directory
NSF Publications
BIO--Director for Biological Sciences
CISE--Director for Computer and Information Science
   & Technology
EHR--Director for Education and Human Resources
ENG--Director for Engineering
GEO--Director for Geosciences
MPS--Director for Math & Physical Sciences
NSB--National Science Board
OIG--Office of the Inspector General
Office of the Director
SBE--Director for Social, Behavioral and Economic Sciences
SRS--Science Resources Studies Division
On-Line STIS System (login as "public")
Other US Government Gopher Services
    About this list
    Extension Service, USDA
    Federal Info Exchange (FEDIX)
    Government in General (maintained by UCI)
    LANL Physics Information Service
    Library of Congress MARVEL
    National Aeronautics and Space Administration
    National Coordination Office for HPCC (NCO/HPCC) Gopher
    National Institute of Standards and Technology (NIST)
    National Institutes of Health (NIH)
    National Oceanic and Atmospheric Administration (NOAA)
    National Science Foundation (NSF)
    Protein Data Bank--Brookhaven National Lab
```

```
U.S. Dept. of Education
US Environmental Protection Agency (EPA)
U.S. Geological Survey
USDA National Agricultural Library Plant Genome
USDA-ARS GRIN National Genetic Resources Program
```

ftp and Gopher Sites by Topic

This section lists a few of the many special-interest topics that have information available on the Internet through ftp and Gopher. Each individual entry lists the method of access and all the information necessary to get access to your topic.

Note: *This section is by no means complete; it's intended simply to give a feel for the types of information available and how to get access to it.*

Gopher and ftp sites are listed for the following topics:

Agriculture	Law
Aviation	Mathematics
Books	Music
Computer Networking	Recipes
Computer Security	Religion
Education	Science (General)
Genealogy	Weather
Health	ZIP Codes
History	

Agriculture

Several different services offer agricultural information on the Internet. Some services are weather- and crop-related; others provide information related to health.

Access method: gopher esusda.gov (192.73.224.100)

Description: This Gopher server, run by the Extension Service of the USDA, provides access to various educational and information services of the Cooperative Extension System, as well as providing links to other agricultural Gopher servers around the country. This Gopher also provides information such as White House press releases, the Clinton health plan, the federal budget, and more.

9

Access method: `ftp ftp.sura.net` (128.167.254.179)

`get file /pub/nic/agricultural.list`

Description: This document, titled "Not Just Cows—A Guide to Internet/Bitnet Resources in Agriculture and Related Sciences," contains pointers to many resources on BITNET and the Internet for the agricultural sciences. This document is fairly large (about 2,700 lines), so you should peruse it on-line when you retrieve it.

Aviation

Access method: `gopher av.eecs.nwu.edu` (129.105.5.6)

Description: This site is run by Northwestern University as a repository for aviation information. Some information is from the USENET `rec.aviation` group, but quite a bit is contributed from individual pilots on the Internet. Stories, pictures, and flight-planning information are available.

Books

Access method: `ftp mrcnext.cso.uiuc.edu` (128.174.201.12)

`cd /pub/etext`

Description: This site maintains an archive of the Project Gutenberg files. Project Gutenberg is aimed at producing 10,000 of the most widely read books in electronic form. Some books already available at this site are *Alice in Wonderland*, *The CIA World Fact Book*, *Roget's Thesaurus*, and *Moby Dick*.

Computer Networking

Access method: `ftp dhvx20.csudh.edu` (155.135.1.1)

`cd global_net`

Description: This site maintains an archive of documents pertaining to the effort to bring network access to lesser-developed nations and the poorer parts of developed nations.

Note: Many other networking documents are available, as described in the host-specific section earlier. The site `ds.internic.net` is a primary source for all documents and information about the Internet and networking in general.

Computer Security

Access method: `ftp ftp.cert.org` (192.88.209.5)

`cd /pub`

Description: The Computer Emergency Response Team (CERT) is a federally funded organization that acts as a clearinghouse for computer security information. On its ftp site are archives of all its security bulletins, some computer security tools, computer virus information, and other computer security related items.

Education

Access method: `gopher nysernet.org` (192.77.173.2)

Description: The Empire Schoolhouse is one option under the Nysernet Gopher server (under the K-12 special collection), but is accessed directly via telnet. This server has information about education from grades kindergarten through 12, including the Educational Resource Information Center and the Empire Internet Schoolhouse.

Genealogy

If you are looking up your roots and need some help, the following sites may be just what you need. They provide information on genealogy, including database programs.

Access method: `ftp wood.cebaf.gov` (129.57.32.165)

`cd genealogy`

Description: This site contains a large amount of information on genealogy, including information on the PAF genealogy program, genealogy database programs, and text files relating to genealogy.

Access method: `ftp vm1.nodak.edu` (134.129.111.1)

`cd roots-l`

Description: This site contains a very large number of text files relating to genealogy. Retrieve the file FAQ.INDEX for a beginning on how to use the information in this directory.

Health

Access method: `gopher gopher.nih.gov` (128.231.2.3)

Description: Run by the National Institutes of Health, this Gopher site has health and clinical information, grants and research information,

9

molecular biology databases, and links to the National Institute of Allergy and Infectious Disease and National Institute of Mental Health Gopher sites. This site also features information about cancer (CancerNet) and AIDS-related information. Access to the National Library of Medicine is also available.

History

Access method: `ftp byrd.mu.wvnet.edu` (129.71.32.152)

`cd /pub/history`

Description: This site offers documents on many different historic categories, including diplomatic, ethnic, maritime, and U.S. history.

Law

Several law schools offer extensive resources on the Internet for lawyers and others interested in the law.

Access method: `gopher fatty.law.cornell.edu` (132.236.108.5)

Description: This site, run by the Cornell University law school, features information such as a directory of legal academia, discussion and LISTSERV archives, U.S. law (primary documents and commentary), foreign and international law (primary documents and commentary), and other legal resources (such as government agencies and Internet sources). This site is very complete and valuable for all legal references.

Access method: `gopher gopher.law.csuohio.edu` (137.148.22.51)

Description: This site, run by the Cleveland State University law school, features information such as electronic forms of many legal sources, legal sources on the Internet, course schedules, and links to other Gopher sites.

Mathematics

Access method: `gopher e-math.ams.com` (130.44.1.100)

Description: This site is run by the American Mathematics Society to provide an electronic forum for AMS members and others interested in mathematics. Topics include mathematical publications, mathematical preprints, mathematical discussion lists and bulletin boards, general information of interest to mathematicians, and professional information for mathematicians.

Music

Musicians have access to several archives of information, including scores, guitar tablature, and lyrics of popular songs.

Access method: `ftp ftp.nevada.edu (131.216.1.11)`

`cd /pub/guitar`

Description: This directory contains tablature or chords written for guitar. People from all over the world submit songs that they have transcribed into tablature form; if you submit something, however, please make sure that it isn't copyrighted.

Access method: `ftp ftp.uwp.edu (131.210.1.4)`

`cd /pub/music`

or `gopher ftp.uwp.edu`

Description: This server has archives of information about music, including articles about music composition, archives of music by artist name, classical music buying guide, folk music files and pointers, lyrics archives, and more.

Recipes

Several Internet mailing lists and USENET groups are devoted to cooking and recipes. Over quite a few years, these recipes have been collected into several archives on the Internet.

Access method: `ftp gatekeeper.dec.com (16.1.0.2)`

`cd /pub/recipes`

Description: The archive at `gatekeeper.dec.com` has many different items of interest. The recipes area has hundreds of items submitted by users over a period of several years. This archive is organized by recipe title.

Access method: `ftp mthvax.cs.miami.edu (129.171.32.5)`

`cd /pub/recipes`

Description: This site holds the archives for the USENET group `rec.food.recipes`. Recipes here are organized by food type—that is, fish, chicken, and so on. Programs for indexing and reading the `rec.food.recipes` archives are also available on this site (for Macintosh and IBM PC); see the file `/pub/recipes/readme` for information.

9

Religion

Many different religious texts and informational files are available on Internet servers. These sites are a good place to find many of these texts.

Access method: `ftp wuarchive.wustl.edu` (128.252.135.4)

   `cd /doc/bible`

Description: Complete editions of the King James Version of the Bible, including cross-references, are available for IBM PCs and Macintoshes. You probably want to get the README file first to understand how to use the files.

Access method: `ftp quake.think.com` (192.31.181.1)

   `cd /pub/etext/koran`

Description: This directory contains an electronically scanned version of M.H. Shakir's translation of the Holy Qur'an, as published by Tahrike Tarsile Qur'an, Inc. There are files for each chapter, and you can retrieve each one individually.

Access method: `ftp nic.funet.fi` (128.214.6.100)

   `cd /pub/doc/bible/hebrew`

Description: This directory contains the Torah from the Tanach in Hebrew, the Prophets from the Tanach in Hebrew, and the Writings from the Tanach in Hebrew. Also included is a program to display Hebrew letters on an IBM PC monitor and a Hebrew quiz with biblical Hebrew-language tutor. This site is in Europe, so you may want to limit your file transfers somewhat.

Science (General)

Access method: `gopher gopher.hs.jhu.edu` (128.220.1.137)

Description: This server is run by the History of Science Department at Johns Hopkins University. Available topics include "scientists on disk"—that is, a collection of important documents by scientists; the history of science (including departmental information such as memos and correspondence); classes about the history of science; and other information in the "grab bag" category. The scientists on disk collection includes papers by Darwin and Oppenheimer and information about the Royal Society of Science.

Weather

Access method: gopher wx.atmos.uiuc.edu (128.174.80.10)

Description: This server is the University of Illinois Weather Machine. It gives Gopher access to weather information for many different regions, including many major cities in the United States. It also allows access to image files from different satellites. These images are in GIF format and may be displayed on your local machine after you retrieve them.

ZIP Codes

Access method: ftp oes.orst.edu (128.193.124.2)
           cd /pub/almanac/misc
           get zipcode

Description: This file gives a list of all ZIP codes for the United States (and territories) as of the current date of the file. The file is of the form zipcode:city (that is, 15001:Aliquippa, PA), which allows for easy searching.

9

Chapter 10

Selected USENET Groups

As discussed in Chapter 1, "Introducing the Internet," you can subscribe to many USENET news groups. This chapter lists some news groups that may be of interest to people using the Internet for business or research purposes.

Unlike many other sources of information on the Internet, a centralized list of the news groups is available within USENET. This list, called the *news groups file*, is available through several different sources. One of the easiest ways to get this list of groups is by reading the news group `news.announce.newusers`. This group is set up to introduce new readers to USENET; every USENET reader should read the articles posted this group at least once. Some of the regularly posted articles are as follows:

- *List of Periodic Information Postings*. A description of the regular postings to various news groups that give information about those groups.

- *Publicly Accessible Mailing Lists*. A list of most of the publicly accessible mailing lists available on the Internet. Mailing lists are discussed in Chapter 11.

- *The USENET Newsgroup Creation Companion*. A document describing the process of creating new netnews groups.

- *USENET Software: History and Sources*. A document on the history of USENET and the software that makes it run.

- *List of Active Newsgroups*. The list of available news groups.

Note: *If the article you are interested in isn't available now at your site, wait a while; the articles in* news.announce.newusers *are posted regularly (usually once a month). Any changes since the last time they were posted also are noted. So if you already have read the articles there, you usually can read just the changes to see what information is new.*

After you have the list of available news groups, you can look for a news group that matches the topics you are interested in. The file lists each news group, one per line, with a brief description of the topics that group covers. So you can read through the list to look for a group that matches your topics. When you find a group that looks promising, you should read some of the articles in that group to see whether the topics being discussed are of interest. You may have to look through several groups before finding one that matches your interests exactly, though.

Note: *When you start a news-reading session, your news-reading software may show you a list of the news groups that have recently been added to your system, and ask whether you want to subscribe them. This way, you automatically can see new groups that you may be interested in.*

This chapter lists a number of interesting USENET groups, with brief descriptions of the topics covered by each group. If a USENET group is moderated, this will be mentioned. In some cases, several USENET groups are related to the same topic. This list is far from complete, as many of the USENET groups have limited appeal or do not appear on many Internet sites (such as groups in the alt hierarchy). The groups listed here, however, are available on most systems that have USENET access.

Aeronautics

Two USENET groups are devoted to the science of aeronautics. The first group, sci.aeronautics, discusses general topics related to the science of aeronautics. The second group, sci.aeronautics.airliners, discusses specific issues related to airliner technology. Both groups are moderated.

10

Agriculture

One USENET group, `sci.agriculture`, is devoted to farming, agriculture, and related topics.

Amiga Computer Systems

Many USENET groups are devoted to discussing specific computer systems from various manufacturers. Several of these groups are devoted to the Amiga computer systems.

News Group	Description
`comp.sys.amiga.advocacy`	Discussion about the merits of Amiga computer systems versus other types of computers.
`comp.sys.amiga.announce`	Announcements about Amiga computers (moderated).
`comp.sys.amiga.applications`	General discussion about programs that run on Amiga systems.
`comp.sys.amiga.audio`	Discussion about music, MIDI, speech synthesis, and other sounds generated on Amiga systems.
`comp.sys.amiga.datacomm`	Discussion about data communications between Amiga systems.
`comp.sys.amiga.emulations`	Discussion specific to various hardware and software emulators for Amiga systems.
`comp.sys.amiga.games`	Discussion of games for Amiga systems.
`comp.sys.amiga.graphics`	Discussion about graphics applications and techniques on Amiga systems.
`comp.sys.amiga.hardware`	Questions, reviews, problem reports, and other information about computer hardware for Amiga computers.
`comp.sys.amiga.introduction`	Information for new users of Amiga systems.
`comp.sys.amiga.marketplace`	Discussion about prices, availability, and sales of Amiga computers and accessories.
`comp.sys.amiga.misc`	General discussion about Amiga systems not covered by other USENET groups.

(continues)

News Group	Description
comp.sys.amiga.multimedia	Discussion about animation, video, and multimedia applications for Amiga systems.
comp.sys.amiga.programmer	Discussion for programmers of Amiga systems.
comp.sys.amiga.reviews	Reviews of Amiga software, hardware, and accessories (moderated).
comp.sources.amiga	Postings of sourcecode for programs that run on Amiga systems (moderated).
comp.binaries.amiga	Postings of executable programs that run on Amiga systems (moderated).

Announcements

Several news groups are devoted to announcements of interest to all USENET readers. Many systems subscribe new users to these groups automatically; new users should probably read these groups regularly.

News Group	Description
news.announce.important	General announcements of interest to all USENET readers (moderated).
news.announce.newgroups	Announcements about the creation of new USENET groups (moderated).
news.announce.newusers	Announcements and information of interest to new USENET readers (moderated).
news.newusers.questions	Questions and answers for readers new to USENET.

Apple II Computer Systems

Several USENET groups are devoted to discussing various aspects of Apple II computers.

News Group	Description
comp.sys.apple2	General discussion about Apple II computers not covered in other USENET groups.
comp.sys.apple2.comm	Discussion specific to data communications between Apple II systems.
comp.sys.apple2.gno	The Apple II-GS system's GNO operating system.
comp.sys.apple2.marketplace	Discussion about buying, selling, and trading Apple II equipment and accessories.
comp.sys.apple2.programmer	Discussion about programming Apple II systems.
comp.sys.apple2.usergroups	Discussion and announcements about Apple II users' groups.
comp.sources.apple2	Postings of program sources for programs that run on Apple II computers (moderated).
comp.binaries.apple2	Postings of executable programs that run on Apple II computers (moderated).

Artificial Intelligence

Several USENET groups are available that discuss the field of artificial intelligence. These groups tend to be oriented toward the application of artificial intelligence in computers and computer software.

News Group	Description
comp.ai	General artificial intelligence discussion not covered in other groups.
comp.ai.edu	Applications of artificial intelligence to education.
comp.ai.fuzzy	Fuzzy set theory, also known as fuzzy logic.
comp.ai.genetic	Genetic algorithms in computing.
comp.ai.jair.announce	Announcements and abstracts of the Journal of AI Research (moderated).

(continues)

News Group	Description
comp.ai.jair.papers	Papers published by the Journal of AI Research (moderated).
comp.ai.nat-lang	Natural language processing by computers.
comp.ai.neural-nets	All aspects of neural networks.
comp.ai.nlang-know-rep	Natural language and knowledge representation (moderated).
comp.ai.philosophy	Philosophical aspects of artificial intelligence.
comp.ai.shells	Artificial intelligence applied to computer command processors (called *shells*).
comp.ai.vision	Artificial intelligence vision research (moderated).

Astronomy

Several USENET groups are devoted to discussing the science of astronomy.

News Group	Description
sci.astro	General discussion and information about astronomy.
sci.astro.fits	Specific issues related to the Flexible Image Transport System used in astronomy.
sci.astro.hubble	Specific discussion about processing Hubble space telescope data (moderated).
sci.astro.planetarium	Discussion about planetariums.

Biology

The science of biology is discussed in several USENET groups under the sci.bio hierarchy.

10

News Group	Description
`sci.bio`	General discussion and information about biology not covered in other USENET groups.
`sci.bio.ecology`	Discussion about research into ecology.
`sci.bio.evolution`	Discussions about evolutionary biology (moderated).
`sci.bio.herp`	Discussions about the biology of amphibians and reptiles.
`sci.bio.technology`	Discussions about any topic related to biotechnology.

Books

One USENET group discusses books about technical topics:
`misc.books.technical`.

Chemistry

The science of chemistry is discussed in two USENET groups. The group `sci.chem` is for general discussion about chemistry and related sciences. The second group, `sci.chem.organomet`, is specifically for discussion about organometallic chemistry.

Consumer Issues

Two USENET groups discuss issues of interest to consumers. The first group, `misc.consumers`, is devoted to general topics of consumer interest, including product reviews, advice, and so forth. The second group is `misc.consumers.house`, which is devoted to issues relating to owning and maintaining a house.

Databases

Several USENET groups are devoted to discussing databases. Many of these groups discuss database products by a particular vendor. The group descriptions tell you which product is discussed.

News Group	Description
comp.databases	General discussion on database and data management issues and theory.
comp.databases.informix	Discussion on the Informix database management software.
comp.databases.ingres	Discussion on issues relating to INGRES database products.
comp.databases.ms-access	Microsoft's Windows-based relational database system, Access.
comp.databases.object	General discussion of object-oriented paradigms in database systems.
comp.databases.oracle	The SQL database products of the Oracle Corporation.
comp.databases.paradox	The Paradox database software for DOS and Microsoft Windows by Borland.
comp.databases.pick	Pick-like, post-relational database systems.
comp.databases.rdb	The relational database software RDB from Digital Equipment Corporation.
comp.databases.sybase	Sybase implementations of the SQL server.
comp.databases.theory	General discussion of advances in database technology.
comp.databases.xbase.fox	Fox Software's XBase system and compatible products.
comp.databases.xbase.misc	Discussion of other XBase products.

Education

Two USENET groups are devoted to discussions about education. The first, misc.education, discusses general topics dealing with the education system. The second group is misc.education.language.english, which is specifically devoted to teaching the English language to speakers of other languages.

Note: *An entire hierarchy is devoted to education in grades kindergarten through 12. This hierarchy, called the* k12 *hierarchy, isn't available at many Internet sites. If your site does not receive this hierarchy, you should contact your site administrator to see whether it can be made available.*

Engineering

Several different USENET groups discuss engineering and the different branches of engineering.

News Group	Description
sci.engr	General discussions about technical aspects of engineering tasks not covered in one of the specific engineering groups.
sci.engr.advanced-tv	Discussions about HDTV/DATV standards, formats, equipment, and practices.
sci.engr.biomed	Discussions specific to the field of biomedical engineering.
sci.engr.chem	Discussions specific to the field of chemical engineering.
sci.engr.civil	Discussions about topics related to the field of civil engineering.
sci.engr.control	Topics related to the engineering of control systems.
sci.engr.lighting	Discussions about light, vision, and color in the fields of architecture, the media, etc.
sci.engr.manufacturing	Discussions about all aspects of manufacturing technology.
sci.engr.mech	Discussions specific to the field of mechanical engineering.

Geology

The science of geology is covered in three USENET groups:

News Group	Description
sci.geo.fluids	Discussion about geophysical fluid dynamics.
sci.geo.geology	Discussion about solid earth sciences.
sci.geo.meteorology	Discussion about the science of meterology and related sciences.

Graphics

The USENET groups that deal with graphics have widely different discussion topics. Some groups talk about technical aspects of graphics; others discuss specific computer graphics software packages.

News Group	Description
comp.graphics	General discussion of computer graphics, art, animation, and image processing.
comp.graphics.algorithms	Technical discussion about algorithms used in producing computer graphics.
comp.graphics.animation	Technical discussion of techniques used in computer animation.
comp.graphics.avs	Discussion about the Application Visualization System.
comp.graphics.data-explorer	Discussion about the Visualization Data Explorer from International Business Machines, Inc.
comp.graphics.explorer	The Explorer modular visualization environment.
comp.graphics.gnuplot	The GNUPLOT interactive function plotter software package.
comp.graphics.opengl	Discussion about the OpenGL 3D application programming interface specification.

News Group	Description
`comp.graphics.research`	Highly technical computer graphics discussion (moderated).
`comp.graphics.visualization`	Information about scientific visualization.

Handicaps/Disabilities

One USENET group, `misc.handicap`, discusses issues of interest to people with physical or mental disabilities. This group is moderated.

Hewlett-Packard Computer Systems

Several USENET groups are devoted to Hewlett-Packard computer products, including calculators and other products:

News Group	Description
`comp.sys.hp`	General discussion about Hewlett-Packard equipment not covered in other USENET groups.
`comp.sys.hp.apps`	General discussion about programs that run on Hewlett-Packard equipment.
`comp.sys.hp.hardware`	Discussion about Hewlett-Packard system hardware of all types.
`comp.sys.hp.hpux`	Discussion about Hewlett-Packard's version of UNIX (HP-UX) and the Hewlett-Packard 9000 series computers.
`comp.sys.hp.misc`	General discussion about Hewlett-Packard equipment.
`comp.sys.hp.mpe`	Discussion about the Hewlett-Packard MPE product and the Hewlett-Packard 3000 series computers.
`comp.sys.hp48`	Discussion about the Hewlett-Packard HP48 and HP28 calculators.

IBM Personal Computer Systems

IBM PC systems (and the systems compatible with them) are tremendously popular, and quite a few netnews groups are devoted to discussing these systems. The IBM PC USENET groups are some of the most popular groups on USENET.

News Group	Description
comp.sys.ibm.pc.demos	Discussion of demonstration software that run on IBM PC systems.
comp.sys.ibm.pc.digest	Discussion of the IBM PC, PC-XT, and PC-AT systems (moderated). The posts are in digest format, where several articles are joined together into one large post.
comp.sys.ibm.pc.games.action	Specific discussion about arcade-style games on PC systems.
comp.sys.ibm.pc.games.adventure	Specific discussion about adventure-style games on PC systems.
comp.sys.ibm.pc.games.announce	Announcements about all types of PC games (moderated).
comp.sys.ibm.pc.games.flight-sim	Specific discussion about flight simulator programs on PC systems.
comp.sys.ibm.pc.games.misc	General discussion about games on PC systems not covered in other USENET groups.
comp.sys.ibm.pc.games.rpg	Specific discussion about role-playing games on PC systems.
comp.sys.ibm.pc.games.strategic	Specific discussion about strategy and planning style games on PC systems.
comp.sys.ibm.pc.hardware	Discussion about XT/AT/EISA type hardware from any PC vendor.
comp.sys.ibm.pc.hardware.cd-rom	Specific discussion about CD-ROM drives and interfaces for PC systems.
comp.sys.ibm.pc.hardware.chips	Discussion about processor, cache, and memory chips for IBM PC systems.
comp.sys.ibm.pc.hardware.comm	Discussion about modems and other communications equipment for IBM PC systems.

News Group	Description
`comp.sys.ibm.pc.hardware.misc`	General discussion about IBM PC hardware not covered by other USENET groups.
`comp.sys.ibm.pc.hardware.networking`	Network hardware and equipment specifically for IBM PC systems.
`comp.sys.ibm.pc.hardware.storage`	Specific discussion about disk drives and other IBM PC storage devices.
`comp.sys.ibm.pc.hardware.systems`	Discussion about entire IBM PC computer and compatible systems.
`comp.sys.ibm.pc.hardware.video`	Specific discussion about video cards and monitors for IBM PC systems.
`comp.sys.ibm.pc.misc`	General discussion about all aspects of IBM PC computer systems.
`comp.sys.ibm.pc.rt`	Discussion about the IBM RT computer system.
`comp.sys.ibm.pc.soundcard`	Discussion about hardware and software related to IBM PC sound cards.
`comp.sys.ibm.ps2.hardware`	Discussion specific to micro channel hardware from any vendor.

Information Retrieval Systems

Several different information retrieval systems are in use on the Internet, and each system has its own USENET group to discuss specific topics for that system. Also, there are groups discussing general topics in information retrieval systems.

News Group	Description
`comp.infosystems`	General discussion about information systems. Specific discussion about a particular information retrieval system should be directed to the group for that specific system.
`comp.infosystems.announce`	Announcements of interest to people concerned with Internet information services (moderated).

(continues)

News Group	Description
comp.infosystems.gis	General discussion about all aspects of Geographic Information Systems.
comp.infosystems.gopher	Discussion specific to the Gopher information retrieval system.
comp.infosystems.wais	Discussion specific to the WAIS full-text search system.
comp.infosystems.WWW	Discussion specific to the World Wide Web information system.

Investing

Investing is discussed in several USENET groups, with the readers of the groups providing advice and experiences to other USENET readers.

News Group	Description
misc.invest	General discussions about investing and handling money.
misc.invest.canada	Discussions specific to investing in Canadian financial markets.
misc.invest.funds	Sharing information about bond, stock, and real estate funds.
misc.invest.real-estate	Discussions about property investments.
misc.invest.stocks	Discussions sharing information about stocks and options.
misc.invest.technical	Technical discussion about analyzing market trends.

Languages (Computer Programming)

Many USENET groups are devoted to the discussion of various computer programming languages. All these USENET groups are under the comp.lang hierarchy and are devoted to discussions on their specific language.

10

News Group	Description
comp.lang.ada	The Ada programming language.
comp.lang.apl	The APL programming language.
comp.lang.asm370	The IBM system 370 assembly language.
comp.lang.basic.misc	General discussion of the BASIC programming language.
comp.lang.basic.visual	Discussion specific to the Microsoft Visual Basic product.
comp.lang.c	The C programming language.
comp.lang.c++	The C++ object-oriented programming language.
comp.lang.clos	The Common LISP Object System.
comp.lang.clu	The CLU programming language.
comp.lang.dylan	The Dylan programming language.
comp.lang.eiffel	The object-oriented Eiffel programming language.
comp.lang.forth	The FORTH programming language.
comp.lang.forth.mac	The Macintosh FORTH programming environment from CSI.
comp.lang.fortran	The FORTRAN programming language.
comp.lang.functional	General discussion about functional programming languages.
comp.lang.hermes	The Hermes programming language.
comp.lang.icon	The ICON programming language.
comp.lang.idl	The Interface Description Language.
comp.lang.idl-pvwave	Discussion about IDL and the PV-Wave system.
comp.lang.lisp	General discussion about the LISP programming language.
comp.lang.lisp.franz	Discussion specific to the Franz Lisp programming system.

(continues)

News Group	Description
comp.lang.lisp.mcl	Discussion specific to Apple's Macintosh Common LISP.
comp.lang.lisp.x	Discussion specific to the XLISP language system.
comp.lang.logo	The Logo teaching and learning language.
comp.lang.misc	Discussion about computer languages that don't have a specific USENET group.
comp.lang.ml	Discussion about the various ML programming languages (moderated).
comp.lang.modula2	The Modula-2 programming language.
comp.lang.modula3	The Modula-3 programming language.
comp.lang.oberon	The Oberon programming language.
comp.lang.objective-c	The Objective-C programming language.
comp.lang.pascal	The Pascal programming language.
comp.lang.perl	The Perl programming system.
comp.lang.pop	The Pop-11 programming language.
comp.lang.postscript	The PostScript page description language.
comp.lang.prolog	The PROLOG programming language.
comp.lang.rexx	The REXX computer command language.
comp.lang.sather	The object-oriented computer programming language Sather.
comp.lang.scheme	The Scheme programming language.
comp.lang.scheme.c	The Scheme C language environment.
comp.lang.sigplan	Information and announcements from the Association for Computer Machinery's SIGPLAN group (moderated).
comp.lang.smalltalk	The SmallTalk 80 programming language.
comp.lang.tcl	The Tcl programming language.
comp.lang.verilog	Discussions about Verilog and PLI.

News Group	Description
`comp.lang.vhdl`	The VHSIC Hardware Description Language.
`comp.lang.visual`	General discussion about visual programming languages.

Legal Issues

Several USENET groups are devoted to discussing the law and legal matters. The readers of these groups often provide information about legal issues.

News Group	Description
`misc.legal`	General discussion about legalities and the ethics of law.
`misc.legal.computing`	Discussions about the legal climate of the computing industry.
`misc.legal.moderated`	Discussions about all aspects of the legal profession and the law (moderated).

Libraries

The USENET group `comp.internet.library` discusses the various electronic libraries on the Internet. This USENET group is moderated.

Macintosh Systems

Apple Macintosh systems are also very popular with users of the Internet. Quite a few groups are devoted to discussing Macintosh systems.

News Group	Description
`comp.sys.mac.advocacy`	Discussion comparing Macintosh computers with systems from other vendors.
`comp.sys.mac.announce`	Important announcements for Macintosh users (moderated).

(continues)

News Group	Description
comp.sys.mac.apps	Discussion about Macintosh software applications.
comp.sys.mac.comm	Discussion about modems and other communications products for Macintosh systems.
comp.sys.mac.databases	Specific discussion about database systems for Macintosh computers.
comp.sys.mac.digest	General Apple Macintosh information and uses in digest form, where several articles are grouped together (moderated).
comp.sys.mac.games	General discussion about games running on Macintosh systems.
comp.sys.mac.graphics	General discussion about graphics, including paint, draw, and CAD applications.
comp.sys.mac.hardware	General discussion about Macintosh hardware.
comp.sys.mac.hypercard	Discussion and information about using the Macintosh HyperCard system.
comp.sys.mac.misc	General discussion about Macintosh systems not covered in other USENET groups.
comp.sys.mac.oop.macapp3	Discussion specific to version 3 of the MacApp object-oriented programming system.
comp.sys.mac.oop.misc	General discussion about object-oriented programming on the Macintosh.
comp.sys.mac.oop.tcl	Discussion specific to the THINK Class Library system from Symantec for object-oriented programming.
comp.sys.mac.portables	Discussion particular to Macintosh laptop systems.
comp.sys.mac.programmer	General discussion about programming Macintosh systems.
comp.sys.mac.scitech	Discussion about using the Macintosh in scientific and technical work.

News Group	Description
comp.sys.mac.system	Discussion about the Macintosh system software.
comp.sys.mac.wanted	Postings from people who want a particular program or product for their Macintosh.
comp.sources.mac	Postings of program sources for the Macintosh systems (moderated).
comp.binaries.mac	Postings of executable programs that can run on a Macintosh (moderated).

Mathematics

Several USENET groups are devoted to discussing the science of mathematics.

News Group	Description
sci.math	General discussion of the science of mathematics.
sci.math.num-analysis	Discussion specific to the mathematical field of numerical analysis.
sci.math.research	Discussion of current mathematical research (moderated).
sci.math.symbolic	Discussion about the mathematical field of symbolic algebra.

Medicine

Medicine is discussed in several USENET groups. Some groups focus on general medical research and information, whereas others are devoted to specific diseases and fields.

News Group	Description
sci.med	General discussion about medicine and related products and regulations.
sci.med.aids	Specific discussion about AIDS, including treatment, the pathology and biology of the HIV virus, and prevention (moderated).
sci.med.dentistry	Discussion about the medical field of dentistry.
sci.med.nursing	Discussion about nursing questions and related topics.
sci.med.nutrition	Discussion about nutrition and its impact on the body and health.
sci.med.occupational	Discussion about occupational injuries, including prevention and treatment.
sci.med.pharmacy	Discussion about the teaching and practice of pharmacy.
sci.med.physics	Issues of physics in medical testing and care.
sci.med.psychobiology	Information and news in psychiatry and psychobiology.
sci.med.telemedicine	Discussion specific to the topic of clinical consulting through computer networks.

Microsoft Windows

Several USENET groups are devoted to discussing Microsoft Windows, one of the most popular window systems running on IBM-compatible systems. Some groups are devoted to programming under the Windows environment, while other groups discuss using the Windows system.

News Group	Description
comp.os.ms-windows.advocacy	Speculation and debate about Microsoft Windows.
comp.os.ms-windows.announce	Announcements relating to Microsoft Windows (moderated).
comp.os.ms-windows.apps	Discussion about computer applications (programs) running under Windows.

News Group	Description
comp.os.ms-windows.misc	General discussion about issues relating to Windows.
comp.os.ms-windows.nt.misc	General discussion about the Microsoft Windows NT environment.
comp.os.ms-windows.nt.setup	Discussion specifically about setting up and configuring Windows NT systems.
comp.os.ms-windows. programmer.misc	General discussion about programming under Microsoft Windows.
comp.os.ms-windows. programmer.tools	Discussion about development tools for programming under Microsoft Windows.
comp.os.ms-windows. programmer.win32	Discussion specifically about programming the 32-bit Windows interface.
comp.os.ms-windows.setup	Discussion specifically about installing and setting up a Microsoft Windows system.
comp.binaries.ms-windows	Postings of programs that run under Microsoft Windows (moderated).

MS-DOS Systems

Although the number of people running MS-DOS systems has been going down in recent years, a great number of MS-DOS systems are still around. Several USENET groups are devoted to MS-DOS, including groups on programming and various applications.

News Group	Description
comp.os.msdos.4dos	Discussion specific to the 4DOS command processor.
comp.os.msdos.apps	Discussion about applications that run under MS-DOS.
comp.os.msdos.desqview	Discussion specific to the DESQview product from Quarterdeck.
comp.os.msdos.mail-news	Discussion about administering mail and USENET news systems under MS-DOS.
comp.os.msdos.misc	General discussion about MS-DOS systems.

(continues)

News Group	Description
comp.os.msdos.pcgeos	Discussion about the GeoWorks PC/GEOS and PC/GEOS-based packages.
comp.os.msdos.programmer	Discussion about programming MS-DOS systems.
comp.os.msdos.programmer. turbovision	Discussion on programming with Borland's Turbo Vision text application libraries.
comp.binaries.ibm.pc	Postings of programs that run under MS-DOS (moderated).
comp.binaries.ibm.pc.d	Discussions about the postings made in comp.binaries.ibm.pc.
comp.binaries.ibm.pc.wanted	Requests for IBM PC and compatible programs.

On-Line Documentation

Two moderated news groups are set up to provide a central location where announcements about documentation or technical reports can be made.

News Group	Description
comp.doc	Announcements about archived public-domain documentation.
comp.doc.techreports	Lists of available technical reports.

Organizations

Several computer organizations have USENET groups devoted to discussions by and about the organization.

News Group	Description
comp.org.acm	Discussion about the Association for Computing Machinery.
comp.org.decus	Discussion about the Digital Equipment Computer Users Society.

News Group	Description
`comp.org.eff.news`	News from the Electronic Frontier Foundation (moderated).
`comp.org.eff.talk`	General discussion about the Electronic Frontier Foundation.
`comp.org.fidonet`	The FidoNews digest, which is the official newsletter of the FidoNet Association (moderated).
`comp.org.ieee`	Discussion and announcements about the Institute of Electronics and Electrical Engineers.
`comp.org.isoc.interest`	Discussion about the Internet Society.
`comp.org.issnnet`	Discussion about the International Student Society for Neural Networks.
`comp.org.sug`	Discussion about the Sun User's Group.
`comp.org.usenix`	Events and announcements about the USENIX Association.
`comp.org.usenix.roomshare`	Discussing finding lodging during USENIX conferences.

OS/2 Systems

Like the MS-DOS and Microsoft Windows USENET groups, several groups are devoted to discussion about the IBM OS/2 operating system.

News Group	Description
`comp.os.os2.advocacy`	Discussion in support of and against OS/2.
`comp.os.os2.announce`	News and announcements related to OS/2 (moderated).
`comp.os.os2.apps`	Discussion about programs that run under the OS/2 system.
`comp.os.os2.beta`	General discussion about beta (preliminary) releases of the OS/2 system software.
`comp.os.os2.bugs`	Reports of problems with OS/2 systems and fixes and workarounds for these problems.

(continues)

News Group	Description
comp.os.os2.misc	General discussion about the OS/2 operating system.
comp.os.os2.multimedia	Discussion about multimedia applications on OS/2 systems.
comp.os.os2.networking	Computer networking in the OS/2 system.
comp.os.os2.programmer.misc	General discussion about programming systems running OS/2.
comp.os.os2.programmer.	Specific discussion about porting porting (translating) software to OS/2 systems.
comp.os.os2.setup	Installing and configuring OS/2 systems.
comp.os.os2.ver1x	Discussion about versions of OS/2 from version 1.0 through 1.3.
comp.binaries.os2	Posting of executable programs that run under the OS/2 operating system.

Patents

One USENET group is devoted to discussing patents of computer technology: comp.patents. This USENET group is moderated.

Physics

The science of physics is discussed in several USENET groups:

News Group	Description
sci.physics	General discussion about physical laws, properties, etc.
sci.physics.accelerators	Discussions about particle accelerators and the physics of beams.
sci.physics.fusion	Information and discussion about fusion, especially "cold" fusion.
sci.physics.research	Information and discussion about current physics research (moderated).

Psychology

The science of psychology is discussed in two USENET groups. The first, `sci.psychology`, is devoted to general discussions about psychology and related topics. The second group, `sci.psychology.digest`, posts articles from PSYCOLOQUY, a refereed journal and newsletter about psychology. The second group is moderated.

Risks of Computer Use

One USENET group, `comp.risks`, is devoted to discussing the risks to the public from computers and their use. This USENET group is moderated, and articles are presented in digest form, where several individual articles are joined together into one larger article.

Security (Computer System)

Four USENET groups discuss computer security related issues. These groups often have announcements about possible security problems with particular computer systems, and the availability of fixes for these problems.

News Group	Description
`comp.security.announce`	Announcements from the Computer Emergency Response Team (CERT) about computer system security (moderated).
`comp.security.misc`	General discussion about security in computer systems and networks.
`comp.security.unix`	Specific discussion about security in computers running the UNIX operating system.
`comp.virus`	Discussion about computer viruses and virus detection software (moderated).

Silicon Graphics Systems

Computer systems from Silicon Graphics are very popular with researchers and business people who use graphics applications. Several USENET groups are devoted to various aspects of Silicon Graphics computer systems.

News Group	Description
comp.sys.sgi.admin	Discussion about systems administration for Silicon Graphic's Iris systems.
comp.sys.sgi.announce	Announcements for the SGI community (moderated).
comp.sys.sgi.apps	Discussion about software applications that run on SGI systems.
comp.sys.sgi.bugs	Reports of problems that have been found on SGI systems, and fixes or workarounds for them.
comp.sys.sgi.graphics	Discussion about graphics packages and techniques for SGI systems.
comp.sys.sgi.hardware	Discussion about SGI hardware and peripherals.
comp.sys.sgi.misc	General discussion about SGI systems not covered in other USENET groups.

Software Engineering

One USENET group is devoted to discussing technical aspects of software engineering and related topics: comp.software-eng.

Space

Several USENET groups discuss topics related to space and space flight.

News Group	Description
sci.space	General discussions about space, space programs, and space-related research.
sci.space.news	Announcements of news items related to the space program (moderated).

News Group	Description
sci.space.policy	Discussion about space policy.
sci.space.science	Discussion about space and planetary science and related technical work (moderated).
sci.space.shuttle	Discussion specific to the U.S. space shuttle program and missions.
sci.space.tech	Discussion of technical and general issues related to space flight (moderated).

Statistics

The science of statistics is discussed in several USENET groups that offer both general and specific information.

News Group	Description
sci.stat.consult	Discussions related to statistical consulting.
sci.stat.edu	Topics related to statistics education.
sci.stat.math	Discussion of statistics from a strictly mathematical viewpoint.

Sun Computer Systems

Computers manufactured by Sun Microsystems Inc. are popular with Internet users. Several USENET groups provide support and information for users of these systems.

News Group	Description
comp.sys.sun.admin	Information for and by administrators of Sun computer systems.
comp.sys.sun.announce	Announcements of interest to users of Sun computer systems.
comp.sys.sun.apps	Discussion of software applications that run on Sun computer systems.

(continues)

News Group	Description
comp.sys.sun.hardware	Information and discussion about Sun system hardware and peripherals.
comp.sys.sun.misc	General discussion about Sun computer systems not covered in other USENET groups.
comp.sys.sun.wanted	Postings by people looking for Sun products and support.

UNIX

UNIX is probably the most popular operating system in use on the Internet today, and the number of USENET groups that provide support for people running UNIX reflects this. There is a USENET group that discusses almost every aspect of UNIX.

News Group	Description
comp.unix.admin	Discussion about administering a system running UNIX.
comp.unix.advocacy	Arguments against and in favor of the UNIX operating system.
comp.unix.aix	Discussions about IBM's version of UNIX, AIX.
comp.unix.amiga	Discussions about Minix, SYSVR4, and other UNIX variants that run on an Amiga system.
comp.unix.aux	Discussions about Apple's UNIX that runs on Macintosh II computers.
comp.unix.bsd	Discussions about the Berkeley Software Distribution of UNIX.
comp.unix.cray	Discussions about Cray computers that run UNIX.
comp.unix.dos-under-unix	Discussions about MS-DOS running under a UNIX system, by whatever means.
comp.unix.internals	Specific discussions about UNIX internals.

10

News Group	Description
comp.unix.large	Discussions about UNIX on mainframe systems and in large networks.
comp.unix.misc	General discussion about UNIX not covered in other USENET groups.
comp.unix.osf.misc	General discussion about the Open Software Foundation UNIX products.
comp.unix.osf.osf1	Discussion specific to the Open Software Foundation's OSF/1 product.
comp.unix.pc-clone.16bit	Discussions about UNIX running on Intel i268 architecture based systems.
comp.unix.pc-clone.32bit	Discussions about UNIX running on Intel i386 and i486 architecture based systems.
comp.unix.programmer	Help for people programming under UNIX.
comp.unix.questions	Help for beginners to the UNIX operating system.
comp.unix.shell	Discussions about using and programming the UNIX shells command processors.
comp.unix.solaris	Discussions about the Solaris operating system.
comp.unix.sys3	UNIX system III discussions.
comp.unix.sys5.misc	General discussion about UNIX system V releases that predate release 3.
comp.unix.sys5.r3	Discussions about UNIX system V release 3.
comp.unix.sys5.r4	Discussions about UNIX system V release 4.
comp.unix.ultrix	Discussions about the ULTRIX system from Digital Equipment Corporation.
comp.unix.unixware	Discussions about Novell's UnixWare products.
comp.unix.user-friendly	Discussions about how user-friendly UNIX is and how to improve it.

(continues)

News Group	Description
comp.unix.wizards	Questions and discussions for experts on the UNIX operating system (moderated).
comp.unix.xenix.misc	General discussion about the XENIX version of UNIX.
comp.unix.xenix.sco	Discussions specific to the XENIX version of UNIX from the Santa Cruz Operation.

Chapter 11

Mailing Lists

One way to have friendly discussions on a topic is to subscribe to a mailing list that discusses the topic you are interested in. Unlike USENET news groups, mailing lists have limited distributions (only to the people who request a subscription), and the tone of conversations is often more serious and cooperative than you find in a news group. Mailing lists are maintained by individuals who volunteer their time and resources to coordinate the lists. The number and topics of mailing lists change constantly as people start and end discussions.

This chapter contains a sampling of the mailing lists that exist on the Internet. The information in this chapter was taken from two large lists available on the Internet: the Publicly Accessible Mailing List maintained by Stephanie da Silva (`arielle@taronga.com`) and Chuq Von Rospach (`chuq@apple.com`), and the Special Interest Groups list available via anonymous ftp on `ftp.nisc.sri.com` in `netinfo/interest-groups`.

The mailing lists described in this chapter are geared toward academic and business interests, and are listed by general topic. Many other mailing lists are described in the two lists that were used as reference material for this chapter. There are other mailing lists for people who are interested in—for example—horses, scuba diving, and Firebirds and Camaros. If you have an interest that isn't covered by the mailing lists in this chapter, you need to search the lists mentioned earlier. More information about getting copies of these lists is given in the next two sections.

Note: *Remember, if you are accessing the Internet from an e-mail only service or from a service that charges you for data transferred or stored, getting copies of the lists can be an expensive proposition (the Special Interest Groups list used while creating this chapter was more than 700 printed pages long). Books that* *contain these lists are available, but they are always somewhat out-of-date because the lists change frequently.*

The Publicly Accessible Mailing List

One major list that was used to create this chapter is the Publicly Accessible Mailing List. The on-line version of this list is periodically posted to the USENET news groups `news.lists`, `news.announce.newusers`, and `news.answers`. It's also available by way of anonymous ftp to `rtfm.mit.edu` in the directory `/pub/usenet/news.announce.newusers` in files starting with the name `Publicly_Accessible_Mailing_Lists`.

The Special Interest Groups List

The Special Interest Groups list describes the special interest mailing lists available on the Internet. You can access this file via anonymous ftp on `ftp.nisc.sri.com` in `netinfo/interest-groups`. A compressed version available in `netinfo/interest-groups.Z` can also be obtained through e-mail by sending a message to `mail-server@nisc.sri.com`, with `send netinfo/interest-groups` in the body of the message.

This list usually is updated on a quarterly basis. An electronic mail server is available to copy the list to those who don't have direct ftp access to the Internet. Send a message to `mail-server@nisc.sri.com` with a line `send netinfo/interest-groups` in the message body. For more information, use the line `send HELP` (the uppercase HELP is important).

Subscribing to a Mailing List

To subscribe to some of the lists, you need only to contact the list maintainer to be added to the distribution, and then send mail to *listname@address* to make submissions to the list. (In the listings, words in *italic* indicate a placeholder, which you need to replace with the proper name for your situation.)

For other lists—mainly, those that use the LISTSERV software—you send messages to the software, which automatically does whatever your message requested (subscribes you, unsubscribes you, submits your message to the list, etc.). Instructions for subscribing to these lists are given as part of the list description.

Note: *Generally, for administrative matters related to a list (such as getting added or deleted, or asking about archive files), you should write to* `list-request@host` *(for example,* `gateway2000-request@sei.cmu.edu`*). This way, you get the coordinator rather than the membership of the entire mailing list. For each list you are interested in, look at the entry to see whether a* `-request` *address is provided (you also can just try to send to the* `-request` *address, since the information may have been left out of the description).*

If the directions given in the description don't work for you, try sending mail to the list coordinator/owner and explain that you want to join the list, but are having problems. Some maintainers will automatically send you information about the list (how to post messages, etc.) when you request a subscription.

Note: *The mailing lists in this chapter were taken from lists that were current at the time this book was printed. Send mail to the list coordinator to see whether the list still exists.*

Mailing List Descriptions

The following mailing lists are in alphabetical order according to subject matter. The entries are in one of two different formats, depending on from which list they were taken .

The format for entries from the Publicly Accessible List Mailing List is

list name
Contact: `contact e-mail address` (contact real name)

Purpose: Description of mailing list focus.

The format for entries from the Special Interest Groups list is

List Name
List address: `subscription address`

Description: The purpose of the list. The description may provide the location and availability of any archives and usually explains how to subscribe to the mailing list.

Coordinator/Owner: The person who maintains the list.

Many of the addresses are shown all uppercase, or with initial caps. In all probability, all lowercase entries will work, but you may want to type the capitalization exactly as given (this is how the entries appeared in the on-line list).

Note: *Some entries in this chapter have been edited for clarity and content.*

Agricultural/Earth Sciences

AG-EXP-L

List address: AG-EXP-L%NDSUVM1.BITNET@CUNYVM.CUNY.EDU

Purpose: Discusses the use of expert systems in agricultural production and management. Primary emphasis is for practitioners, Extension personnel, and Experiment Station researchers in the land grant system.

To subscribe to this list, send the LISTSERV command SUB AG-EXP-L *Jon Doe* (with your name substituted for *Jon Doe*) as the first text line of a message to LISTSERV%NDSUVM1.BITNET@CUNYVM.CUNY.EDU. To be removed from the list, send the command SIGNOFF AG-EXP-L. For example: SUB AG-EXP-L Jon Doe would be the only line in the body (text) of mail sent to subscribe Jon Doe to the list.

Monthly public logs of mail to AG-EXP-L are kept on LISTSERV for a few months. For a list of files, send the Index AG-EXP-L command to LISTSERV%NDSUVM1.BITNET@CUNYVM.CUNY.EDU.

Coordinator: Sandy Sprafka (NU020746%NDSUVM1.BITNET@CUNYVM.CUNY.EDU)

Agmodels-l

Contact: jp@unl.edu (Jerome Pier)

Purpose: A forum for the discussion of agricultural simulation models of all types. Plant growth, micro-meteorological, soil hydrology, transport, economic, farm systems, and many other models may be discussed. Problems and advantages of computer simulation models for agriculture as well as the role played by models in the future of agriculture. The list is unmoderated.

To subscribe, send e-mail to listserv@unl.edu with the one-line message sub agmodels-l *your name*.

ethology

Contact: `saarikko@cc.helsinki.fi` (Jarmo Saarikko)

Purpose: An unmoderated mailing list for the discussion of animal behavior and behavioral ecology. Possible topics could be new or controversial theories, new research methods, and equipment. Announcements of books, papers, conferences, new software for behavioral analysis, etc., with possible experiences, are also encouraged.

Forest Management DSS

Contact: `listserv@pnfi.forestry.ca` (Tom Moore)

Purpose: This discussion group is a forum for rapid exchange of information, ideas, and opinions related to the topics of decision support systems and information systems for forest management planning. Also welcome are announcements of meetings, calls for papers, calls for proposals, help wanted, employment wanted, resumes, book reviews, and copies of papers or speeches.

Although this is being sponsored as part of a Canadian research program, participation from the international community is welcome. Please pass this information on to your colleagues.

To subscribe, send e-mail to `listserv@pnfi.forestry.ca` with the message `SUBSCRIBE FMDSS-L` *FirstName LastName*.

Park Rangers

Contact: `60157903@wsuvm1.csc.wsu.edu` (Cynthia Dorminey)

Purpose: This list is primarily for anyone working or interested in working as a ranger (general, interpretive, etc.) for the National Park Service (U.S.A.), but rangers from state and county agencies as well as other countries are also welcome. The group discusses numerous topics related to this profession.

SEISM-L

List address: `SEISM-L%BINGVMA.BITNET@MITVMA.MIT.EDU`

Description: Seismological topics of general interest.

To subscribe, send the following command to `LISTSERV%BINGVMB.BITNET@MITVMA.MIT.EDU: SUBSCRIBE SEISM-L` *your_full_name*. To unsubscribe, send `UNSUBSCRIBE SEISM-L`.

Coordinator: Jim Blake (`AS0JEB%BINGVMA.BITNET@MITVMA.MIT.EDU`)

Soils-l
Contact: `jp@unl.edu` (Jerome Pier)

Purpose: A forum for the discussion of all subjects dealing with soil science. Soil physics, chemistry, genesis, classification, mineralogy, fertility, conservation, etc. may be discussed within this unmoderated group. The formation of this group has been sanctioned by The American Society of Agronomy and the Soil Science Society of America.

Subscription: Send e-mail to `listserv@unl.edu` containing the one-line message sub `soils-l` *your name*.

wildnet
Contact: `wildnet-request@access.usask.ca` (Eric Woodsworth)

Purpose: This list is concerned with computing and statistics in fisheries and wildlife biology. Relevant topics include G.I.S., ecological modeling, software, etc.

WXSPOT
List address: `WXSPOT%UIUCVMD.BITNET@VM1.NODAK.EDU`

Description: Mailing list for discussions about severe storm spotter training, spotter networks, training materials, upcoming training, methods of transmitting weather data, and local community programs. The list will be used for discussions only and will not carry current weather data. It's hoped that through these discussions, better community severe storm spotter training and public awareness programs can be developed.

To join the list, send the command SUB `WXSPOT` *your_full_name* (where *your_full_name* is your real name, not your login ID) as the only line in the body of a message to `LISTSERV%UIUCVMD.BITNET@VM1.NODAK.EDU` (for example: SUB `WXSPOT` John Q. Publicas).

Coordinator: Chris Novy (`AXVSCCN%UICVMC.BITNET@VM1.NODAK.EDU`)

Business and Management Topics
BDGTPLAN
List address: `BDGTPLAN%UVMVM.BITNET@VM1.NODAK.EDU`

Description: Discussion of college and university budget and planning issues including—but not limited to—economic and enrollment forecasting, relationships with state governments, innovative approaches to integrating planning and budgeting, strategies for increasing participation, cost center analysis, use of financial databases for modeling and reporting, endowment spending policies, tuition pricing, resource reallocation, financial reporting to boards and legislators, etc.

To join the list, send the command SUBSCRIBE BDGTPLAN *your full name* (where *your full name* is your real name, not your login ID) as the only line in the body of a message to LISTSERV%UVMVM.BITNET@VM1.NODAK.EDU.

Coordinator: Dayna Flath (DMF%UVMVM.BITNET@VM1.NODAK.EDU)

econ-dev

Contact: majordomo@csn.org

Purpose: To share information and to network with professionals who are in economic development or are pursuing some of the same informational goals.

We here at the economic development department in Littleton, Colorado, use information as the cornerstone of our program. Littleton's New Economy Project works primarily with small, innovative companies trying to give them the sophisticated tools they need to compete in the new global environment. Rather than "hunt" for faraway companies and offer incentives to try to get them to locate in Littleton, we concentrate on adding value to existing local companies, or "garden." Services include using commercial databases to provide a variety of strategic information.

We are also actively interested in systems thinking, chaos, and complexity as they apply to economics. We look forward to hearing from those of you out there who use information, and who are involved with businesses. To subscribe, send the following to majordomo@csn.org:

```
subscribe econ-dev
```

This should be sent in the body of the message. The subject is ignored.

International Trade and Commerce

Contact: info-request@tradent.wimsey.bc.ca

Purpose: Discussions of international trade, commerce, and the global economy, including postings of company profiles, trade leads, and topics pertaining to entrepreneurial ventures.

MARKET-L
List address: `MARKET-L@UCF1VM.CC.UCF.EDU`

Description: Mailing list open to any marketing academics or practitioners of marketing who want to discuss marketing-related topics.

Log files will be kept on a monthly basis.

To subscribe, send the command `SUB MARKET-L` `Your_full_name` (where `Your_full_name` is your real name, not your user ID) as the body of a message to `LISTSERV@UCF1VM.CC.UCF.EDU`; for example, `SUB MARKET-L John Doe.`

Coordinator: UCF Postmaster (`POSTMAST@UCF1VM.CC.UCF.EDU`)

project-management
Contact: `project-management-request@smtl.demon.co.uk`

Purpose: This list aims to discuss project management techniques generally, not just project management software and programs.

You can join the list by sending e-mail to

`project-management-request@smtl.demon.co.uk`

with the subject line of `subscribe`.

QUALITY
List address: `LISTSERV@PUCC.PRINCETON.EDU`

Description: `QUALITY@PUCC.PRINCETON.EDU` is the electronic communications network for discussing Total Quality Management (TQM) in the manufacturing and service industries. TQM refers to an organization-wide effort to achieve quality. It can be described as a philosophy that is intended to involve everyone in the organization in a quest for quality, with customer satisfaction as the driving force.

The topics for discussion on QUALITY are grouped into three areas:

- Quality Systems: quality control, quality assurance, statistical process control, employee involvement, JIT, and others.

- Quality Standards: ISO 9000 (European and international), Baldrige (U.S.), Deming (Japanese), and JIS (Japanese).

■ Case Studies and Research Papers

Present activities of QUALITY:

■ When a user subscribes to QUALITY, he/she may send mail to the list for distribution to all its members. All members of the mailing list will receive a copy of each piece of mail sent to the list. All mail that is received and redistributed by the list is cataloged and stored in a log file (for example, QUALITY LOG9303) that can be searched or retrieved by individuals with access to QUALITY.

To prevent "rapid-fire" random e-mail transmissions, all messages are relayed to the QUALITY editor for a once- or twice-weekly batch mail release in digest form. Also, each subscriber may disable the automatic QUALITY e-mail transmission to his/her site and download log files of each month's e-mail traffic.

■ QUALITY Filelist Datafiles are available for downloading. The objective is to develop a clearinghouse of information on TQM.

Potential/future activities include an electronic business newsletter, electronic user directories, bibliographies of current business research, and a job bank.

To receive the current listing of files, send the following to `LISTSERV@PUCC.PRINCETON.EDU` (not to QUALITY), with the command `GET QUALITY FILELIST`:

■ File downloads (`GET` *filename filetype*). For example, `GET QUALITY INTRO`.

■ File subscriptions. Specialized information or information that's too large for normal e-mail is placed in QUALITY data files for downloading by subscribers. A more complete description of the files are contained in the file QUALITY INDEX.

You may subscribe to a data file (such as QUALITY INDEX) in one of two ways:

1. Automatic downloading of the entire file to your address with each update.

2. Automatic notification that the file has been updated. You may terminate this file subscription on demand.

Send the following to `LISTSERV@PUCC.PRINCETON.EDU` (not to QUALITY):

- To download one file, one time, without subscribing: `GET filename filetype` (for example, `GET QUALITY INDEX`)

- To receive automatic file downloads (AFD=automatic file distribution) on file updates: `AFD ADD filename filetype` (for example, `AFD ADD QUALITY INDEX`)

- To cancel automatic file downloads: `AFD DEL filename filetype`

- To receive automatic file update information (FUI): `FUI ADD filename filetype`

- To cancel automatic file update information: `FUI DEL filename filetype`

- To receive a list of files to which you are subscribed: `AFD LIST` or `FUI LIST`

To subscribe to QUALITY, send e-mail to `LISTSERV@PUCC.PRINCETON.EDU` (not to QUALITY) with the body containing the appropriate command:

- To add yourself, `SUB QUALITY yourfirstname yourlastname`

- To remove yourself, `SIGNOFF QUALITY`

Direct any questions to the list editor:

> James W. Reese, QUALITY Editor
> Associate Professor of Economics
> University of South Carolina, Spartanburg
> 800 University Way
> Spartanburg, SC 29303
> *Voice:* 803-472-4527
> *Fax:* 803-472-3754
> or `R505040@UNIVSCVM.CSD.SCAROLINA.EDU`

Role Modeling

Contact: `majordomo@taskon.no`

Purpose: The Role Modeling mailing list is concerned with the use of roles as a concept in object-oriented systems design. Topics include:

- Role modeling in OO software development

- Role models in business process modeling

- Methodologies based on role modeling, such as:

    The OOram methodology, an object-oriented software development method that uses role modeling.

    Using state machines to describe and/or specify certain aspects of an object's behavior.

    Related subjects

The list is managed by `cepe@taskon.no`.

To subscribe to the list, send mail to `majordomo@taskon.no`. The body of the message should contain the line

```
subscribe role-modeling
```

If you need to get in touch with a human, send mail to `role-modeling-owner@taskon.no`.

Computers

386users
Contact: `386users-request@udel.edu` (William Davidsen Jr.)

Purpose: Topics are 80386-based computers, and all hardware and software that is either 386-specific or has special interest on the 386.

Amiga CDROM
Contact: `cdrom-list-request@ben.com`

Purpose: For Amigans who use or are interested in CD-ROM drives and discs. Questions or comments about the list can be sent to me (`ben@ben.com`). Questions about CD-ROMs (installation, troubleshooting, etc.) should be sent to the list and not me directly. I am archiving all posts to the list.

Commodore-Amiga
Contact: `subscribe@xamiga.linet.org`

Purpose: For Commodore Amiga computer users. Weekly postings of hardware reviews, news briefs, system information, company progress, and information for finding out more about the Commodore and Amiga.

Send subscription requests to `subscribe@xamiga.linet.org`, using this format:

```
#commodore youraccount@youraddress;
```

CSAA

Contact: `announce-request@cs.ucdavis.edu` (Carlos Amezaga)

Purpose: The Comp.Sys.Amiga.Announce mailing list has been created for those folks who have no access to USENET. I provide the gate between the USENET news group C.S.A.A. and mail.

This group distributes announcements of importance to people using the Commodore brand Amiga computers. Announcements may contain any important information, but most likely will deal with new products, disk library releases, software updates, reports of major bugs or dangerous viruses, notices of meetings or upcoming events, and so forth. A large proportion of posts announce the upload of software packages to anonymous ftp archive sites. To subscribe, unsubscribe, or to send comments on this mailing list, send mail to `announce-request@cs.ucdavis.edu`, and your request will be taken care of.

ctf-discuss

Contact: `ctf-discuss-request@cis.upenn.edu` (Dave Farber)

Purpose: This mailing list is targeted at stimulating discussion of issues critical to the computer science community in the United States (and, by extension, the world). The Computer Science and Telecommunications Board (CSTB) of the National Research Council (NRC) is charged with identifying and initiating studies in areas critical to the health of the field. Recently one such study—"Computing the Future"—has generated a major discussion in the community and has motivated the establishment of this mailing list to involve broader participation. This list will be used in the future to report and discuss the activities of the CSTB and to solicit opinions in a variety of areas.

DECnews-PR

Contact: `decnews-pr-request@pa.dec.com` (Russ Jones)

Purpose: DECnews for Press and Analysts is an Internet-based distribution of all Digital press releases. It is provided as a courtesy to analysts, members of the press, and the consulting community. This is a one-way mailing list, with approximately 8 press releases per week.

To subscribe, send mail to `decnews-pr@pa.dec.com` with a subject line of `subscribe`. Please include your name and telephone number in the body of the subscription request.

dg-users
Contact: `dg-users-request@ilinx.wimsey.com`

Purpose: The mailing list is concerned with the technical details of Data General, its O/Ss, and the various cornucopia of hardware it supplies and supports.

The administrator's e-mail address is `brian@ilinx.wimsey.com`.

ECTL
Contact: `ectl-request@snowhite.cis.uoguelph.ca` (David Leip)

Purpose: A list dedicated to researchers interested in computer speech interfaces.

Emplant
Contact: `subscribe@xamiga.linet.org`

Purpose: For the Emplant Macintosh Hardware Emulator. Emplant is a hardware board that allows Amiga users to run any Macintosh programs, in color. The mailing list will provide any info on compatibility and software upgrades.

Send subscription requests to `subscribe@xamiga.linet.org`, using this format:

```
#emplant username@domain;
```

es
Contact: `es-request@hawkwind.utcs.toronto.edu` (Chris Siebenmann)

Purpose: Discussion of the es shell. Es is simple yet highly programmable. By exposing many of the internals and adopting constructs from functional programming languages, Paul Haahr and Byron Rakitzis have created a shell that supports new paradigms for programmers. The es shell and the mailing list archives are available on `ftp.sys.utoronto.ca`, directory `/pub/es`.

Futurebus+ Users

Contact: `majordomo@theus.rain.com`

Purpose: A discussion group for users of Futurebus+. Topics include the design, implementation, integration, and operation of the hardware and software that are related to Futurebus+.

To subscribe, mail to `majordomo@theus.rain.com` with `subscribe fbus_users` *youraccount@youraddress* in the body of the text.

Gateway 2000

Contact: `gateway2000-request@sei.cmu.edu` (Tod Pike)

Purpose: A good source of information about Gateway 2000 products. The Gateway 2000 Mailing List is *not* owned by Gateway 2000, Inc. of North Sioux City, SD. It (along with the news group `alt.sys.pc-clone.gateway2000`) is run for and by Gateway 2000 *users*.

Imagen-L

Contact: `listserv@bolis.sf-bay.org`

Purpose: This list is a discussion forum for all aspects of Imagen laser printers. Any discussion pertaining to Imagen printers is welcome, including software compatibility, hardware interfacing, LAN attachment capabilities, imPRESS programming, or methods used to create spooling and accounting software.

To subscribe, send an e-mail message to `listserv@bolis.sf-bay.org` containing the line `subscribe Imagen-L`, and you will be added to the list.

INFO-CONVEX

List address: `INFO-CONVEX@PEMRAC.SPACE.SWRI.EDU`

Description: Mailing list for sharing ideas, questions, bug fixes, and so forth concerning any aspect of the hardware and software products produced by Convex Corp. Initially, this group will not be moderated.

All requests to be added to or deleted from this list, problems, questions, etc., should be sent to `info-convex-request@PEMRAC.SPACE.SWRI.EDU`.

Coordinator: `karen@pemrac.space.swri.edu` (Karen Birkelbach)

info-encore

Contact: `info-encore-request@cs-gw.D.UMN.EDU` (Dan Burrows)

Purpose: Mailing list for discussion of issues involving hardware and software issues of Encore computers and EtherNet terminal servers.

This mailing list is also gatewayed into the inet list `comp.sys.encore`.

info-fortune

Contact: `info-fortune-request@csd4.csd.uwm.edu` (Thomas Krueger)

Purpose: This mailing list is for users of UNIX-based microcomputers produced by Fortune Systems. Any subject pertaining to Fortune computers is allowed.

INFO-MAC

List address: `INFO-MAC@SUMEX-AIM.STANFORD.EDU`

Description: Network interest group for the Apple Macintosh computer. This list is SUMEX's contribution to the community of research and instructional developers and users of the Macintosh; all submissions of messages and programs in this spirit are welcome.

For those sites with ftp access to SUMEX-AIM, archives for INFO-MAC are kept under `{SUMEX-AIM}/info-mac/digest/infomacv`M`-`NNN, where M is the volume number and NNN is the digest number. (These numbers have little to no bearing on reality.)

Programs submitted to the bulletin board, along with documentation files and other references, are stored in the `info-mac` directory. With ftp access as user "anonymous" and any password, you can bring these files over to your host and download them to your Macintosh. USENET and some other networks that copy `info-mac` will see sources redistributed at the time they are mentioned in the digest distributions.

11

Messages to `INFO-MAC@SUMEX-AIM.STANFORD.EDU` are scanned to filter out any list requests, questions previously answered, pure speculation or opinion, or messages obviously not in line with the stated purpose of the list.

All requests to be added to or deleted from this list, problems, questions, etc., should be sent to `INFO-MAC-REQUEST@SUMEX-AIM.STANFORD.EDU`. Due to the size of this list, INFO-MAC sends only to relays—that is, addresses such as `INFOMAC@yoursite.whatever`, which then distributes it locally. Please check with your local gurus to gain access to your local relay.

Moderators: Bill Lipa (`Info-Mac-Request@SUMEX-AIM.STANFORD.EDU`) and Jon Pugh (`Info-Mac-Request@SUMEX-AIM.STANFORD.EDU`)

Info-PGP
Contact: `info-pgp-request@lucpul.it.luc.edu`

Purpose: Discussion of Phil Zimmerman & Co.'s Pretty Good Privacy (PGP) public key encryption program for MS-DOS, UNIX, SPARC, VMS, Atari, Amiga, and other platforms. Mirror of `alt.security.pgp` and related articles on `sci.crypt`.

info-prime
Contact: `info-prime-request@blx-a.prime.com`

Purpose: INFO-PRIME is the discussion group/mailing list for users and administrators of Prime Computer equipment: 50-series (PRIMOS) and EXL series (UNIX). This mailing list is gatewayed to the USENET news group `comp.sys.prime`.

info-solbourne
Contact: `info-solbourne-request@acsu.buffalo.edu` (Paul Graham)

Purpose: Discussions and info about Solbourne computers.

info-stratus
Contact: `Info-Stratus-Request@mike.lrc.edu` (Richard Shuford)

Purpose: This electronic mailing list is a user-centered and user-conducted forum for discussing the fault-tolerant machines produced by Stratus Computer Corporation and their cousins, the IBM System/88 and Olivetti CPS-32.

Info-Stratus is not intended to replace the vendor-provided support channels but to complement them. Subscribers to Info-Stratus will exchange technical information and tap the collective experience of a host of other professionals who use or develop software on Stratus-architecture systems, or who configure and maintain hardware in the Stratus environment.

INFO-VAX

List address: INFO-VAX@SRI.COM

Description: INFO-VAX is a discussion of the Digital Equipment Corporation VAX series of computers. Typically, the material is question-and-answer, where someone wants information on some program, bug, or feature. Both UNIX and VAX/VMS operating systems are discussed; however, the list is primarily about VAX/VMS. This list is gatewayed to the USENET group COMP.OS.VMS.

Archived messages are kept at CRVAX.SRI.COM in the files [ANONYMOUS.INFO-VAX]INFO-VAX-ARCHIVE.*yymmdd*. For a list of the archive files, send a mail message to INFO-VAX-REQUEST@SRI.COM with the subject DIRECTORY.

All requests to be added to or deleted from this list, problems, questions, etc., should be sent to INFO-VAX-REQUEST@SRI.COM. Internet subscribers can join by sending a mail message with a subject of ADD. To be removed from the list, the subject should be REMOVE.

Coordinator: Ramon Curiel (Ray@SRI.COM)

info-tahoe

Contact: info-tahoe-request@uwm.edu (Jim Lowe)

Purpose: Discussions pertaining to the Tahoe type of CPU. These include the CCI Power 6/32, the Harris HCX/7, and the Sperry 7000 series computers.

The info-tahoe mailing list is set up as a mail reflector. This mailing list is also gatewayed into the inet list comp.sys.tahoe.

info-tandem

Contact: info-tandem-request@zorch.sf-bay.org

Purpose: Discussion of systems from Tandem Computers Inc. Includes both open and proprietary lines.

Linux-Activists

Contact: `linux-activists-request@niksula.hut.fi` (Ari Lemmke)

Purpose: LINUX operating system hacking. LINUX is now on a hackers-only stage. More information is available by ftp from `nic.funet.fi` in the file `/pub/OS/Linux/README`.

MachTen

Contact: `MachTen-request@tenon.com` (Leonard Cuff)

Purpose: Discuss topics of interest to users of MachTen, a Mach/BSD UNIX for all Macintoshes from Tenon Intersystems. This list includes programming tips and examples, configuration questions, and discussion of problems and workarounds. People not currently using MachTen and wanting either general information or specific questions answered should not subscribe, but write to `info@tenon.com`.

MACPROG

List address: `MACPROG@WUVMD.WUSTL.EDU`

Description: Hosted by Washington University, the MACPROG list is the Internet answer to the excellent USENET programming forum. Hopefully, the easier access of an Internet-based list will promote even better communication between Macintosh developers of commercial, in-house, and shareware software. This list also will move some of the more technical topics out from lists devoted to user-oriented issues.

I will be moderating the list remotely from Wayne State University. I'm not a Mac programming expert per se, but I am one of those sadistic individuals who—convinced life alone wasn't handing me enough problems—decided to take up Mac programming for the sheer fun of it. Luckily, I found a job where they'd pay me to have fun. (Actually, I'm a systems analyst, but they give me in-house programming time for good behavior.)

The list will be moderated in a digest format (Info-mac style). I'll collect submissions into one digest and crank one out every day or two as traffic dictates. If the initial membership is any indication, this list should have heavy traffic: 30 people have subscribed already, with 40 more inquiries, without even having officially announced the list.

The focus of MacProg will be to discuss mainstream language coding techniques. What's a mainstream language? C and Pascal principally, although other languages such as Lisp, Prologue, FORTRAN, BASIC, HyperTalk, and application scripting are certainly welcome. Besides Q & A, I'd like to have other features running. For example, I'd like participants to report errors in documentation from Apple or other sources. There have been times when I've felt like terminating execution of my program with a 16-pound, chrome-plated sledgehammer simply because of an error I was getting, caused by errant specifications from Apple. Also, I'd like participants to offer quick reviews on books they've read, seminars they've attended, or interactive courses they've used that have been particularly good or bad. Since no one can ever know everything about Mac programming, and since system compatibility is a constantly moving target, sources of programming information are important for beginners and experts alike.

So if you think you'd like to use this informative service for Macintosh developers, send mail to `LISTSERV@WUVMD.WUSTL.EDU` with the following command in the BODY of the mail: `SUBSCRIBE MACPROG` *your name*.

Special thanks to Eric Oberle of Washington University for setting this all up on his mainframe. But what do you mean when you say, "I have to pay the electric bill?"

Owner and Moderator: Bill Brandt (`WBRANDT@WAYNEST1.BITNET`)

Note: *This is not a valid Internet address if your site doesn't understand BITNET addressing.*

Multicast
Contact: `Multicast-Request@Arizona.EDU` (Joel Snyder)

Purpose: For discussion of multicast and broadcast issues in an OSI environment. Archives of the list and a database of contributed documents are also available on `Arizona.EDU`.

Ncube
Contact: `ncube-users-request@cs.tufts.edu` (David Krumme)

Purpose: Exchange of information among people using NCUBE parallel computers.

netblazer-users
Contact: `netblazer-users-request@telebit.com`

Purpose: To provide an unmoderated forum for discussions among users of Telebit NetBlazer products. Topics include known problems and workarounds, features discussions, and configuration advice.

neuron

Contact: `neuron-request@cattell.psych.upenn.edu` (Peter Marvit)

Purpose: Neuron-Digest is a moderated list (in digest form) dealing with all aspects of neural networks (and any type of network or neuromorphic system). Topics include connectionist models (artificial neural networks) and biological systems ("wetware"). Back issues and limited software is available via ftp from `cattell.psych.upenn.edu`. The digest is gatewayed to USENET's `comp.ai.neural-nets`.

NeXT-L

List address: `NeXT-L@ANTIGONE.COM`

Description: Mailing list for discussion of the NeXT Computer.

To subscribe, send a message to `LISTSERV@ANTIGONE.COM` with the text `SUBSCRIBE NEXT-L` *Your Full Name.*

List owner: Michael Ross (`NEXT-L-REQUEST@ANTIGONE.COM`)

ntp

Contact: `ntp-request@trantor.umd.edu`

Purpose: Discussion of the Network Time Protocol.

numeric-interest

Contact: `numeric-interest-request@validgh.com` (David Hough)

Purpose: Discussion of issues of floating-point correctness and performance with respect to hardware, operating systems, languages, and standard libraries.

rc

Contact: `rc-request@hawkwind.utcs.toronto.edu` (Chris Siebenmann)

Purpose: Discussion of the rc shell, designed by Tom Duff to replace the venerable Bourne shell in Plan 9. It provides similar facilities to sh, with some small additions and mostly less idiosyncratic syntax. Most of the discussion on the list is about Byron Rakitzis' free reimplementation of the shell. See the rc FAQ for more details; get it from `rtfm.mit.edu` as `/pub/usenet/comp.unix.shell/rc-FAQ`.

scoann
Contact: `scoann-request@xenitec.on.ca` (Ed Hew)

Purpose: The SCO Announce mailing list is a moderated announcements list providing product update and new product announcements supplied by SCO or by developers offering SCO-based products.

Submissions for the list should be addressed to `scoannmod@xenitec.on.ca`.

The scoann mailing list is bidirectionally gatewayed with the USENET `biz.sco.announce` news group.

scogen
Contact: `scogen-request@xenitec.on.ca` (Geoff Scully)

Purpose: This group will be beneficial to anyone interested or currently using Santa Cruz Operation products. This mailing list is a single area where discussions and information can be exchanged regarding *all* SCO products.

The scogen mailing list is bidirectionally gatewayed with the USENET `biz.sco.general` news group.

scoodt
Contact: `scoodt-request@xenitec.on.ca` (Ed Hew)

Purpose: The SCO Open Desktop electronic mailing list is intended to provide a communications vehicle for interested parties to provide, request, submit, and exchange information regarding the configuration, implementation, and use of the SCO Open Desktop operating system as available from the Santa Cruz Operation.

All submissions will be posted as received with appropriate author attribution. Questions are welcome. Someone may even answer them.

The scoodt mailing list is bidirectionally gatewayed with the USENET `biz.sco.opendesktop` news group.

SOMWPS
Contact: `SOMWPS-Info@knex.via.mind.org`

Purpose: SOMWPS is a mailing list for people interested in the technical aspects of IBM's System Object Model and associated object technologies such as CORBA and the OS/2 WorkPlace Shell. It's primarily aimed at developers but may be interesting for technically advanced users as well.

IBM's System Object Model is a language neutral framework for object-oriented programming. The first implementation is part of IBM's OS/2 operating system. SOM is compliant with the Object Management Group's (OMG) Common Object Request Broker Architecture. There are also extensions to SOM for distributed object-oriented design, DSOM.

The OS/2 WorkPlace Shell is the most famous application of SOM. As such, we will be discussing its technical underpinnings as well as discussing WPS programming techniques. For the most part, if it is related to SOM, we are interested in discussing it.

To subscribe, send the following commands to `Mail-Server@knex.via.mind.org`:

```
SUBSCRIBE SOMWPS FirstName LastName
OPTION SOMWPS ALIAS your_email_address
```

Note: *The* `Subject:` *header line is ignored. The command must appear in the body of the e-mail text.*

sun-386i

Contact: `sun-386i-request@ssg.com` (Rick Emerson)

Purpose: Discussion and information about the 386i-based Sun machines.

sun-nets

Contact: `sun-nets-request@umiacs.umd.edu`

Purpose: Discussion and information on networks using Sun hardware and/or software.

sunflash (aka The Florida SunFlash)

Contact: `flash@sun.com` (John J. McLaughlin)

Purpose: To keep Sun users informed about Sun via press releases, product announcements, and technical articles. This is a one-way mailing list. Each month, 25 to 35 articles are posted. More than 110,000 Sun users subscribe. Requests to be added to the list should go to `sunflash-request@Sun.COM`. For more info, send mail to `info-sunflash@Sun.COM`.

transputer
Contact: `transputer-request@tcgould.tn.cornell.edu`

Purpose: The Transputer mailing list was created to enhance communication among those who are interested in the Transputer and Transputer-based systems.

Submissions should be of non-proprietary nature and be concerned with, but not limited to

- Algorithms

- Current development efforts (hardware and software)

- INMOS and third-party systems (Meiko, FPS, etc.)

- Interfaces

- Dedicated computational resources

- Occam and non-Occam language development

Archives of submissions are available by anonymous ftp from the host `tcgould.tn.cornell.edu` (user ID `anonymous`, password is of the form *user@host*) and through UUCP on a per-request basis.

The list is maintained as a mail reflector. Submissions therefore are sent out as they are received.

Unisys
Contact: `unisys-request@bcm.tmc.edu` (Richard H. Miller)

Purpose: Discussion of all Unisys products and equipment.

Computer Administration

alpha-osf-managers
Contact: `alpha-osf-managers-request@ornl.gov`
`majordomo@ornl.gov`

Purpose: Fast-turnaround troubleshooting tool for managers of DEC Alpha AXP systems running OSF/1.

bbones

Contact: `mail-bbones-request@yorku.ca`

Purpose: A list discussing the construction of mail backbones for organizations and campuses. Created as a follow-up to a discussion at the 1992 spring Interop hosted by Einger Stefferud.

cisco

Contact: `cisco-request@spot.colorado.edu` (David Wood)

Purpose: This list is for discussion of the network products from Cisco Systems, Inc.—primarily the AGS gateway, but also the ASM terminal multiplexor and any other relevant products. Discussions about operation, problems, features, topology, configuration, protocols, routing, loading, serving, etc., are all encouraged. Other topics include vendor relations, new product announcements, availability of fixes and new features, and discussion of new requirements and desirables.

cm5-managers

Contact: (machine) `listserv@boxer.nas.nasa.gov`
(human) `jet@nas.nasa.gov` (J. Eric Townsend)

Purpose: Discussion of administrating the Thinking Machines CM5 parallel supercomputer. To subscribe, send a message to `listserv@boxer.nas.nasa.gov` with a *body* of `subscribe cm5-managers` *your_full_name*.

decstation-managers

Contact: `decstation-managers-request@ornl.gov`
`majordomo@ornl.gov`

Purpose: Fast-turnaround troubleshooting tool for managers of RISC DECstations.

HDESK-L

List address: `HDESK-L@WVNVM.WVNET.EDU`

Description: Mailing list for the discussion of Help Desks. Staff and management of Help Desks are encouraged to exchange experiences with the startup and operation of Help Desks at their sites, as well as their experiences with problem-tracking software.

BITNET users may subscribe by sending the command SUBSCRIBE HDESK-L *Your full name* (where *Your full name* is your real name, not your login ID) in a message to LISTSERV@WVNVM.WVNET.EDU.

Coordinator: Roman J. Olynyk (U0BA9@WVNVM.WVNET.EDU)

HP Patch
Contact: hpux-patch-request@cv.ruu.nl

Purpose: This is the official announcement of the HP Patch Descriptions Mailing List. In short, the purpose of the mailing list is this:

- If somebody receives a patch from HP, he/she can post the *description* of that patch to the mailing list.

- Other members now know that a patch exists and can ask HP for "patch *xxxx*" if they think they have a problem.

- The patches themselves are *never* posted!!!!!!!!!

- This list exists only as long as HP itself doesn't supply a list of available patches.

To reach ALL MEMBERS of the list, send e-mail to

　　hpux-patch@cv.ruu.nl

This is what you might want to do if you receive a new patch :-)

To subscribe, send e-mail to hpux-patch-request@cv.ruu.nl. Please include your e-mail address in the message. Not all mailers generate proper return addresses.

INFO-UNIX
List address: INFO-UNIX@BRL.MIL

Description: INFO-UNIX is intended for question/answer discussion, where "novice" system administrators can pose questions. Also, much of the discussion of UNIX on small (micro) computers may be moved from INFO-MICRO, INFO-CPM, etc., into INFO-UNIX. Hopefully, enough people who know some answers will subscribe so that the list serves a purpose; some overlap is expected with the UNIX-WIZARDS list.

All requests to be added to or deleted from this list, problems, questions, etc., should be sent to INFO-UNIX-REQUEST@BRL.MIL.

Moderator: Mike Muuss (mike@BRL.MIL)

mtxinu-users

Contact: dunike!mtxinu-users-request

mtxinu-users-request@nike.cair.du.edu

Purpose: Discussion and bug fixes for users of the 4.3+NFS release from the Mt. Xinu folks.

PCSUPT-L

List address: PCSUPT-L%YALEVM.BITNET@CUNYVM.CUNY.EDU

Description: A users' group for the discussion of issues that address end-user support for IBM PCs and similar microcomputers. By providing a central forum for users worldwide, the group will foster the timely communication of solutions to problems with hardware, operating systems, and applications. The group is to include technical support professionals as well as those who find themselves in the role of ad hoc "PC expert." Participants in the group will determine what specific issues are discussed; topics the group is likely to address are

- Institutional procedures (for example, hard disk backups within departments, software evaluation for institutional support, etc.)

- Exchange of tips and tricks for getting the most from PCs

- Equipment quality and reliability (e.g., which hard disks are most reliable and which are least)

- Differences with new releases of DOS (new commands, changes in command syntax, etc.)

- Comparisons of clones to IBM PCs and PSs in price/performance terms

- Viruses and vaccines

To subscribe, send the command SUBSCRIBE PCSUPT-L *Your_Full_Name* (where *Your_Full_Name* is your real name, not your user ID) to LISTSERV%YALEVM.BITNET@CUNYVM.CUNY.EDU. To unsubscribe, send the command UNSUBSCRIBE PCSUPT-L.

Coordinator: Bob Boyd (RWBOYD%YALEVM.BITNET@CUNYVM.CUNY.EDU)

POP

Contact: pop-request@jhunix.hcf.jhu.edu (Andy S. Poling)

Purpose: This list was formed out of desperation for an organized source of information to discuss Post Office Protocol (POP2 and POP3—described in RFCs 918, 937, 1081, and 1082) and implementations thereof.

The driving interest was lack of easily obtained knowledge of available POP2 and POP3 servers and clients. This mailing list is meant to provide this information. Anyone—consumer or product provider—is invited to participate.

pubnet

Contact: `pubnet-request@chinacat.unicom.com` (Chip Rosenthal)

Purpose: The administration and use of public-access computer systems—primarily UNIX systems. The list membership includes a large number of people who run sites listed in the world-famous NIXPUB listing. If you have questions about setting up or running a public-access system, this is the place to be.

scribe

Contact: `scribe-hacks-request@decwrl.dec.com`

Purpose: This list is designed for persons who perform the role of Scribe database administrator at their installation. Discussion will be about Scribe features, bugs, enhancements, performance, support, and other topics of interest to Scribe DBAs. The list will *not* be moderated, but will simply consist of a mail reflector—that is, if you send a message to the list, it will be rebroadcast to everyone on the list. Discussion at the level of "How do I get a paragraph to indent 5 spaces instead of 3?" is specifically discouraged.

Solaris

List address: `LISTSERV@IndyCMS.IUPUI.Edu`

Description: Solaris is dedicated to discussing the Solaris operating system produced by SunSoft, a Sun Microsystems company. Solaris (the list) is completely independent of Solaris (the operating environment), SunSoft (the manufacturer), and Sun Microsystems (the parent corporation).

Solaris (the list) is owned and coordinated by a computing professional (Phillip Gross Corporon) and an interested layperson (John B. Harlan).

Solaris (the list) is bidirectionally gatewayed to the inet news group `comp.unix.solaris`.

To subscribe to the Solaris e-mail list, send mail to `LISTSERV@IndyCMS.IUPUI.Edu` with the following command in the BODY of the mail:

```
SUB SOLARIS yourfirstname yourlastname
```

List owners/coordinators: Phillip Gross Corporon (`phil@CSE.ND.Edu`) John B. Harlan (`JBHarlan@IndyVAX.IUPUI.Edu`)

sun-managers

Contact: `sun-managers-request@eecs.nwu.edu`

Purpose: Information of special interest to managers of sites with Sun workstations or servers.

SYS7-L

List address: `LISTSERV@UAFSYSB.UARK.EDU`

Description: SYS7-L is dedicated to the discussion of issues related to the installation, configuration, features, and product compatibilities of the Macintosh Operating System Version 7.0. Full discussion of all topics related to this subject are appropriate for the list, which will be unmoderated unless moderation becomes necessary to reduce traffic to a reasonable level. To receive a list of files, send the command INDEX LISTNAME to `LISTSERV@UAFSYSB.UARK.EDU`.

To subscribe to SYS7-L, send the following command to `LISTSERV@UAFSYSB.UARK.EDU` via mail text: SUBSCRIBE SYS7-L *Your_full_name*; for example: SUBSCRIBE SYS7-L Joe Shmoe.

Owner: David Remington (`DAVIDR@UAFSYSB.UARK.EDU`)

UNIX-WIZARDS

List address: `UNIX-WIZARDS@BRL.MIL`

Description: Distribution list for people maintaining machines running the UNIX operating system.

All requests to be added to or deleted from this list, problems, questions, etc., should be sent to `UNIX-WIZARDS-REQUEST@BRL.MIL`.

Coordinator: Mike Muuss (`mike@BRL.MIL`)

XGKS

Contact: `xgks-request@unidata.ucar.edu` (Steve Emmerson)

Purpose: A mailing list for the maintenance, enhancement, and evolution of the XGKS package, created by the University of Illinois under contract with IBM and distributed as part of X11R4. The XGKS package is a full 2C GKS implementation and allows GKS applications to operate in an X Window system environment.

xopen-testing

Contact: `xopen-testing-request@uel.co.uk` (Andrew Josey)

Purpose: This list provides a forum for discussion of issues related to testing operating systems for conformance to the X/OPEN Portability Guide (XPG), including Issue 3 (XPG3) and later.

The scope of this newsletter is the discussion of items associated with the testing of the X/Open Portability Guide, including but not limited to test suite technology (X/Open's VSX and other third-party test suites for the XPG), latest news on X/Open Branding, and other related issues. These issues can include problems related to test suites in general, testability of various features of the XPG, and portability of the test suites.

Computer Language

AMOS

Contact: `subscribe@xamiga.linet.org`

Purpose: For the AMOS programming language on Amiga computers. Features source, bug reports, and help from users around the world, but mainly European users. Most posts will be in English, but there are no limitations to the language used, since AMOS is very popular in most European countries.

Send subscription requests to `subscribe@xamiga.linet.org`, using this format:

```
#amos username@domain;
```

Basic programming

Contact: `basic-request@ireq.hydro.qc.ca` (Robert Meunier)

Purpose: Discussion and exchange on using BASIC as a programming language.

BETA

Contact: `usergroup-request@mjolner.dk` (Elmer Soerensen Sandvad)

Purpose: A discussion forum for BETA users. BETA is a modern object-oriented programming language with powerful abstraction mechanisms including class, subclass, virtual class, class variable, procedure, subprocedure, virtual procedure, procedure variable, coroutine, subcoroutine, virtual coroutine, coroutine variable, and many more, all unified to the ultimate abstraction mechanism: the pattern. Other features include general block structure, coroutines, concurrency, strong typing, part objects, separate objects, and classless objects.

C-IBM-370

Contact: `C-IBM-370-request@dhw68k.cts.com` (David Wolfskill)

Purpose: The C on IBM mainframes mailing list is a place to discuss aspects of using the C programming language on s/370-architecture computers—especially under IBM's operating systems for that environment.

info-ccc

Contact: `xurilka!info-ccc-request@uunet.uu.net` (Luigi Perrotta)

Purpose: The info-ccc mailing list is devoted to the Concurrent C and Concurrent C++ programming languages. However, discussions can be anything relevant to concurrent programming.

lang-lucid

Contact: `lang-lucid-request@csl.sri.com` (R. Jagannathan)

Purpose: Discussions on all aspects related to the language Lucid, including (but not restricted to) language design issues, implementations for personal computers, implementations for parallel machines, language extensions, programming environments, products, bug reports, and bug fixes/workarounds.

Logo

Contact: `logo-friends-request@aiai.ed.ac.uk`

Purpose: Discusses the Logo computer language.

posix-ada

Contact: `posix-ada-request@grebyn.com` (Karl Nyberg)

Purpose: To discuss the Ada binding of the Posix standard. This is the IEEE P1003.5 working group.

posix-testing

Contact: `posix-testing-request@mindcraft.com` (Chuck Karish)

Purpose: This list will provide a forum for discussion of issues related to testing operating systems for conformance to the various POSIX standards and proposed standards (IEEE 1003.x and whatever derivative standards may emerge from the NIST, ANSI, ISO, and so on).

These issues include problems related to test suites in general, testability of various features of the standards, and portability of the test suites to the many very different POSIX implementations we expect to see in the near future. We'll focus on the test suites themselves rather than on the standards to which they test (notably POSIX p1003.3).

think-c

Contact: `think-c-request@ics.uci.edu` (Mark Nagel)

Purpose: This list exists to discuss the Think C compiler for the Macintosh. Acceptable topics include discussion of compiler problems and solutions/workarounds, discussion of object-oriented programming and Macintosh programming, and the sharing of source code. Associated with this list is an archive stored on `ics.uci.edu` accessible via ftp, and a mail archive server (`archive-server@ics.uci.edu`). Submissions to the archive should go to `think-c-request`.

TurboVision

Contact: `listserv@vtvm1.cc.vt.edu`

Purpose: For TurboVision programmers (a library that comes with Borland C++ and Pascal compilers). Both languages are discussed. You can subscribe by sending the message `subscribe turbvis My Name` to `listserv@vtvm1.cc.vt.edu`.

TURBOC-L

List address: `TURBOC-L@UCF1VM.CC.UCF.EDU`

Description: The TURBOC-L list is for Turbo C questions, tips, code, bug reports, and any other Turbo C related areas of interest.

Log files will be kept on a monthly basis.

To subscribe, send the command SUB TURBOC-L *Your_full_name* (where *Your_full_name* is your real name, not your user ID) as the body of a message to LISTSERV@UCF1VM.CC.UCF.EDU; for example: SUB TURBOC-L John Doe.

Coordinator: UCF Postmaster (POSTMAST@UCF1VM.CC.UCF.EDU)

VISBAS-L
List address: LISTSERV@tamvm1.tamu.edu

Description: A list to discuss the Visual Basic software. To subscribe, send a message or e-mail to LISTSERV@tamvm1.tamu.edu with the following in the BODY:

    SUB VISBAS-L *yourfirstname yourlastname*

Owner: Chris Barnes (x005cb@tamvm1.tamu.edu)

x-ada
Contact: x-ada-request@expo.lcs.mit.edu

Purpose: To discuss the interfaces and bindings for an Ada interface to the X Window system.

Computer Security

mac-security
Contact: mac-security-request@world.std.com (David C. Kovar)

Purpose: This mailing list is for people interested in Macintosh security. This can be used to discuss

- Existing security problems in various Macintosh applications

- Security applications, hardware, and solutions

- Potential problems and their solutions

- Just about anything else related to Macintosh security and access control

security
Contact: security@rutgers.edu

Purpose: Discussion group for all aspects of computer security.

11

VIRUS-L

List address: VIRUS-L%LEHIIBM1.BITNET@CUNYVM.CUNY.EDU

Description: Virus-L is a forum specifically for the discussion of computer virus experiences, protection software, and other virus-related topics. The list is currently open to the public and is a non-digest format list.

Archives are available, as is a file called DIRTY DOZEN, which lists a number of viruses, Trojan horses, and pirated programs for the IBM PC. All submissions to VIRUS-L are stored in weekly log files that any user on (or off) the mailing list can download. There is also a small archive of some of the public anti-virus programs that are now available (this archive also can be accessed by any user). All this is handled automatically by the LISTSERV.

To find out what files are available on the LISTSERV, send mail to LISTSERV%LEHIIBM1.BITNET@MITVMA.MIT.EDU, saying INDEX VIRUS-L. Note that filenames/extensions are separated by a space, and not by a period. Once you decide which file(s) you want, send mail to the LISTSERV address, saying GET *filename filetype*. For example, GET VIRUS-L LOG8804 would get the file called VIRUS-L LOG8804 (which happens to be the monthly log of all messages sent to VIRUS-L during April 1988). Note that, starting June 6, 1988, the logs are weekly. The new file format is VIRUS-L LOG*yymmx*, where *yy* is the year (88, 89, etc.), *mm* is the month, and *x* is the week (A, B, etc.). Readers who prefer digest format lists should read the weekly logs and sign off the list itself.

Readers who prefer digest format lists should periodically read the public backlogs of submissions, available from the LEHIIBM1 LISTSERV via a GET command as described above (e.g., GET VIRUS-L LOG8806A for the first week of activity during June 1988). Mail sent to VIRUS-L%LEHIIBM1.BITNET@CUNYVM.CUNY.EDU will automatically be redistributed to everyone on the mailing list. By default, you will NOT receive a copy of your own letters. If you want to, send mail to the LISTSERV, saying SET VIRUS-L REPRO.

To subscribe, send mail with the following command in the message body to LISTSERV%LEHIIBM1.BITNET@MITVMA.MIT.EDU: SUB VIRUS-L *Your_Full_Name* (where *Your_Full_Name* is your real name, not your user ID). To unsubscribe, send SIGNOFF VIRUS-L.

All other requests, problems, questions, etc., should be sent to the coordinator.

Coordinator: Kenneth R. van Wyk (LUKEN@VAX1.CC.LEHIGH.EDU)

Databases

big-DB
Contact: big-DB@midway.uchicago.EDU (Fareed Asad-Harooni)

Purpose: Discussions pertaining to large databases (generally greater than 1 million records) and large database management systems such as IMS, DB2, and CCA's Model/204. Anyone having interests in large database issues is welcome.

FOXPRO-L
List address: FILESERV@POLARBEAR.RANKIN-INLET.NT.CA

Description: The FOXPRO-L mailing list is designed to foster information sharing between users of the FoxPro database development environment now owned and distributed by Microsoft. New and experienced users of FoxPro are welcome to join in the discussions.

Topics that may be discussed in the FOXPRO-L mailing list include (but are not necessarily limited to) the following: ideas for applications, exchanging code snippets, problem solving, product news, and just about anything else related to the FoxPro development environment.

Archives of FOXPRO-L and related files are stored in the /pub/coneill subdirectory at ftp.rahul.net (IP = 192.160.13.1) and are available for anonymous ftp access. If you don't have ftp capability, the same files are available in the /files/foxpro subdirectory via a file server at the mailing list's home site (polarbear.rankin-inlet.nt.ca). To receive the current index of files available from both sites, send an empty message to FOXPROINDEX@POLARBEAR.RANKIN-INLET.NT.CA, or send a message to FILESERV@POLARBEAR.RANKIN-INLET.NT.CA with the first line containing the words GET /FILES/FOXPRO/FOXPRO-L.IDX.

Note: *The FOXPRO-L mailing list is not affiliated with Microsoft Inc. in any way. Perhaps a few folks from the FoxPro Division at Microsoft will join the mailing list, but there are absolutely no guarantees this will happen. In other words, the FOXPRO-L mailing list is an "informal" support group, not an official "organ" of Microsoft.*

To subscribe to the FOXPRO-L mailing list, send an e-mail message to `FILESERV@POLARBEAR.RANKIN-INLET.NT.CA` with the following in the body:

```
JOIN FOXPRO-L
QUIT
```

info-ingres

Contact: `info-ingres-request@math.ams.com`

Purpose: To discuss the commercial version of Ingres.

informix-list

Contact: `informix-list-request@rmy.emory.edu` (Walt Hultgren)

Purpose: An unmoderated list for the discussion of Informix software and related subjects. Topics include all Informix offerings, from C-ISAM to WingZ, plus third-party products. Membership is open to anyone, including end users, vendors, and employees of Informix Software, Inc. An optional gateway service of Informix-related articles from `comp.databases` is offered. Not affiliated with Informix Software, Inc.

ORACLE-L

List address: `ORACLE-L%SBCCVM.BITNET@CUNYVM.CUNY.EDU`

Description: This list is for discussion of all issues relevant to the ORACLE database management system. ORACLE is a registered trademark of ORACLE corporation.

To subscribe to this list on the Internet, send a mail message to `LISTSERV@CCVM.SUNYSB.EDU`. The message should contain the following text:

```
SUBSCRIBE ORACLE-L your full name
```

SQLINFO

List address: `SQLINFO%UICVM.BITNET@CUNYVM.CUNY.EDU`

Description: Mailing list for discussions about SQL/DS and general database topics.

All requests to be added to or deleted from this list, problems, questions, etc., should be sent to `INFO%UICVM.BITNET@CUNYVM.CUNY.EDU`.

Coordinator: Glori A. Chadwick (`GLORI%UMDD.BITNET@CUNYVM.CUNY.EDU`)

11

SQL-sybase
Contact: sybase-request@apple.com

Purpose: This is an semi-unmoderated mailing list for sharing information about the Sybase SQL server and related products.

UUG-dist
Contact: uug-dist-request@dsi.com (Syd Weinstein)

Purpose: Discussion of Unify Corporation's database products, including Unify, Accell/IDS, Accell/SQL, and Accell/"generic database engine."

Desktop Publishing

CDPub
Contact: CDPub-Info@knex.via.mind.org

Purpose: CDPub is an electronic mailing list for folks engaged or interested in CD-ROM publishing in general and desktop CD-ROM recorders and publishing systems in particular.

Topics of interest to the list include information on the various desktop publishing systems for premastering using CD-R media and tapes (DAT, e.g.), replication services, various standards of interest to publishers (ISO9660, RockRidge, etc.), retrieval engines, platform independence issues, etc.

Discussions on all platforms are welcome, be it MS-DOS-based PCs, Apple, UNIX, Amiga, etc. Also of interest will be publishing for platforms such as CD-I, 3DO, et al. In short, if it relates to CD-ROM publishing, we want to talk about it, exchange information, inform, and be informed.

To subscribe, send the following command to Mail-Server@knex.via.mind.org:

```
SUBSCRIBE CDPub FirstName LastName
```

ctt-Digest
List address: LISTSERV@SHSU.edu

Description: ctt-Digest is a (most probably) multipart daily digest of activity on the comp.text.tex news group. ctt-Digest is *not* intended to include

- Posts to `comp.text.tex` originating on INFO-TeX

- Those periodicals included on TeX-Pubs (i.e., Texhax Digest, UKTeX Digest, TeXMaG, the "Frequently Asked Questions" and "FAQ Supplement" posts from `comp.text.tex`, and TUG's "TeX and TUG News"). When these periodicals are removed, it's noted at the end of that issue.

Daily digests are designed to keep distribution parts under 42K in size to accommodate as many mailers as possible. Efforts are made to keep each `comp.text.tex` post in whole between parts (although certain size constraints may preclude this as a universal rule). In general, each day's distribution has been between 1 and 3 parts, but the number of parts will vary directly with `comp.text.tex` activity, as well as how spontaneously our news feed keeps up with traffic to SHSU. The ctt-Digest distribution is automatically processed and forwarded to subscribers at approximately 0200 Central Standard/Daylight Time (U.S.).

The address `ctt-Digest@SHSU.edu` is restricted with respect to posting as it is purely a redistribution list. The posting address via mail to access `comp.text.tex` remains `INFO-TeX@SHSU.edu`, although posts to INFO-TeX will not appear in ctt-Digest.

If you would like to subscribe to ctt-Digest, please include the command `SUBSCRIBE ctt-Digest "Your Real Name in Quotes"` in the body of a mail message to `LISTSERV@SHSU.edu`.

If you have any questions or comments about this new service (or any of our TeX-related services), please contact me directly.

George D. Greenwade, Ph.D.
Department of Economics and Business Analysis
College of Business Administration
P.O. Box 2118   *Voice:* (409) 294-1266
Sam Houston State University   *Fax:* (409) 294-3612
Huntsville, TX 77341   *Internet:* `bed_gdg@SHSU.edu`

DTP-L

List address: `LISTSERV@YALEVM.BITNET`

Description: Many users throughout the Internet, BITNET, and elsewhere have expressed an interest in starting a digest to exchange information on desktop publishing in general, and on the subtleties and complexities of specific programs, including but not limited to Quark-Xpress, Aldus PageMaker and FreeHand, Adobe Illustrator, Ventura Publisher, FrameMaker, Interleaf, and Fontographer. Please note that these would not be system-level discussions; they would deal more at the user-level. Also, technical discussions of PostScript for its own sake (and not how it relates to these programs) would be covered in the PostScript forums and digests.

Caveats aside, every user of these and other programs has discovered some excellent workarounds, irritating problems, or elegant solutions. These could be shared for the benefit of all. I have also set up contacts with Quark, and I'm receiving quick shipment of Zappers and other software to be available to list members and the net community at large. Hopefully, similar agreements can be made with other publishers.

Some emphasis will be placed on use of service bureaus and medium- to high-resolution output devices (Linotronics, Agfas, Varitypers, etc.) without becoming overly technical. The list organizers (myself and Jeff Wasilko of RIT) also have conventional typesetting backgrounds, and we manage service bureaus at our schools.

The list is called DTP-L. To subscribe, send e-mail to `listserv@yalevm.ycc.yale.edu` that contains as its first and only line (substitute your name for *firstname*, etc.):

```
subscribe dtp-l firstname middleinit lastname
```

Because this is a digest, items of interest should *not* be sent to the listserver for efficiency's sake. Send submissions to `glenn_fleishman@yccatsmtp.ycc.yale.edu`, or to `jjwcmp@ultb.isc.rit.edu`. These submissions will be edited and compiled. When collected items reach 30K, they will be distributed through the listserver mechanism to all subscribers.

If you can't subscribe through conventional means, please contact Glenn Fleishman at the above address. Put `subscription` in the subject field of the memo.

Owners: Jeff Wasilko, Rochester Institute of Technology Communications Dept.; Glenn Fleishman, Yale University Printing Service

emtex-user

Contact: `emtex@chemie.fu-berlin.de` (Vera Heinau and
Heiko Schlichting)

`emtex-user-request@chemie.fu-berlin.de`

Purpose: Information about emTeX, an implementation of TeX for
MS-DOS and OS/2. This list is meant for everyone who wants to discuss
problems concerning installation and/or use of the emTeX package and
to be informed about bugs, fixes, and new releases. It sometimes has a
traffic of about 5-10 mails per day, so if you (or your host) can't handle
such a quantity of mail, please don't sign on. The list is maintained "by
hand," so please be patient if a request is not answered immediately.

Conversation language: English

framers

Contact: `framers-request@uunet.uu.net` (Mark Lawrence)

Purpose: Framers is a users' forum for sharing experiences and information about the FrameMaker desktop publishing package from Frame
Technology.

Hyperbole, Hyperbole-announce

Contact: `hyperbole-request@cs.brown.edu` (Bob Weiner)

Purpose: Hyperbole is for discussion of the Hyperbole systems and
the related topics of hypertext and information retrieval. Hyperbole-
announce announces new releases and bug fixes for Hyperbole. Anyone
on Hyperbole is automatically subscribed to Hyperbole-announce, so
you should request subscription to only one of the two lists.

Hyperbole is a flexible hypertext manager developed at Brown University
that sits atop GNU Emacs and provides efficient point-and-click information access and full customizability in GNU Emacs Lisp. Hyperbole allows
hypertext buttons to be embedded within unstructured and structured
files, mail messages, and news articles. It also provides point-and-click
access to ftp archives, Wide Area Information Servers (WAIS), and the
World Wide Web (WWW) hypertext system.

Use the following format on your `Subject:` line to execute requests (include the period at the end of the line):

```
Add firstname-lastname <user@domain> to mail-list-name-without-
domain.
```

For example: `Add Joe Smith <joe@mot.com> to hyperbole.`

leaf

List address: `leaf%TEKSCE.SCE.TEK.COM@RELAY.CS.NET`

Description: Discussions on all aspects related to the Interleaf publishing environment, including (but not restricted to) the Interleaf language, user environment, implementations on new platforms, user-written enhancements, and filters, bug reports, and workarounds.

We have a registered domain in the UUCP zone, and you can find us in the UUCP maps. `user@ILEAF.COM` is equivalent to `ileaf!user@EDDIE.MIT.EDU` (10 Canal Park), and `user@HQ.ILEAF.COM` is equivalent to `leafusa!user@UUNET.UU.NET` (25 First Street). Note that, at least in the `hq.ileaf.com` subdomain, you can mail to most users at Interleaf via a first initial and last name alias (for example, I am reachable as `sfreedman@hq.ileaf.com`). Finally, using explicit UUCP paths inside Interleaf is unnecessary, since the alias files on our gateways should resolve the user anyway.

All requests to be added to or deleted from this list, problems, questions, etc., should be sent to `leaf-request%TEKSCE.SCE.TEK.COM@RELAY.CS.NET`.

metacard-list

Contact: `listserv@grot.starconn.com`

Purpose: Discussion of the MetaCard product from MetaCard Corporation. MetaCard is an application development system, similar to Apple's HyperCard product, that runs on a variety of popular platforms in a UNIX/X11/Motif environment.

To subscribe to the metacard-list, send mail to

```
listserv@grot.starconn.com
```

with the following commands in the body of the message:

```
subscribe metacard-list firstname lastname
quit
```

Replace *firstname lastname* with your name, not your e-mail address.

Administrative messages other than subscription and unsubscription should be sent to `metacard-list-owner@grot.starconn.com`.

PAGEMAKR
List address: `PAGEMAKR@INDYCMS.IUPUI.EDU`

Description: Mailing list for PageMaker users to share their ideas and problems with. The list is for desktop publishers who use PageMaker in either the MAC or PC environment. Since the program runs exactly the same in both settings, all PageMaker users are invited to subscribe.

To subscribe, send the command `SUBSCRIBE PAGEMAKR` *Your full name* (where *Your full name* is your real name, not your login ID) in a message to `LISTSERV@INDYCMS.IUPUI.EDU`.

Coordinator: Cindy Stone (`stonec@GOLD.UCS.INDIANA.EDU`)

VPIEJ-L
List address: `VPIEJ-L@VTVM1.CC.VT.EDU`

Description: VPIEJ-L is a discussion list for electronic publishing issues, especially those related to Scholarly Electronic Journals. Topics for discussion include SGML, PostScript, and other e-journal formats, as well as software and hardware considerations for creation of, storage, and access to e-journals. Publishers, editors, technical staff, programmers, librarians, and end users are welcome to join.

One goal of the list is to provide better feedback from users to creators, so we are very interested in receiving any archival issues. This should give those of us involved in publishing an idea as to what distribution methods work and how end users are accessing and using these publications. Current readers of and contributors to VPIEJ-L have discussed readability and screen display, copyright, and advertising (non-commercial).

Archives of VPIEJ-L are available. A listing may be retrieved by sending the command `INDEX VPIEJ-L` in the *body* of e-mail or a message to `LISTSERV@VTVM1.CC.VT.EDU`. To subscribe, send the following command to `LISTSERV@VTVM1.CC.VT.EDU` in the body of mail (*not* subject): `SUB VPIEJ-L` *your_full_name*, where *your_full_name* is your name (for example: `SUB VPIEJ-L Joan Doe`).

Owner: James Powell (`JPOWELL@VTVM1.CC.VT.EDU`)

wais-discussion

Contact: wais-discussion-request@think.com

Purpose: WAIS stands for Wide Area Information Servers, an electronic publishing project lead by Thinking Machines.

WAIS-discussion is a digested, moderated list on electronic publishing issues in general and Wide Area Information Servers in particular. There are postings every week or two.

wais-talk

Contact: wais-talk-request@think.com

Purpose: WAIS stands for Wide Area Information Servers, an electronic publishing project lead by Thinking Machines.

WAIS-talk is an open list (interactive, not moderated) for implementors and developers. This techie list is not meant as a support list. Please use the alt.wais news group for support, and send bug fixes, etc., to bugwais@think.com.

Documentation and Writing

COPYEDITING-L

Contact: listserv@cornell.edu

Purpose: COPYEDITING-L is an open mailing list for copy editors and other defenders of the King's English who want to discuss editorial problems, client relations, Internet resources, dictionaries, or whatever.

To subscribe to COPYEDITING-L, send the following command to listserv@cornell.edu as the body of a mail message: SUBSCRIBE COPYEDITING-L *Your full name* (for example, SUBSCRIBE COPYEDITING-L Joe Shmoe).

Owner: Carol Roberts (cjr2@cornell.edu)

JOURNET

List address: JOURNET@QUCDN.QUEENSU.CA

Description: Mailing list for discussion of topics of interest to journalists and journalism educators.

Anyone wanting to write longer contributions (about three screens) for inclusion in a proposed monthly electronic digest should send them directly to the coordinator for editing and compiling.

To join the list, send the command Subscribe JOURNET *your full name* (where *your full name* is your real name, not your login ID) as the only line in the text/body of a message to JOURNET@QUCDN.QUEENSU.CA.

11

Coordinator: George Frajkor (FRAJKOR%CARLETON.CA@VM1.NODAK.EDU)

TECHWR-L
Contact: listserv@vm1.ucc.okstate.edu

Purpose: Techwr-l is a new list for technical communicators and related issues. Anything related to any facet of technical communication (practice, research, teaching) is appropriate for this list.

Some possible topics or questions could include the following:

- How do you handle uncooperative engineers or programmers?

- What do others do about making technical writing a priority in their companies?

- I am researching user documentation (vendor-ware) and would like to contact anyone who has written after-market documentation for any platform.

- I still can't decide how to include commands in sentences without either confusing readers, ignoring rules of English use, or both. Help!

- What is vendor-ware?

- I can't seem to convince my students of the importance of audience analysis when writing proposals. Does anyone have exercises or real-life examples that might help?

- I am a new technical writer at a company manufacturing heavy equipment. My employer insists on using terminology that isn't consistent with industry standards. Users have said it's confusing. How might I persuade this company to change the policy?

■ I just spent three months working on a new user's manual for ULTRIX. If anyone would like a copy for reference or to adapt with attribution, please contact me at `generous@very.very.nice`.

■ Does anyone have any experience using the new tech writing textbook by anonymous? I couldn't find a review in Tech Comm.

■ I am trying to decide if my company should use FrameMaker or PageMaker for medium-length manuals. Has anyone had particularly good or bad experiences with doing manuals on either one?

To subscribe,

1. Address a message to `listserv@vm1.ucc.okstate.edu`.

2. Leave the subject line blank.

3. On the first line of the message, type `subscribe techwr-1` **`Your_first_name Your_last_name`** (for example, `subscribe techwr-1 Jane Doe`).

4. Send the message.

Owner: Eric J. Ray (`ejray@okway.okstate.edu`)
Technical Information Analyst
OSU Computer Center, MS 113
Oklahoma State University
Stillwater, OK 74078
(405) 744-6301

WRITERS
List address: `WRITERS%NDSUVM1.BITNET@VM1.NODAK.EDU`

Description: On-line discussion group for professional writers and those who aspire to be writers. Discussions center around the art, craft, and business of writing, and keeps members informed about new and varied opportunities for writers. To list archives of WRITERS back issues, send the following command to `LISTSERV%NDSUVM1.BITNET@VM1.NODAK.EDU` via mail: `INDEX WRITERS`.

To subscribe, send the command SUB WRITERS *your full name* (where *your full name* is your real name, not your login ID) as the only line in the body of a message to LISTSERV%NDSUVM1.BITNET@VM1.NODAK.EDU.

Coordinator: Ray Wheeler (DS001451@VM1.NODAK.EDU)

Education
AI-ED
List address: AI-ED@SUN.COM

Description: Discussions related to the application of artificial intelligence to education. This includes material on intelligent computer-assisted instruction (ICAI) or intelligent tutoring systems (ITS), interactive encyclopedias, intelligent information retrieval for educational purposes, and psychological and cognitive science models of learning, problem solving, and teaching that can be applied to education.

Issues related to teaching AI are welcome. Topics may also include evaluation of tutoring systems, commercialization of AI-based instructional systems, description of actual use of an ITS in a classroom setting, user-modeling, intelligent user-interfaces, and the use of graphics or videodisk in ICAI. Announcements of books, papers, conferences, new products, public domain software tools, etc., are encouraged.

If several people at one site are interested, users should try to form a local distribution system to lessen the load on SUN.COM.

Archives of messages are kept on host SUN.COM.

All requests to be added to or deleted from this list, problems, questions, etc., should be sent to AI-Ed-Request@SUN.COM.

Moderators: J.R. Prohaska (prohaska@SUN.COM)
Stuart Macmillan (smacmillan@SUN.COM)

BI-L
List address: BI-L%BINGVMB.BITNET@VM1.NODAK.EDU

Description: BI-L is a computer conference dedicated to discussing ways of assisting library users in effectively and efficiently exploiting the resources available in and through the libraries of the 1990s.

Contributors to the forum deal with the practical, theoretical, and technical aspects of what has been called Bibliographic Instruction, Library Use Instruction, Library Orientation, and several other names. We examine, explore, critique, appraise, and evaluate strategies, programs, and equipment that we have found to be valuable (or not) in working toward the goal of the self-sufficient library user.

To join BI-L, send the following e-mail message to
`LISTSERV%BINGVMB.BITNET@VM1.NODAK.EDU: SUBSCRIBE BI-L`
`Your Name`. (Put your first and last name where it says `Your Name`.)

To contribute to BI-L, send your e-mail message to
`BI-L%BINGVMB.BITNET@VM1.NODAK.EDU`.

Note: *You send your message to the* list, *not to the list server.*

For more information about BI-L, contact

> Martin Raish
> Coordinator of Bibliographic Instruction
> State University of New York at Binghamton
> Box 6012
> Binghamton, New York 13902-6012
> (607) 777-4385 or `MRAISH@BINGVMA.BITNET`
> (`MRAISH%BINGVMA.BITNET@CUNYVM.CUNY.EDU`)

CREWRT-L
List address: `CREWRT-L@UMCVMB.MISSOURI.EDU`

Description: This list was created as a place to discuss how and why creative writing is being taught at colleges and universities, including the role it plays in the curriculum, the history of creative writing programs, the shape and flavor of creative writing courses, and the influence it has or should have on students' lives. Any teacher who has ever taught a creative writing course (poetry or fiction) and any student who has ever taken such a course should feel welcome to participate.

The list is open and unmoderated, so discussion can range as far and wide as members want, from ethereal theory to classroom strategies and anything remotely tangential to either. However, this list is not intended to be a place for sharing creative work—not that such sharing is in any way forbidden, but there are other lists designed for that purpose.

To subscribe, send mail to `LISTSERV@UMCVMB.MISSOURI.EDU` and include the command

    SUB CREWRT-L *Your Name*

Owner: Eric Crump (`LCERIC@UMCVMB.MISSOURI.EDU`)

CTI-L
List address: `LISTSERV@IRLEARN.UCD.IE`

Description: CTI-L is an unmoderated list to facilitate the discussion of issues in the use of computers in teaching. The list is intended to promote discussion on how computers can be used in learning and teaching via the following: CTI (Computers in Teaching Initiative), CAT (Computer Aided Teaching), CBT (Computer Based Training), CAL (Computer Aided Learning), CBL (Computer Based Learning), and TBT (Technology Based Training).

To subscribe, send a message to `LISTSERV@IRLEARN.UCD.IE` with the following line of text in the *body*:

    SUB CTI-L *Your_full_name*

where *Your_full_name* is your first and last name.

List coordinator: Claron O'Reilly (`CLARON@IRLEARN.UCD.IE`)

EdLaw
List address: `LISTSERV@UKCC.uky.edu`

Description: EdLaw is designed for those who teach and practice law concerning public education, private education, and colleges and universities. It's intended to be an exchange of information on legislation and litigation and their various components. It should not be viewed as legal advice in any form, but rather as a conversation among those knowledgeable in the field.

Archives of EdLaw are stored in the EdLaw FILELIST. To receive a list of files, send the command `INDEX EdLaw` to `LISTSERV@UKCC.uky.edu`.

To subscribe to EdLaw, send the following command to `LISTSERV@UKCC.uky.edu` via mail (in the *body* of the mail):

    SUBSCRIBE EdLaw *your full name*

For example: `SUBSCRIBE EdLaw Joe Shmoe`

Owner: Virginia Davis-Nordin (`NORDIN@ukcc.uky.edu`)

home-ed

Contact: `home-ed-request@think.com` (David Mankins)

Purpose: This mailing list is for the discussion of all aspects and methods of home education. These methods include the "unschooling" approach, curricula-based home-schooling, and others. The list is currently unmoderated and welcomes everyone interested in educating their children at home, whatever the reasons.

home-ed-politics

Contact: `home-ed-politics-request@mainstream.com` (Craig Peterson)

Purpose: To discuss political issues dealing with home education. This includes government intrusion into families, public schooling as it influences home education, legislation in various states and the federal level, etc. This list is managed by listproc.

K12ADMIN

List address: `LISTSERV@SUVM.SYR.EDU`

Description: A worldwide discussion group has been set up to provide a discussion base for K-12 school administrators: principals, vice principals, superintendents, assistant superintendents, central and county office administrators, and others involved with K-12 school administration.

Conversation on this list will focus on the topics of interest to the school administrator community, including the latest on school management, curriculum, services, operations, technology and activities. K12ADMIN is a discussion group for administrative practitioners helping other administrative practitioners, sharing ideas, helping to solve problems, telling each other about new publications and upcoming conferences, asking for assistance or information, and linking administrators for information, and sharing resources.

This discussion is open to *all* school administrators and people involved with the school administration field—worldwide. We want to keep the activity and discussion focused on school administration, K-12. But the group can be used by members for many different things—to ask for input, share ideas and information, link programs that are geographically remote, make contacts, etc.

The K12ADMIN list is operated by several volunteers, including Mike Eisenberg, director of the ERIC Clearinghouse on Information Resources at Syracuse University; Mary Lou Finne, user services coordinator of the ERIC Clearinghouse on Educational Management at the University of Oregon; and Peter Milbury, librarian of Pleasant Valley High School, Chico, California.

To subscribe to K12ADMIN,

1. Compose an e-mail message to `listserv@suvm.syr.edu`.

2. In the body of the message, enter **subscribe K12ADMIN *Your Name*** (example: `subscribe K12ADMIN Jane Doe`).

3. Send the message. You will receive a subscription confirmation from K12ADMIN.

Owners: Mike Eisenberg (`ERIC04@SUVM.SYR.EDU`), ERIC Clearinghouse on Information Resources at Syracuse University

Mary Lou Finne (`MARY_LOU_FINNE_AT_CATE@CCMAIL.UOREGON.EDU`), ERIC Clearinghouse on Educational Management at the University of Oregon

Peter Milbury (`PMILBUR@EIS.CALSTATE.EDU`), Pleasant Valley High School, Chico, California

KIDSNET
List address: `KIDSNET@VMS.CIS.PITT.EDU`

Description: A mailing list formed to provide a global network for the use of children and teachers in grades K-12. It is intended to provide a focus for technological development and for resolving the problems of language, standards, etc., that inevitably arise in international communications.

All requests to be added to or deleted from this list, problems, questions, etc., should be sent to `KIDSNET-REQUEST@VMS.CIS.PITT.EDU`.

Coordinator: Bob Carlitz (`carlitz@VMS.CIS.PITT.EDU`)

LAWSCH-L
List address: `LAWSCH-L%AUVM.BITNET@VM1.NODAK.EDU`

Description: A forum to discuss matters that affect all law students. It's also designed to allow for interaction between students and law schools to lessen the gap between them. The list is based at American University Law School.

To subscribe, send the command SUB LAWSCH-L *your_full_name* (where *your_full_name* is your real name, not your login ID) in the body of a message to LISTSERV%AUVM.BITNET@VM1.NODAK.EDU.

Coordinator: Ed Kania (EKANIA%AUVM.BITNET@VM1.NODAK.EDU)

TIPS

List address: LISTSERV@FRE.FSU.UMD.EDU

Description: A forum for the open discussion of all aspects of teaching in psychology. Although the psychological sciences are the primary content focus of this group, membership is open to all who share an interest in exchanging ideas and information about teaching. The primary goal of this computer conference is to foster growth in teaching by providing a forum for teachers to talk to each other. Topics such as the exchange of experiences, teaching demonstrations, reviews of teaching materials, and the sharing of teaching resources are encouraged. Announcements regarding teaching conferences are welcome as well.

The list is structured so that replies go to the entire list in an effort to stimulate discussion.

To subscribe to TIPS, send e-mail to LISTSERV@FRE.FSU.UMD.EDU on the Internet, with the following command in the *body* of mail:

    SUBSCRIBE TIPS *Yourfirstname Yourlastname*

For example: SUBSCRIBE TIPS John Doe
To send e-mail to TIPS, send your message to TIPS@FRE.FSU.UMD.EDU on the Internet, or use the REPLY command if supported by your system.

Owner: Bill Southerly (TIPSOWNER@FRE.FSU.UMD.EDU)
or TIPSOWNER@FRE.TOWSON.EDU

Engineering

aeronautics

Contact: aeronautics-request@rascal.ics.utexas.edu

Purpose: The aeronautics mailing list—a news-to-mail feed of the sci.aeronautics news group—is a moderated discussion group dealing with atmospheric flight, specifically aerodynamics, flying qualities, simulation, structures, systems, propulsion, and design human factors.

Subscribers can participate in real-time with the main group.

AVIATION-THEORY

List address: AVIATION-THEORY@MC.LCS.MIT.EDU

Description: Mailing list dedicated to the more theoretical side of aerospace engineering. The intent is to discuss aerospace technology; calls for papers, announcements for seminars, etc., also can be sent to the list. Although the list has its origin in the AVIATION digest, subjects related to aviation theory—like space flight technology—may be discussed as well. Topics open for discussion are calls for papers, aerodynamics aircraft structures, seminar announcements, flight mechanics, aircraft materials, books to be published, stability and control, and others.

A mailing list for the Internet and BITNET has been created already, and we are looking for someone who would like to create the USENET group, so we can create digests from those messages.

All requests to be added to or deleted from this list, problems, questions, etc., should be sent to aviation-theory-request@MC.LCS.MIT.EDU.

Moderator: Rob A. Vingerhoeds (ROB%BGERUG51.BITNET@MITVMA.MIT.EDU)

Embedded Digest

Contact: embed-request@synchro.com (Chuck Cox)

Purpose: The Embedded Digest is a forum for the discussion of embedded computer system engineering. Suitable topics include embedded hardware and software design techniques, development and testing tool reviews, product announcements, etc.

FASE

Contact: `fase@cs.uh.edu`

Purpose: FASE (Forum for Academic Software Engineering) provides a forum for communication among academic educators who teach software engineering. Submissions are compiled and mailed to subscribers approximately monthly.

INFO-VLSI

List address: `INFO-VLSI@THINK.COM`

Description: Mailing list for the exchange of information on all aspects of integrated circuit (IC) design. The list is gatewayed to/from the USENET group `comp.lsi`.

Archived messages are kept at `Think.COM` in the files `mail/info-vlsi.archive*`.

All requests to be added to or deleted from this list, problems, questions, etc., should be sent to `INFO-VLSI-REQUEST@THINK.COM`.

Coordinator: Bruce Walker (`bruce@THINK.COM`)

MECH-L

List address: `MECH-L%UTARLVM1.BITNET@CUNYVM.CUNY.EDU`

Description: Mailing list for discussion of any topics pertinent to the mechanical engineering communities such as meeting announcements, software evaluation, composite material research, and others. MECH-L welcomes any suggestions and comments and encourages faculty/students in ME-related areas (such as aerospace and civil) to join the list.

To subscribe, send the text `SUB MECH-L` *your_full_name* (where *your_full_name* is your name) in the body of a message to `LISTSERV%UTARLVM1.BITNET@CUNYVM.CUNY.EDU`.

Coordinator: S. Nomura (`B470SSN%UTARLVM1.BITNET@CUNYVM.CUNY.EDU`)

softpats

List address: `softpats@uvmvm.uvm.edu`

Description: A mailing list for the discussion of software patents and related issues. The mailing list, called `softpats@uvmvm.uvm.edu`, is run by a list server, so to subscribe, send the text `sub` `softpats` *your-name* in the *body* of a message to `listserv@uvmvm.uvm.edu`.

This mailing list is, for the time being, *not* moderated. Expected topics include legality and desirability of software patents, announcements of new patents granted, and actions taken by various groups for and against the patenting of software. To keep noise to a minimum, discussion of look-and-feel issues will *not* be considered acceptable; the USENET group `gnu.misc.discuss` is probably a more appropriate vehicle.

11

List Owner: Garrett A. Wollman (`wollman@emily.uvm.edu`)

Testing-Research
Contact: `Testing-Research-Request@cs.uiuc.edu` (Brian Marick)

Purpose: Testing-Research is a forum for testing researchers to discuss current and future research. Since testing is one of the most down-to-earth kinds of software engineering research, testing practitioners are welcomed. Messages about practice should be the kind that can guide or improve research; messages that can improve practice should go in the USENET group `comp.software-eng`. This list is unmoderated.

WELDCOMP
List address: `WELDCOMP@CASCADE.CARLETON.CA`

Description: SIG for computer modeling welds, run from CASCADE (Centre for Advanced Studies in Computer Aided Design and Engineering) at Carleton University. Messages related to computer modeling welds and the following topics would be especially welcome (if traffic warrants, anyone of them could become a Special Interest Group (SIG) or distribution list):

- Weld pool physics

- Weld microstructures

- Residual stress and distortion

- Sensors and control

- Failure mechanisms and analysis

All requests to be added to or deleted from this list, problems, questions, etc., should be sent to `WELDCOMP-REQUEST@CASCADE.CARLETON.CA`.

Coordinator: Warren Hik (`hik@CASCADE.CARLETON.CA`)

Film Industry

filmmakers

Contact: `filmmakers-request@grissom.larc.nasa.gov`

Purpose: The Filmmakers' mailing list deals with all aspects of motion picture production, with an emphasis on technical issues. Heavily stressed are construction and design issues for those working on tight budgets. It should be emphasized that the subject is film, not video.

stagecraft

Contact: `stagecraft-request@jaguar.cs.utah.edu` (Brad Davis)

Purpose: This list is for the discussion of all aspects of stage work, including (but not limited to) special effects, sound effects, sound reinforcement, stage management, set design and building, lighting design, company management, hall management, hall design, and show production. This is not a forum for the discussion of various stage productions (unless the discussion pertains to the stagecraft of a production), acting or directing methods (unless you know of ways to get actors to stand in the right spots), or film or video production (unless the techniques can be used on the stage). The list will not be moderated unless problems crop up. Archives will be kept of the discussion (send mail to `stagecraft-request` for copies).

VIDPRO-L

List address: `VIDPRO-L@UXA.ECN.BGU.EDU`

Description: A discussion list for individuals interested in all aspects of video production and operations. The focus of discussion will be professional video production at all levels. However, anyone with an interest in video production or equipment operations is invited to subscribe and join the discussion. The list can also serve as a point for asking questions about equipment purchases, equipment problems, production problems, etc.

As the list grows, it may also become a location for posting verifiable positions in video production. If you are aware of positions, send them directly to me for posting. The list is currently moderated to avoid duplication and junk mail from reaching the subscribers.

Again, anyone with an interest in video is welcome to subscribe. To subscribe to VIDPRO-L, send a message to `LISTSERV@UXA.ECN.BGU.EDU`; leave the subject line blank; in the body of the message, type

> `SUBSCRIBE VIDPRO-L` *`first-name last name`*

Owner: P. Gordon Sroufe (`cfpgs1@uxa.ecn.bgu.edu`)

Fine Arts Research

FINEART

List address: `FINEART%ecs.umass.edu@RELAY.CS.NET`

Description: The FINEART Forum is dedicated to international collaboration between artists and scientists. It is subsidized by the International Society for the Arts, Science, and Technology (ISAST), 2020 Milvia, Berkeley, CA 94704. The purpose of this bulletin board is to disseminate information regarding the use of computers in the fine arts. Topics to be included are

- Computers used in the design of works of art

- Computers used to fabricate works of art

- Computers used within works of art

- Computers used to analyze works of art

- Computers used to criticize art

- Computers used to distribute art

General areas of interest include

Art and AI	Interactive Video
Computer Aided Fabrication	Picture Networks
Computer Animation	Paint Systems
Design Rule Systems	Sensory Environments
Image Rendering	Shape Grammars
Image Synthesis	Style Simulation

Send submissions and requests for list membership to

> FINEART%ecs.umass.csnet@RELAY.CS.NET
> *Phone:* (413) 545-1902

Moderator: Ray Lauzzana (lauzzana%ecs.umass.edu@RELAY.CS.NET)

Music-Research
Contact: Music-Research-Request@prg.oxford.ac.uk (Stephen Page)

Purpose: The Music-Research electronic mail redistribution list was established after a suggestion made at a meeting in Oxford in July 1986 to provide an effective and fast means of bringing together musicologists, music analysts, computer scientists, and others working on applications of computers in music research.

As with any forum for discussion, certain subject areas are of particular interest to the group of people on this list. Initially, the list was established for people whose chief interests concern computers and their applications to music representation systems, information retrieval systems for musical scores, music printing, music analysis, musicology, ethnomusicology, and tertiary music education. The following areas are not the principal concern of this list, although overlapping subjects may well be interesting: primary and secondary education, sound generation techniques, and composition. Articles on electronic music, synthesizers, MIDI, etc., will be rejected at the request of the readers of the list.

Graphics, Video Imaging, and Multimedia
af
Contact: af-request@crl.dec.com

Purpose: Discussion of AudioFile, a client/server, network transparent, device independent audio system.

Direct-L
List address: LISTSERV@uafsysb.uark.edu

Description: The DIRECT-L list was formed to provide a forum for discussions of the software program MacroMind Director for the Macintosh. Possible discussion topics include but are not limited to

Programming in Lingo

Hardware configurations

Use with other software packages

Video sources, techniques, methods

Kiosk development

Device drivers

This list will be unmoderated with archives. Archives of DIRECT-L will be stored in the DIRECT-L FILELIST. To receive a list of files, send the command INDEX DIRECT-L to LISTSERV@uafsysb.uark.edu.

To subscribe to DIRECT-L, send the following command to LISTSERV@uafsysb.uark.edu via mail text:

    SUBSCRIBE DIRECT-L *Your_full_name*

where *Your_full_name* is your name. For example:

    SUBSCRIBE DIRECT-L Rita Someone

Owner: CB Lih (CBLIH@uafsysb.uark.edu)

DVI-list
Contact: dvi-list-request@calvin.dgbt.doc.ca (Andrew Patrick)

Purpose: This mailing list is intended for discussions about Intel's DVI (Digital Video Interactive) system. These discussions cover applications and programming with DVI.

FRAC-L
List address: FRAC-L%GITVM1.BITNET@CUNYVM.CUNY.EDU

Description: Mailing list dedicated to the computer graphical generation of fractal images.

In conjunction with the list, an archive of programs submitted by users will be maintained. Mr. Homer Smith of Art Matrix in Ithaca, New York, has donated a program library, which will soon be available from LISTSERV at GITVM1.

To add yourself to the list, send the command `SUBSCRIBE FRAC-L` `Your_Full_Name` via mail to `LISTSERV%GITVM1.BITNET@CUNYVM.CUNY.EDU` (where `Your_Full_Name` is your real name, not your user ID). To remove yourself from the list, send the command `UNSUBSCRIBE FRAC-L`.

All other problems, questions, etc., should be sent to the coordinator.

Coordinator: David D. Lester (`CC100DL%GITVM1@CUNYVM.CUNY.EDU`)

INFO-GRAPHICS
List address: `INFO-GRAPHICS@ADS.COM`

Description: Discussion of graphics hardware, software, and any topic related to graphics. Basically, a free-wheeling exchange of information, much like INFO-CPM.

All requests to be added to or deleted from this list, problems, questions, etc., should be sent to `INFO-GRAPHICS-REQUEST@ADS.COM`.

Coordinator: Andy Cromarty (`andy@ADS.COM`)

iti151
Contact: `iti151-request@oce.orst.edu` (Paul O'Neill)

Purpose: For users of Imaging Technology's series 150 and 151 image processing systems and ITEX151 software. The goal is to share algorithms, code, tricks, pitfalls, advice, etc., in an effort to decrease development time and increase functionality for the users of these systems. (Also, despite their good support, we customers may want to gang up on ITI someday!!)

Lightwave
Contact: `subscribe@xamiga.linet.org`

Purpose: For Video Toaster users, supporting the NewTek 3-D object modeler/ray tracer and hardware involved in video editing, such as time base correctors and VCR equipment. This mail is echoed from another site.

Send subscription requests to `subscribe@xamiga.linet.org`, using this format:

```
#lightwave username@domain;
```

mmos2-l

Contact: `Mail-Server@knex.via.mind.org`

Purpose: The list's primary goal is to discuss programming of multimedia elements under IBM's OS/2, authoring tools and multimedia peripherals such as audio boards, motion video subsystems and devices such as CD-ROM, VideoDiscs, etc. The list welcomes the participation of and contribution from programmers, multimedia designers, and presentation experts and novices, as well as content creators such as CBT authors, computer musicians, animators, etc. Users of multimedia programs and publications are also welcome.

mmos2-l redistributes submissions as they come in as individual articles.

To subscribe to the list, send mail to

        `Mail-Server@knex.via.mind.ORG`

where the body of the message is

        `subscribe Mmos2-L` *FirstName LastName*

PHOTO-CD

Contact: `listmgr@info.kodak.com` (Don Cox)

Purpose: The Kodak Photo-CD Mailing List provides libraries of information on Kodak CD products or technology and closely related products. Information in the library section is posted and maintained by Kodak. The mailing list is an open discussion area to talk with other Internet users interested in our CD technology and products. Kodak will participate in message conversations on occasion. Kodak does not guarantee the accuracy of information passed between mailing list users.

PHOTO-CD is a public mailing list. Those who want to subscribe to it should send mail to the following address:

        `listserv@info.kodak.com`

with the command

        `SUBSCRIBE PHOTO-CD` *first-name last-name*

on a line by itself in the body (and no other text). Substitute your first name and last name where indicated; these will be used to identify you when you submit a message to the list. Your electronic mail address will be derived from this subscription request message.

Health and Medical

ADA-Law

Contact: wtm@bunker.afd.olivetti.com

Purpose: Discussion of the Americans with Disabilities Act (ADA) and other disability-related legislation, not only in the United States but in other countries as well.

To subscribe, send the message Subscribe ADA-Law *your name* to listserv@vm1.nodak.edu, or send mail to wtm@bunker.afd.olivetti.com.

AI-MEDICINE

List address: AI-MEDICINE@MED.STANFORD.EDU

Description: AI-MEDICINE is an unmoderated mailing list serving Internet and BITNET domains since September 1990. Current readership consists mainly of computer scientists and engineers with interest in biomedical and clinical research, and of physicians with interest in medical informatics.

AI in Medicine is a broad subject area that encompasses almost all research areas in artificial intelligence. For the purposes of this mailing list, AI in Medicine may be defined as "computer-based medical decision support" (or "computer-assisted medical decision making").

This definition may be expanded to include AI-based approaches to computer-assisted medical instruction. According to this definition, topics such as billing systems and hospital/medical office information retrieval systems clearly remain outside the scope of this forum.

Some borderline topics can't readily be classified under AI in Medicine, yet have clear connections to both artificial intelligence and medical practice. Processing and interpretation of medical images and signals are among those subject areas, and the current readership of this list contains a substantial number of researchers working in these fields. These borderline subject areas will remain within the scope of the list, as long as the focus lies on the artificial intelligence aspects, and not the detailed engineering principles.

Any individual or organization with Internet or BITNET mailing addresses may join.

Requests for subscription may be sent to

ai-medicine-request@med.stanford.edu

List address for unmoderated distribution of messages:

ai-medicine@med.stanford.edu

List coordinator: Serdar Uckun, M.D., Ph.D. (uckun@hpp.stanford.edu)

11

ANEST-L

List address: LISTSERV@UBVM.CC.BUFFALO.EDU

Description: This list was formed to serve as a vehicle for discussing topics related to anesthesiology and collecting any information related to anesthesiology.

Archives of ANEST-L and related files are stored in the ANEST-L FILELIST. To receive a list of files, send the command INDEX ANEST-L to LISTSERV@UBVM.CC.BUFFALO.EDU as the first line in the body of a mail message (not the Subject: line).

To subscribe to ANEST-L, send the command SUB ANEST-L *yourfirstname yourlastname* to LISTSERV@UBVM.CC.BUFFALO.EDU via a mail message (again, as the first line in the body of the mail, not the Subject: line). For example: SUB ANEST-L John Doe.

Owner: Andrew M. Sopchak
        Internet: sopchaka@vax.cs.hscsyr.edu
        Department of Anesthesiology
        SUNY Health Science Center
        750 East Adams Street
        Syracuse, NY 13210

aids

Contact: aids-request@cs.ucla.edu (Daniel R. Greening)

Purpose: A distribution list for people who can't read sci.med.aids. Covers predominately medical issues of AIDS. Some discussion of political and social issues. Postings to AIDSNEWS and Health InfoCom News mailing lists are also carried.

Postings to aids@cs.ucla.edu are NON-confidential and are moderated. The average number of postings to aids is about 2 per day. The average size of articles is very large (statistics, news summaries, etc.).

Blind News Digest

Contact: wtm@bunker.afd.olivetti.com

Purpose: This is a moderated mailing list in digest format that deals with all aspects of the visually impaired/blind.

To subscribe, send the message

```
Subscribe BlindNws your name
```

to listserv@vm1.nodak.edu, or send mail to wtm@bunker.afd.olivetti.com.

CUSSNET

Contact: cussnet-request@stat.com

Purpose: Computer Users in the Social Sciences is a discussion group devoted to issues of interest to social workers, counselors, and human service workers of all disciplines. The discussion frequently involves computer applications in treatment, agency administration, and research. Students, faculty, community-based professionals, and just good ol' plain folks join in the discussion. Software, hardware, and ethical issues associated with their use in human services generate lively and informative discussions. Please join us. Bill Allbritten, Ph.D., moderator (director, Counseling and Testing Center, Murray State University, Murray, KY 42071)

To join the list, send e-mail to listserv@stat.com. The first line of text should be

```
subscribe cussnet
```

Down Syndrome

Contact: wtm@bunker.afd.olivetti.com

Purpose: For discussion of any issue related to Down Syndrome. This list is open to parents, siblings, relatives, friends, teachers, and professionals, as well as to people with Down Syndrome.

To subscribe, send the message

    Subscribe Down-Syn *your name*

to listserv@vm1.nodak.edu, or send mail to wtm@bunker.afd.olivetti.com.

GRADNRSE
List address: ISTSERV@KentVM.Kent.EDU

Description: The GradNrse is a discussion group for practicing nurses. Moderated by Linda Q. Thede, RN, MSN, it originates at Kent State University in Ohio. It is intended to provide practicing nurses worldwide a place to give and get information about practice situations from their colleagues. Broad ideas for discussion include

- Actual practice problems and/or solutions (e.g. "I have a patient with *XX* disease; what experiences does anyone else have with this situation?")

- Nursing law in one's state

- Nursing ethics situations

- Nursing policies/politics

- Staff development or patient education

- Short summaries and or reactions to news articles affecting nursing

Naturally, it isn't limited to the above topics; these are just suggestions. In short, anything that would be of interest to practicing nurses is great! To subscribe, send an e-mail message to Listserv@KentVm.Kent.Edu.

Leave the name and subject blank. The message should be

    sub gradnrse *YourFirstName YourLastName*

Owner: Linda Thede (LThede@KentVm.Kent.Edu)

handicap
Contact: wtm@bunker.shel.isc-br.com

Purpose: The Handicap Digest provides an information/discussion exchange for issues dealing with the physically/mentally handicapped. Topics include, but are not limited to, medical, education, legal, technological aids, and the handicapped in society.

MEDCONS
List address: `MEDCONS%FINHUTC.BITNET@VM1.NODAK.EDU`

Description: This list isn't intended for non-professionals or patients, who still are welcome to follow the activity on the list. It is intended for physicians and investigators in the medical field to allow medical consulting on a voluntary basis. The final responsibility for the care of patients is always that of the personal physician exclusively.

Short descriptions of cases "hard to solve" in the form anamnesis status and laboratory findings (question: what bothered the patient?) followed by the diagnosis and cure are encouraged. Real bedside problem solving could also be enlightened by short descriptions of the most exotic and puzzling cases colleagues have encountered.

Absolute anonymity for the patients is required. Please favor Latin and professional terminology to make it easier to keep laymen from obstructing the list. Contributions from the field of so-called alternative medicine are obsolete and will not be redistributed to the subscribers.

To join, send the command `SUBSCRIBE MEDCONS` *Your_full_name* (where *Your_full_name* is your real name, not your login ID) in the body of a message to `LISTSERV%FINHUTC.BITNET@VM1.NODAK.EDU`.

Coordinator: Dr. Mikael Peder (`PEDER@CC.HELSINKI.FI`)

medphys
Contact: `medphys-request@radonc.duke.edu`

Purpose: An attempt to foster electronic communication between medical physicists, open to interested others. Medical physics is a somewhat opaque but widely used synonym for radiological physics—the physics of the diagnostic and therapeutic use of radiation in medicine. At present, most subscribers are involved in radiotherapy.

NeXT-Med
Contact: `next-med-request@ms.uky.edu`

Purpose: NeXT-Med is open to end users and developers interested in medical solutions using NeXT computers and/or 486 systems running NEXTSTEP. Discussions on any topic related to NeXT use in the medical industry or relating to health care is encouraged.

NRSING-L

List address: `LISTSERV@NIC.UMASS.EDU`

Description: The NRSING-L list is primarily for the discussion of nursing and health care informatics topics. However, any and all topics relating to nursing are welcomed. This is a warm virtual room of nursing and other experts from around the world.

To subscribe, e-mail to `listserv@nic.umass.edu`. First line in body: `Subscribe nrsing-l` *your real name*.

This list is running on a UNIX box using UNIX ListServer Version 6.0 by Anastasios C. Kotsikonas. To get help, e-mail to

> `listserv@nic.umass.edu`

First line in the body of the message: `HELP`

List Owner: `larrivee@umassmed.ummed.edu`

nucmed
Contact: `nucmed-request@uwovax.uwo.ca`
`trevorc@uwovax.uwo.ca` (Trevor Cradduck)

Purpose: A discussion of nuclear medicine and related issues. Of particular concern is the format of digital images.

Pharmacy Mail Exchange
Contact: `pharm@dmu.ac.uk`

Purpose: Pharmacy Mail Exchange is a distribution list for pharmacists and workers in related subjects. To subscribe or request further details, send mail to

> `pharm-request@dmu.ac.uk`

Owner: Paul Hodgkinson (`phh@dmu.ac.uk`), Dept. of Pharmacy, De Montfort University

Scientific Research

anneal
Contact: `anneal-request@cs.ucla.edu` (Daniel R. Greening)

Purpose: Discussion of simulated annealing techniques and analysis, as well as other related issues (stochastic optimization, Boltzmann machines, metricity of NP-complete move spaces, etc.).

Membership is restricted to those doing active research in simulated annealing or related areas. Current membership is international, and about half the members are published authors. The list itself is unmoderated.

Biomch-L

Contact: `listserv@nic.surfnet.nl` (Ton van den Bogert)

Purpose: This list is intended for members of the International, European, American, Canadian, and other Societies of Biomechanics, ISEK (International Society of Electrophysiological Kinesiology), and for all others with an interest in the general field of biomechanics and human or animal movement. For the scope of this list, see the *Journal of Biomechanics* (Pergamon Press), the *Journal of Biomechanical Engineering* (ASME), or *Human Movement Science* (North-Holland).

Biomch-L is operated under the patronage of the International Society of Biomechanics.

Technical help can be obtained by sending the command `send biomch-l guide` to `LISTSERV@NIC.SURFNET.NL`, or by contacting one of the list owners.

Subscribe by sending `subscribe biomch-l` *first_name last_name* to `listserv@nic.surfnet.nl`.

DEEPSEA

List address: `LISTSERV@UVVM.UVIC.CA`

Description: DEEPSEA's purpose is to serve the world's community of deep-sea and hydrothermal vent biologists working in the areas of evolution, ecology, biogeography, paleontology, systematics, phylogenetics, and population genetics.

To subscribe to the DEEPSEA list, send e-mail to `LISTSERV@UVVM.UVIC.CA`, with the *body* containing the command

```
SUB DEEPSEA yourfirstname yourlastname
```

For example: `sub deepsea Jacques Cousteau`

Owner: Andrew McArthur (`AMCARTHU@UVVM.UVIC.CA`)

electromagnetics

Contact: `EM-request@decwd.ece.uiuc.edu`

Purpose: Discussion of issues relating to electromagnetics. This may take the form of book reviews, code problems, techniques, etc.

hyperchem

11

Contact: `hyperchem-request@autodesk.com` (Mark Davies)

Purpose: The group is designed for, but not limited to, HyperChem users. Any and all scientific and technical issues related to the use of HyperChem are appropriate for discussion on this group. The group is unmoderated, so any message sent to the group is sent automatically to all other members of the group. Any information on this group is to be taken "as is," without representation or warranty of any kind, either express or implied. The user assumes the entire risk as to the use of this information.

NA-net

Contact: `na.join@na-net.ornl.gov`

Purpose: Numerical analysis discussions. To join the NA-net, send mail and in the message body specify the following three fields in any order:

```
Lastname:
Firstname:
E-mail:
```

NPLC

Contact: `tout@genesys.cps.msu.edu` (Walid Tout)

Purpose: To establish this network for rapid communication among researchers in the field of plant lipids. This network can serve as a means to make announcements (such as post-doc positions) to the field. It also can be used to query co-workers regarding techniques, resources, etc. Also, we hope that research results will be disseminated more rapidly by the posting of abstracts for publications that have been accepted and are "in press." Finally, the NPLC newsletter and announcements regarding NPLC meetings, business, etc., will be posted on the network. The NPLC welcomes plant lipid researchers from anywhere in the world to use this network.

To subscribe, send the message

```
SUB NPLC Your_full_name
```

to listproc@genesys.cps.msu.edu.

OPTICS

List address: OPTICS@TOE.TOWSON.EDU

Description: OPTICS is an open list devoted to the interchange of ideas, discussions and meeting announcements in the field of optics—for example, if you will be giving a lecture (colloquium), organizing a scientific meeting in some optic related discipline, or just like to comment in some specific area of optics. You are welcome to send any newsworthy item to OPTICS@TOE.TOWSON.EDU, and it will be forwarded to the mailing list.

The schedule of the National Capital Section of the Optical Society of America will post its meeting schedule on the list as well as send mailings to the membership.

To add your name to the list, send a mail message to MAILSERV@TOE.TOWSON.EDU with the command

```
SUBSCRIBE OPTICS
```

To remove your name from the list, send a mail message to MAILSERV@TOE.TOWSON.EDU with the command

```
UNSUBSCRIBE OPTICS
```

This list is *not* LISTSERV-based.

ORGCHE-L

List address: LISTSERV%RPICICGE.BITNET@CUNYVM.CUNY.EDU

Description: Organic Chemistry mailing list. To facilitate the interchange of ideas, information, computer programs, papers, and to announce opportunities for doing collaborative efforts (teaching and/or research activities) between specialists in organic chemistry and related areas.

To subscribe to the list, send mail with the following line to LISTSERV%RPICICGE.BITNET@CUNYVM.CUNY.EDU:

```
SUBS ORGCHE-L Your_Real_Name
```

If you don't receive mail confirming your subscription, contact `MSMITH%AMHERST.BITNET@CUNYVM.CUNY.EDU`, and he will add your name to the list.

Coordinator: Asuncion Valles
(`D3QOAVC0%EB0UB011.BITNET@CUNYVM.CUNY.EDU`)

physics
Contact: `physics-request@qedqcd.rye.ny.us` (Mike Miskulin)

Purpose: Physics is a newly created digest to cover current developments in theoretical and experimental physics. Typical topics might include particle physics, plasmaphysics, astrophysics. Discussions related to all branches (large and small) of physics are welcome.

TheoryNet
Contact: `TheoryNet@IBM.COM`

Purpose: Mailing list for theoretical computer science. The TheoryNet list now contains around 200 individuals and some 30 local mailing lists. Messages are mailed to ~90 different institutions in 10 countries.

Internet users wanting to be added to or deleted from this list should send mail to `TheoryNet-Request@IBM.COM`.

All other requests, problems, questions, etc., should be sent to `TheoryNet-Request@IBM.COM` (CSNet and Internet).

Moderator: Victor Miller (`TheoryNet-Request@IBM.COM`)

Social Science and Humanities Research
AMLIT-L
List address: `LISTSERV@UMCVMB.MISSOURI.EDU`

Description: The American Literature Discussion List has been created for the discussion of topics and issues in the vast and diverse field of American literature among a worldwide community interested in the subject. You can expect consultations, conferences, and an ongoing exchange of information among scholars and students of American literature on this list. In addition, announcements of relevant conferences and calls for papers are welcome and encouraged.

To subscribe, send a message to `listserv@umcvmb.missouri.edu`. In the body of the message, state `SUB AMLIT-L` *your full name*; for example, `SUB AMLIT-L E. Allen Poe`. If you have any questions, please contact the owner.

Owner: Michael O'Conner (`ENGMO@UMCVMB.MISSOURI.EDU`)

ANCIEN-L
List address: `LISTSERV@ULKYVM.LOUISVILLE.EDU`

Description: ANCIEN-L is a forum for debate, discussion, and the exchange of information by students and scholars of the history of the Ancient Mediterranean. ANCIEN-L is ready to distribute newsletters from study groups, and to post announcements of meetings and calls for papers, short scholarly pieces, queries, and other items of interest.

The list currently doesn't maintain a ftp directory, nor is archiving available. Hopefully, this will change in the near future. ANCIEN-L is associated with the general discussion list HISTORY and cooperates fully with other lists similarly associated.

To subscribe, send a message to `LISTSERV@ULKYVM.LOUISVILLE.EDU`. In the body of the message, state

```
SUB ANCIEN-L yourfirstname yourlastname
```

adding your full name. Postings should be made to `ANCIEN-L@ULKYVM.LOUISVILLE.EDU`.

If you have any questions, please contact the owner.

Owner: James A. Cocks (`JACOCK01@ULKYVM.LOUISVILLE.EDU`)

ANSAXNET
List address: `U47C2@WVNVM.WVNET.EDU`

Description: ANSAXNET is a SIG (Special Interest Group) for scholars of the culture and history of England before 1100 C.E. Scholars interested in the later English Middle Ages and those interested in the early medieval period throughout Europe are also encouraged to join the list.

Members receive a directory of all our members to facilitate telecommunications, and a monthly electronic report to which they are encouraged to contribute announcements and information. This report often provides members with new information about the use of computers in some aspect of their disciplines, as well as news of more conventional developments in the field. We also have projects under way to encode databases that members may use in their own work. To this end, we are now working on the details of distributing to the membership a database of all manuscripts written or owned in England before 1100. We would be glad to add your name to our directory and thus to make you a member of ANSAXNET.

Anyone who wants to be a member of ANSAXNET should send e-mail to the coordinator, including a conventional mailing address and some information about your particular interests in early medieval cultural studies.

Coordinator: Patrick W. Conner (U47C2@WVNVM.WVNET.EDU)

HISLAW-L

List address: LISTSERV@ULKYVM.LOUISVILLE.EDU

Description: HISLAW-L is a forum for debate, discussion, and the exchange of information by students and scholars of the history of the law (feudal, common, canon). HISLAW-L is ready to distribute newsletters from study groups, and to post announcements of meetings and calls for papers, short scholarly pieces, queries, and other items of interest.

The list currently doesn't maintain an ftp directory, nor is archiving available. Hopefully, this will change in the near future.

HISLAW-L is associated with the general discussion list HISTORY and cooperates fully with other lists similarly associated.

To subscribe, send a message to LISTSERV@ULKYVM.LOUISVILLE.EDU. In the body of the message, state SUB HISLAW-L *yourfirstname yourlastname*, adding your full name. Postings should be made to HISLAW-L@ULKYVM.LOUISVILLE.EDU.

If you have any questions, please contact the owner.

Owner: James A. Cocks (JACOCK01@ULKYVM.LOUISVILLE.EDU)

LANTRA-L
List address: `LANTRA-L%FINHUTC.BITNET@CUNYVM.CUNY.EDU`

Description: A forum for all aspects of translation and interpreting of natural languages including, but not restricted to, computer aids for translation and interpreting. All translators, interpreters, educators, and other people who are interested in this fascinating subject are welcome. Topics which can be discussed are

- Computer-aided translation

- Terminology

- Lexicography

- Intercultural communication

- Sociolinguistics

- Psycholinguistics

- Professional ethics for interpreters and translators

- Education and training of interpreters and translators, etc.

To add or remove yourself from the list, send a message to `LISTSERV%FINHUTC.BITNET@CUNYVM.CUNY.EDU`. The Sender of the message you send must be the name (e-mail address) you want to add or remove from the list. The text body of the message should be `SUBSCRIBE LANTRA-L` *your_full_name* or `SIGNOFF LANTRA-L`, where *your_full_name* is your normal name, not your e-mail address.

Coordinator: Helge Niska (`HNISKA%QZCOM.BITNET@CUNYVM.CUNY.EDU`)

LINGUIST
List address: `LINGUIST@UNIWA.UWA.OZ.AU`

Description: A new list has been formed that will serve as a place of discussion for those issues that concern the academic discipline of linguistics and related fields. The list, international in orientation, hopes to provide a forum for the community of linguists as they exist in different countries. Though the list is moderated and all submissions are subject to editorial discretion, it has no areal, ideological, or theoretical bent, and discussion of any linguistic subfield are welcomed. Membership of the list is open to all.

To subscribe to this list, please send a message to `LINGUIST-REQUEST@UNIWA.UWA.OZ.AU`, containing as its first and only line the following: `SUBSCRIBE LINGUIST`

Any other questions may be directed to `LINGUIST-EDITORS@UNIWA.UWA.OZ.AU`.

11

MEDIEV-L
List address: `LISTSERV@UKANVM.CC.UKANS.EDU`

Description: An unmoderated discussion list for scholars and students of the Middle Ages, which, for our present purposes, comprise the period A.D. 283-1500. Although announcements are in English, subscribers are encouraged to use the language in which they feel most comfortable.

Subscribers are reminded that discussion lists are intended to facilitate discussion rather than provide services. The benefits that participants derive from a list depends entirely on what they are willing to contribute.

To subscribe, e-mail `LISTSERV@UKANVM.CC.UKANS.EDU` with the body of the mail containing the command

```
SUB MEDIEV-L your name
```

e.g., `SUB MEDIEV-L John Doe`

MEDIEV-L discussions are not archived, but UKANVM History Lists maintains an anonymous/guest ftp site named MALIN. To reach MALIN,

```
FTP KUHUB.CC.UKANS.EDU
Userid: ANONYMOUS
Password: YOURUSERID
CD DUA9: [MALIN]
DIR
```

Updated catalogs named `MALIN.CAT` are periodically posted. MALIN invites the submission of materials that UKANVM History List subscribers consider appropriate for MALIN to maintain, and is happy, within the limits of its capacity, to serve as a repository for newsletters and similar materials. MALIN works cooperatively with ftp `ra.msstate.edu`.

MEDIEV-L@UKANVM is affiliated with the international HISTORY network and cooperates actively with all other lists similarly affiliated.

If you encounter any difficulties, contact

Jeff Gardner (`JGARDNER@UKANVM.CC.UKANS.EDU`)

Lynn Nelson (`LHNELSON@UKANVM.CC.UKANS.EDU`)

POSCIM

Contact: `UPS500@ibm.rhrz.uni-bonn.de` (Markus Schlegel)

Purpose: The Political Sciences Mailing list is intended as a forum of those researching, teaching, or studying the subject as well as the practicians of politics. As a private list, POSCIM tries to be free of the "noises" common to public lists or news groups related to politics. Exchange over research programs, results, projects, and the arrangement of special events or congresses are only a few of the various options of communication via POSCIM.

To join POSCIM, please contact

```
UPS500@ibm.rhrz.uni-bonn.de
markus@uni-bonn.de
```

RENAIS-L

List address: `LISTSERV@ULKYVM.LOUISVILLE.EDU`

Description: RENAIS-L is a forum for debate, discussion, and the exchange of information by students and scholars of the history of the Renaissance. RENAIS-L is ready to distribute newsletters from study groups and to post announcements of meetings and calls for papers, short scholarly pieces, queries, and other items of interest.

The list currently does not maintain a ftp directory, nor is archiving available. Hopefully, this will change in the near future.

RENAIS-L is associated with the general discussion list HISTORY and cooperates fully with other lists similarly associated.

To subscribe, send a message to `LISTSERV@ULKYVM.LOUISVILLE.EDU`. In the body of the message, state:

```
SUB RENAIS-L yourfirstname yourlastname
```

adding your full name. Postings should be made to RENAIS-
L@ULKYVM.LOUISVILLE.EDU.

If you have any questions, please contact the owner.

Owner: James A. Cocks (JACOCK01@ULKYVM.LOUISVILLE.EDU)

SEMIOS-L
List address: LISTSERV@ULKYVM.LOUISVILLE.EDU

Description: The list TELESI-L has been changed to SEMIOS-L, and the
scope of discussion has been expanded. SEMIOS-L is a discussion group
for those interested in semiotics, verbal and non-verbal communication,
language behavior, visual issues, and linguistics.

To subscribe, send the command SUB SEMIOS-L *Firstname Lastname* to
LISTSERV@ULKYVM.LOUISVILLE.EDU.

Owner: Steven Skaggs, S0SKAG01@ULKYVM.LOUISVILLE.EDU (same)

SLLing-L
Contact: listserv@yalevm.ycc.yale.edu

Purpose: SLLing-L (formerly ASL-LING) is for discussions of Sign
Language Linguistics.

The discussion of deaf culture, education, medical advancements in the
studies of deafness, etc., will be discouraged, except as they are pertinent
to the discussion of sign linguistics.

listserv@yalevm.ycc.yale.edu is the server. cromano@uconnvm.bitnet
(owner) and mosko@matai.vuw.ac.nz are the humans.

Note: *cromano@uconnvm.bitnet is not a valid Internet address if your site
doesn't understand BITNET addressing.*

Software Applications
apE-info
Contact: apE-info-request@ferkel.ucsb.edu (Jim Lick)

Purpose: Discussion of the scientific visualization software package apE.

biosym

Contact: `dibug-request@comp.bioz.unibas.ch` (Reinhard Doelz)

Purpose: For users of Biosym Technologies software. This includes the products InsightII, Discover, Dmol, Homology, Delphi, and Polymer. The list is not run by Biosym.

bx-talk

Contact: `bx-talk-request@qiclab.scn.rain.com` (Darci L. Chapman)

Purpose: bx-talk has been created for users of Builder Xcessory (BX) to discuss problems (and solutions!) and ideas for using BX. BX is a graphical user interface builder for Motif applications, sold by ICS. Please note that this list is not associated with ICS (the authors of BX) in any way. This list is unmoderated.

data-exp

Contact: `stein@watson.ibm.com`

Purpose: The mail list server provides an open forum for users to discuss the Visualization Data Explorer Package. It contains three files at the moment:

- FAQ—frequently asked questions

- Summary—a summary of the software, user interface, executive, data architecture

- Forum—continuing forum of questions and answers about the software

Additionally, internal forum questions and answers are also posted to it by me.

fsuucp

Contact: `fsuucp-request@polyslo.calpoly.edu` (Christopher J. Ambler)

Purpose: The FSUUCP mailing list is for the discussion, bug hunting, feature proposing, and announcements of the availability and release dates of FSUUCP, an MS-DOS UUCP/mail/news package. FSUUCP is shareware, and includes uucico/uuxqt (with support for rmail and rnews—single, batched, and compressed batch), as well as readnews, postnews, mail, expire, uuq, uusnap, uulog, and a host of utilities.

Imagine
Contact: `imagine-request@email.sp.paramax.com` (Dave Wickard)

Purpose: The IML is dedicated to the 3-D computer rendering package Imagine by Impulse Inc. Currently, this package is available on the Amiga computer and for MS-DOS. Subject matter spans most areas and packages in 3-D rendering, but mostly in comparison to Imagine. Many professional artists are using the IML, and the tone is light and friendly. All levels of knowledge and experience are welcome here, and everyone is encouraged to participate. We have held contests, and a frequently asked questions list and full archives since the list's inception in January 1991 are available on request. Merely send a note to the above address with the word `subscribe` in the subject line.

bang address
A type of e-mail address that separates host names in the address with exclamation points. Used for mail sent to the UUCP network.

Note: Bang addressing *is not supported, so please include your Internet-style quest (e.g.,* `somebody@someplace.edu`*).*

improv
Contact: `improv-request@bmt.gun.com` (Timothy Reed)

Purpose: Questions, comments, and bug reports relating to the Improv spreadsheet for NeXTSTEP and Windows, published by Lotus Corp. Some mail includes attachments that may be read with mail readers compatible with NeXT Computer's NeXTmail format.

info-gnu
Contact: `info-gnu-request@prep.ai.mit.edu`

Purpose: To distribute progress reports on the GNU Project, headed by Richard Stallman, and to ask members for various kinds of help. The list is gated both ways with the alternative news group `gnu.announce`, and is filtered (weakly moderated) by Leonard H. Tower Jr.

GNU, which stands for Gnu's Not UNIX, is the name for a complete UNIX-compatible software system whose sources can be given away free to everyone. Major parts have already been written; major parts still remain undone. Project GNU has additional mailing lists to distribute information about specific GNU programs, and to report bugs in them. Contact us at the above address for details.

Info-LabVIEW
Contact: `info-labview-request@pica.army.mil`

Purpose: Info-LabVIEW is an Internet mailing list for the discussion of the use of National Instruments' LabVIEW package for Macintosh, Windows, and Sparcstation environments. LabVIEW is a graphical software system for developing high-performance scientific and engineering applications. LabVIEW acquires data from IEEE-488 (GPIB), RS-232/422, and modular (VXI or CAMAC) instruments and plug-in data acquisition boards.

LabVIEW programs, called *virtual instruments* (VIs), are created by using icons instead of conventional, text-based code. A VI consists of a front panel and a block diagram. The front panel (with knobs, switches, graphs, and so on) is the user interface. The block diagram, which is the executable code, consists of icons that operate on data connected by wires that pass data between them.

The list is being run as a simple redistribution of all submitted messages. ftp archives are on `ftp.pica.army.mil`, `/pub/labview`.

intergraph
Contact: `nik@ingr.ingr.com`

Purpose: Discussion of all Intergraph CADCAM software and hardware. This mailing list is a bidirectional gateway to `alt.sys.intergraph`.

khoros
Contact: `khoros-request@chama.unm.edu`

Purpose: To discuss the khoros software package, developed by Dr. Rasure, his staff, and his students at the University of New Mexico. Khoros is an integrated software development environment for information processing and visualization, based on X11R4.

Matlab
Contact: `matlab-users-request@mcs.anl.gov` (Chris Bischof)

Purpose: Discussion group for users and potential users of the MATLAB numeric computation software from The MathWorks. MATLAB is an interactive matrix-oriented product for linear algebra, digital signal processing, equation solving, control system design, and other engineering and scientific applications. This mail group is administered by the independent MATLAB User Group.

next-gis

Contact: `sstaton@deltos.com` (Steven R. Staton)

`listserv@deltos.com` (send SUBSCRIBE *name* message to join)

Purpose: Discussion of GIS and cartographic-related topics on the NeXT and other workstation computers. Some moderated reposting of `comp.infosys.gis` occurs as well.

nqthm-users

Contact: `nqthm-users-request@cli.com`

`nqthm-users-request@inf.fu-berlin.de`

Purpose: Discussion of theorem proving using the Boyler-Moore theorem prover, NQTHM. Offers lore, advice, information, discussion, help, and a few flames.

pcgeos-list

Contact: `listserv@pandora.sf.ca.us`

Purpose: Discussion forum for users or potential users of PC/GEOS products, including GeoWorks Ensemble, GeoWorks Pro, GeoWorks POS, and third-party products. Topics include general information, tips, techniques, applications, experiences, etc.

Word-Mac

Contact: `word-mac-request@alsvid.une.edu.au` (Roger Debrecency)

Purpose: Word-Mac is a mailing list dedicated to serving users of the Microsoft Word package in its various versions on the Apple Macintosh platform. The list is available in digest form, and archives of all digests are available by anonymous ftp from `/pub/archives/word-mac/digests` on `alsvid.une.edu.au`. Gopher access is also available by pointing your gopher to `alsvid.une.edu.au` (port 70).

To subscribe, mail to `listserv@alsvid.une.edu.au` with the text `subscribe word-mac` *your_first_name your_surname* in the body of the e-mail.

11

Student Information

LAWSCH

List address: `LAWSCH-L%AUVM.BITNET@VM1.NODAK.EDU`

Description: A forum to discuss matters of concern that affect all law students. It's also designed to allow for interaction between students and law schools to lessen the gap between them. The list is based at American University Law School.

To subscribe, send the command `SUB LAWSCH-L` *your_full_name* (where *your_full_name* is your real name, not your login ID) in the body of a message to `LISTSERV%AUVM.BITNET@VM1.NODAK.EDU`.

Coordinator: Ed Kania (`EKANIA%AUVM.BITNET@VM1.NODAK.EDU`)

Meteorology Students

Contact: `dennis@metw3.met.fu-berlin.de`

Purpose: A new mailing list has been created. It is open to everyone but particularly intended as a communication facility for meteorology students. At the moment, 20 people from three continents subscribe to the list.

Beside the usual chatting, subjects of discussion could be student-related topics such as scholarships, summer schools, conferences, and conditions of studying meteorology at a particular university. There is also the option to ask the community for help in meteorology-related questions. There are freshman as well as grad students who will be available to answer your questions in this field.

If enough people are interested, we could organize a kind of project, too.

So that members can get to know each other, a short questionnaire is available. Although no obligation exists to fill it out, it would be nice if all new subscribers would at least answer the basic questions about their name, address, and university. New answered forms are posted to the list; old ones are available on request.

Administrative mail such as subscription or questionnaire requests should be sent to `dennis@metw3.met.fu-berlin.de`.

Although the list is situated in Germany, the language is English, of course. I hope for strong participation.

PSYCGRAD
List address: PSYCGRAD@ACADVM1.UOTTAWA.CA

Description: Now, graduate students of psychology can communicate among each other efficiently and free of charge because of a list on the Listserv called PSYCGRAD (Psychology Graduate Students Discussion Group List). Its main purpose is to provide a medium through which graduate students in the field of psychology can communicate.

If you are studying in a graduate-level psychology program, you are invited to join this list. It is asked that conversation topics be relevant to being a graduate student in psychology. As you probably can see, this is a very open category and not too rigorously defined. Virtually, anything goes except junk-mail advertisements. (Junk mail has been a terrible problem for many users in the past.) The list will not be moderated and subscriptions are open. Corporations, businesses, agencies, publishers, etc., are not invited to the list.

To subscribe, mail the command SUB PSYCGRAD *Yourfirstname Yourlastname* to LISTSERV@ACADVM1.UOTTAWA.CA (don't forget to capitalize and lowercase *Yourfirstname* and *Yourlastname*).

Owner: Matthew Simpson (054340@ACADVM1.UOTTAWA.CA)

SGANet
List address: SGANET%VTVM1.BITNET@CUNYVM.CUNY.EDU

Description: SGANet, developed and implemented at Virginia Polytechnic Institute and State University, is an international mailing network for student government associations, student representative councils, student parliaments, etc., to use in discussing issues faced by such organizations worldwide.

SGANet is easy to use and will be the host of many interesting discussions that will be of great interest to your organization. SGANet is open to any student government association at any university worldwide.

SGANet is an automated mailing list located at Virginia Tech. Let's say, for example, that a student government association from a university in Australia wants to share some of the issues it's working on. The group would simply write its article and send it via mail to one of the addresses above. SGANet then receives its mail and sends copies of it to every organization on the list. There is no limit to mail usage, and anyone on the list can submit an article for distribution. It's that simple, and it's very low in cost—in many cases, *free*.

To become a member of SGANet, send the following message to `LISTSERV%VTMV1.BITNET@CUNYVM.CUNY.EDU`:

```
subscribe SGANet Your organization's full name
```

You will receive acknowledgment and instructions on receipt of your subscription.

Send articles, comments, anecdotes, etc., to `SGANet%VTMV1.BITNET@CUNYVM.CUNY.EDU`. They will be automatically sent to everyone on the list. This allows for really good interactive discussions.

SNURSE-L

List address: `LISTSERV@UBVM.CC.BUFFALO.EDU`

Description: This list has been established as an effort to initiate undergraduate nursing students to a world of electronic health data.

SNURSE-L has a number of different goals lined up:

- The collection and processing of health data
- Discussion of trends and issues in nursing
- Enhanced communication between undergraduate student nurses
- An area for communication among nursing student leaders

Any users who want to join this list should send the following command to `LISTSERV@UBVM.CC.BUFFALO.EDU` via e-mail as the first line in the body of the mail message (not the subject line):

```
SUB SNURSE-L your full name (for example: SUB SNURSE-L Jane Doe)
```

Send the `HELP` or `INFO` commands to `LISTSERV@UBVM.CC.BUFFALO.EDU` for more information.

Owner: Dan Fisher, senior BSN student (`FISHERD@SCSUD.CTSTATEU.EDU`)

ugrad-forum

Contact: `ugrad-forum@yorku.ca`

11

Purpose: An electronic mail server aimed at undergraduates in any discipline anywhere in the world! This mail server (mailing list) is intended to provide an international and interdisciplinary forum for undergraduates to discuss topics of interest and concern to them.

Please note that this mail server is not an IBM-style listserv. Any administrative business (subscribe, unsubscribe) dealing with this mail server should be mailed to `ugrad-forum-request@yorku.ca`, where it will be dealt with by a human. Please include your name and e-mail address in the body of your message as the following example shows:

```
JDoe@school.edu (Jane Doe)
```

Postings to forum participants are made by e-mailing to

```
ugrad-forum@yorku.ca
```

When you make a posting, please keep in mind and respect that you are in conversation with other people. At present, this forum is unmoderated, meaning that all postings are sent to everyone—uncensored. All postings are automatically archived and, from time to time, will be made available via anonymous ftp (file transfer protocol).

It is always good practice to include your signature at the end of your message, as it can be difficult sometimes to glean a sender's address from the mail header alone. This will also facilitate the spawning of private conversations, which may not be of interest to all members of the forum.

Owner: Ian Lumb (`ian@vortex.yorku.ca`)
Earth and Atmospheric Science, York University
North York, Ontario M3J 1P3, Canada
Voice: (416) 736-5245; *Fax:* (416) 736-5817

XCULT-L
List address: `XCULT-L%PSUVM.BITNET@CUNYVM.CUNY.EDU`

Description: An international, intercultural newsletter written by undergraduate and graduate students at Penn State University who are enrolled in Speech Communication 497B: Cross-cultural Communication. Each week, students write on a topic being discussed in class. Topics range from non-dominant cultures in the U.S. to corporate cultures to the use of non-verbal communication in international communication. Participants who receive the newsletter are encouraged to join in the discussions or contribute their own topics and issues.

To subscribe, either send a note to the editor or subscribe directly by sending a mail message with the command subscribe XCULT–L Your Full Name to LISTSERV%PSUVM.BITNET@CUNYVM.CUNY.EDU.

Editor: Joyce Neu (JN0%PSUVM.BITNET@CUNYVM.CUNY.EDU)

Chapter 12

Other Internet Resources

This chapter contains a number of other resources available on the
Internet, including access to on-line library catalogs, on-line books,
on-line newsletters and journals, and BBS resources. There is no
central repository for most of this information—you have to find it
in other lists that currently exist. One of the best places to look for
information about available resources is to read the USENET news
group `alt.internet.services`, if you have access to it.

On-Line Library Catalogs

A large number of libraries are accessible from the Internet. Many of
them are university libraries, but some are public libraries. If you search
an on-line catalog and find a book or other resource you are interested
in, you probably can arrange an interlibrary loan through your university
or public library.

Access method:	telnet access.usask.ca (128.233.3.1)
Log in:	hytelnet
or	telnet info.ccit.arizona.edu (129.196.76.201)
Log in:	hytelnet
or	telnet laguna.epcc.edu (192.94.29.3)
Log in:	library

Description: The hytelnet servers (additional ones are available in other
countries) provide links to many libraries and other information services

around the world. hytelnet is an easy-to-use, menu-driven way to explore many of the Internet's resources. Services provided include library catalogs, other resources (such as archie, electronic books, and others), an Internet glossary, and help on the library catalogs. This resource is very valuable for new Internet users!

Access method: `telnet liberty.uc.wlu.edu (137.113.10.35)`

> *Log in:* `lawlib`

or `gopher liberty.uc.wlu.edu`

or `ftp liberty.uc.wlu.edu`
`cd /pub/lawlib`

Description: Run by Washington and Lee University, this site is very well run and set up. It not only provides access to W & L's law library (with a very large amount of information on-line), but also has connections to a great number of other libraries and information sources on the Internet. The Gopher interface is easier to work with, but the telnet interface is usable also, if you don't have access to Gopher.

Access method: `ftp ariel.unm.edu (129.24.8.1)`
`get file /library/internet.library`

Description: This document lists all the libraries accessible from the Internet. It is very large (more than 8,800 lines) and should be viewed on-line if possible—it's too big to print easily!

Access method: `telnet marvel.loc.gov (140.147.2.69)`

> *Log in:* `marvel`

or `gopher marvel.loc.gov`

Description: This site, run by the Library of Congress, has information about the library, Congress, the federal government, and copyright and employee information. It also has the Global Electronic Library, with information on subjects such as library science, philosophy and religion, the arts, social sciences, law, economics, and others.

Access method: `telnet nessie.cc.wwu.edu (140.160.240.11)`

> *Log in:* `LIBS`

Description: This site has menus of on-line library catalogs organized by state (and country, for non-U.S. libraries). From the state and country menus, you can connect to any of the libraries listed.

Access method: `telnet pac.carl.org` (192.54.81.128)

       Log in: Enter **PAC** at the prompt on the initial screen, and then enter your terminal type (you may want to try vt100, one of the most common types, if you don't know your terminal type).

Description: This site, known as CARL, the Colorado Association of Research Libraries, allows open access to several features (some can be used only by registered users). The open access features include access to the catalogs of libraries in Colorado and a number of other states, and access to UNCOVER, a catalog of the contents of almost 14,000 journals.

12

Bulletin Board Systems

A number of BBS systems on the Internet allow anyone to connect to them. Some of these systems provide access to discussion groups for specific topics, but most of them provide access to databases or information.

Agriculture

Several different services offer agricultural information on the Internet. Some services are weather- and crop-related, whereas others provide information related to health.

Access method: `telnet caticsuf.csufresno.edu` (129.8.100.15)

       Log in: `super`

Description: This service, the Advanced Technology Information Network, provides information about agriculture and biotechnology. It is located in California, so the information is somewhat biased toward that area, but it's useful for people in other areas also. Information offered includes daily agricultural market reports; weather, labor, and job reports; safety information; and event schedules.

Access method: `telnet psupen.psu.edu` (128.118.36.4)

       Log in: `state code`

Description: This service, PENpages, is provided by Penn State University. It provides access to agricultural prices and commodity reports, as well as USDA and 4-H information. Also available is the International Food & Nutrition Database, as well as a rich assortment of weather information.

Calculators

Access method: telnet hpcvbbs.cv.hp.com (192.6.221.13)

  Log in: new

Description: This bulletin board system is for owners of Hewlett-Packard calculators. It features conferences with information and programs for HP calculators, plus real-time conversations with other HP users.

Databases

Access method: telnet columbia.ilc.com (198.242.1.100)

  Log in: cas

Description: The ILC server provides a search and purchase database for books, VHS video cassettes, music CDs, laser discs, and UNIX software. You must have a verified account to order merchandise, but browsing the database is open to anyone.

Access method: telnet holonet.net (157.151.0.1)

  Log in: cdc

Description: This system provides an on-line search and purchase database for compact discs of all types. If you have a credit card, you can order discs.

Access method: telnet nessie.cc.wwu.edu (140.160.240.11)

  Log in: LIBS

Description: This sitehas menus that let you access various Internet databases. The menus are organized by topic (much like this chapter is).

Geography

Access method: telnet martini.eecs.umich.edu 3000 (141.212.99.9)

Description: This server holds U.S. Geological Survey and U.S. Postal Service information about U.S. cities, counties, and states. You can perform searches by ZIP code or city name, and the server returns information such as population data, latitude, longitude, ZIP code, and so on.

Access method: telnet glis.cr.usgs.gov (152.61.192.54)

Log in: guest

Description: The Global Land Information System offers land use maps of the United States, along with graphs and data. Using a PC client or an X Window client, you can display maps and information on your local system.

Government

Access method: telnet fedix.fie.com (192.111.228.33)

Description: The Federal Information Exchange offers information on federal opportunities, minority college and university capabilities, and higher education opportunities for minorities and women.

Access method: telnet fdabbs.fda.gov (150.148.8.48)

Log in: bbs

Description: This site, run by the Food and Drug Administration, contains information about drug enforcement reports, drug and device approvals, the center for devices and radiological health, current information about AIDS, the FDA consumer magazine index (with selected articles), and other information. You can search the FDA files for summaries of FDA information and also retrieve the text of testimony at FDA congressional hearings. Even veterinary medicine news is available.

History

Several different servers provide information of interest to historians. Information about the history of the United States, as well as the rest of the world, is represented.

Access method: telnet ukanaix.cc.ukans.edu (129.237.33.1)

Log in: history

Description: The University of Kansas HNSource is a central information server for historians. From the main menu, you can get information on ftp sites with historical information and databases, information about discussion lists, and bibliographic information.

Access method: `telnet clus1.ulcc.ac.uk` (192.12.72.60)

      Log in: `ihr-uk`

   Password: `ihr-uk`

Description: This site gives on-line resources for historians in the London, England, area, as well as on-line resources for historians in the United Kingdom and the rest of the world. It uses a well-organized hypertext system to let you locate resources and information easily.

Mathematics

Access method: `telnet e-math.ams.com` (130.44.1.100)

      Log in: `e-math`

   Password: `e-math`

Description: This site is run by the American Mathematics Society to provide an electronic forum for AMS members and others interested in mathematics. Topics include mathematical publications, mathematical preprints, mathematical discussion lists and bulletin boards, general information of interest to mathematicians, and professional information for mathematicians.

Seismology

Access method: `telnet geophys.washington.edu` (128.95.16.50)

      Log in: `quake`

   Password: `quake`

Description: This server gives recent earthquake information, reported by the USGS National Earthquake Information Center or by the University of Washington. Information includes the date, time, and magnitude of the earthquake, and the latitude, longitude, and *Description* of the location.

Access method: `telnet bison.cc.buffalo.edu` (128.205.2.22)

                select `INDX` followed by `QKLN`

Description: This site offers the NCEER Quakeline Earthquake resource database. You can search for information on earthquakes, earthquake engineering, natural hazards mitigation, and related topics.

Space

Space flight in general—and information from NASA in particular—has been extremely popular on the Internet for quite a few years. Many NASA sites are directly on the Internet; the sites listed here are only a sampling of the ones available.

Access method: `telnet spacelink.msfc.nasa.gov (192.149.89.61)`

Description: This site, run by NASA, provides the latest NASA news. It includes schedules of space shuttle launches and information about satellites and other topics. You are asked for information and assigned a login name and password that you can use for future login sessions.

Access method: `telnet stinfo.hq.eso.org (134.171.8.4)`

    Log in: `stinfo`

Description: This site is run by the European Space Organization and provides status reports on the Hubble space telescope and European HST news.

Access method: `telnet lpi.jsc.nasa.gov (192.101.147.11)`

    Log in: `envnet`

    Password: `henniker`

Description: This site, run by the NASA Lunar and Planetary Institute (LPI), contains information about the LPI, including the Lunar and Planetary Bibliography database, the image retrieval and processing system (IRPS), and the Mars exploration bulletin board system.

Access method: `telnet ned.ipac.caltech.edu (134.4.10.119)`

    Log in: `ned`

Description: This site offers access to the NASA Extragalactic Database. It provides search capabilities into the database of more than 200,000 astronomical objects and information about astronomical publications.

Stock Market Reports

Access method: `telnet a2i.rahul.net (192.160.13.1)`

      Log in: `guest`

      select n and set your terminal characteristics
(you are prompted for this information)

Description: This site is an Internet access provider and has many interesting items available. The stock market reports are under the current system information menu. Other information is also available about the Internet and the A2I site.

Weather

Everyone is interested in the weather, and you can find out current weather information at several sites on the Internet. Weather maps, forecasts, and historical data are among the data you can find.

Access method: `telnet exnet.iastate.edu (129.186.20.200)`

      Log in: `flood`

Description: This server, run by the Iowa State University Extension, contains articles on flooding and dealing with the results of floods. The server allows you to read or download the information.

Access method: `telnet downwind.sprl.umich.edu 3000`

      or   `telnet 141.212.196.177 3000`

Description: This server, running at port 3000 on the listed site, returns the current forecast for given cities. If you know the city code for the desired location, you can enter it at the prompt; otherwise, you should press Enter and use the menu system. Other information available are a national weather summary, ski conditions, and severe weather and hurricane advisories.

Access method: `telnet wind.atmos.uah.edu 3000`

      or   `telnet 146.229.8.2 3000`

Description: This server is similar to the preceding `downwind` site, but it doesn't have the initial prompt for your city code. In addition to the general information available from the `downwind` site, the `wind` server allows access to the "wx" weather system, which can display weather maps and other information on your local computer if you are running the X Window system.

On-Line Journals and Newsletters

The entries in this section are similar to the listings in Chapter 11, "Mailing Lists," in that some of the entries were taken from the two lists used in Chapter 11 (the Publicly Accessible Mailing List maintained by Stephanie da Silva and Chuq Von Rospach, and the Special Interest Groups list available via anonymous ftp on `ftp.nisc.sri.com` in `netinfo/interest-groups`). Although the entries in Chapter 11 have two different formats (depending on which list they were taken from), all the entries in the following list have been made to conform to the same format:

List Name
List address: The subscription address.

Description: The purpose of the list. The **_Description_** may provide the location and availability of any archives and often explains how to subscribe to the newsletter.

Coordinator/Owner: The person who maintains the list.

Note: *Many addresses are shown all uppercase, or with initial caps. In all probability, all lowercase entries will work, but you may want to type the capitalization exactly as given; this is how the entries appeared in the on-line list.*

To subscribe to some of the journals, you only need to contact the list maintainer to be added to the distribution. For other entries (mainly, those that use the LISTSERV software), you send messages to software that automatically does whatever your message requested (subscribes you, unsubscribes you, and so forth). Instructions for subscribing to these newsletters are given as part of the newsletter **_Description_**.

If the directions given in the **_Description_** don't work for you, try to send mail to the list coordinator/owner to explain that you want to receive the journal but are having problems.

In the listings, words in *italic* indicate a placeholder, which you need to replace with the proper name for your situation.

Note: *Some entries have been edited for clarity and content.*

CATALYST
List address: LISTSERV@VTVM1.CC.VT.EDU

Description: *CATALYST*, a refereed print journal that has been serving community college educators for more than 20 years, is distributed as an electronic journal in addition to its print version. Subscriptions to the electronic version of the journal are now available free of charge via BITNET and the Internet, according to Dr. Darrel A. Clowes, editor of the journal and faculty member at Virginia Polytechnic Institute and State University.

The quarterly journal is published by the National Council on Community Services and Continuing Education, an affiliate council of the American Association of Community, Junior and Technical Colleges. The journal is being made available in its electronic form by the Scholarly Communications Project of Virginia Tech.

Initiated in 1971, *CATALYST* is the second oldest continuously published journal in the community college field. It publishes practitioner-oriented articles on practices in continuing/community education as delivered by community colleges, including papers on research in the field. *CATALYST* currently is distributed in print form to dues-paying members of the Council, as a benefit of their membership, and to libraries and other non-members at subscription prices of $20 per year in the U.S., $25 outside the U.S.

To subscribe to the electronic journal, send the command SUBSCRIBE CATALYST *first name last name* by electronic mail to the address LISTSERV@VTVM1.CC.VT.EDU. Electronic subscribers will receive instructions on how to order a list of available articles, to retrieve the full text of those articles, and to cancel their subscriptions.

Electronic subscribers, in addition to having access to past issues of the journal, will be sent the tables of contents of future issues as those issues are published; the subscribers then may order full text by electronic mail of any and all articles they want to read. Now, all articles from issue numbers 3 and 4 of volume 21 (1991) are available on-line. Consideration will be given to adding all articles from the remaining back issues to the archive.

Coordinator: For further information, contact Lon Savage (SAVAGE@VTVM1.CC.VT.EDU).

DECnews-EDU

List address: LISTSERV@ubvm.cc.buffalo.edu

Description: DECNEWS for Education and Research is a monthly electronic publication from Digital Equipment Corporation's Education Business Unit for the education and research communities worldwide.

To subscribe, send a message to LISTSERV@ubvm.cc.buffalo.edu. The message should be this command:

```
SUB DECNEWS Firstname Lastname (e.g. SUB DECNEWS John Jones)
```

The command is the text of your message; the subject is ignored by LISTSERV.

Coordinator: Anne Marie McDonald (decnews@mr4dec.enet.dec.com)

DECnews-UNIX

List address: decnews-unix@pa.dec.com

Description: DECnews for UNIX—published electronically by Digital Equipment Corporation for Internet distribution every three weeks—contains product and service information of interest to the Digital UNIX community.

To subscribe, send mail to decnews-unix@pa.dec.com with a subject line of subscribe abstract. Please include your name and telephone number in the body of the subscription request.

Coordinator: Russ Jones (decnews-unix-request@pa.dec.com)

decuserve-journal

List address: frey@eisner.decus.org

Description: An alternative method of distribution for the DECUServe Journal, a monthly digest of technical discussions that take place on the DECUS conferencing system. The Journal (and list) is open to anyone who is interested in Digital Equipment topics, "third-party" topics, and connectivity topics.

Contact: Sharon Frey (frey@eisner.decus.org)

Earth and Sky
List address: Majordomo@lists.utexas.edu

Description: This is a weekly on-line publication for the public to learn more about earth science and astronomy. It consists of transcripts of radio programs aired daily on the Earth & Sky Radio Series, which is hosted by Deborah Byrd and Joel Block. The series broadcasts on more than 500 stations in the United States and on a variety of other stations across the globe. For more info, write to Earth & Sky at P.O. Box 2203, Austin, TX 78768.

To add yourself to the EARTHANDSKY mailing list, send

    subscribe EARTHANDSKY *yourname@host.domain.name*

in an e-mail message to

    Majordomo@lists.utexas.edu

HOTT
List address: listserv@ucsd.edu

Description: HOTT is a monthly electronic newsletter that provides summaries of articles on technological advances from a number of different sources, including news magazines, trade magazines, business magazines, and some USENET news groups and Internet mailing lists. It also contains information about upcoming technical conferences and trade shows, lists of newly published technical books, and interviews.

To subscribe, send a mail message to listserv@ucsd.edu. Leave the Subject: line blank. In the body of the message, type **SUBSCRIBE HOTT-LIST**. Don't include your first or last name following this command.

This list is managed with automated software. If you need to get in touch with a human, contact hott@ucsd.edu.

Editor-in-chief: David Scott Lewis (d.s.lewis@ieee.org)

IBJ-L
List address: IBJ-L@poniecki.berkeley.edu

Description: The Internet Business Journal Distribution List is now accepting subscribers. This LISTSERV list distributes the electronic text

of The Internet Business Journal, under the sponsorship of the
Wladyslaw Poniecki Foundation.

The electronic version contains only the table of contents, article
abstracts, editorial, letter from the publisher, and the column "Access—
Ability" (by Dr. Norm Coombs). This e-version is freely available in low
ASCII text and will soon be available as a PostScript file. The IBJ e-version
will also be available via ftp and Gopher.

To subscribe to the Internet Business Journal Distribution List, send the
command

```
SUB IBJ-L your name
```

to `listserv@poniecki.berkeley.edu`

Send the command in the *body* of the mail message, not in the subject
line. Replace `your name` with your full name.

Subscribers to IBJ-L will receive notice of new table of content/abstract
editions, new on-line documents relevant to the business community,
and related information. There is no subscription fee for IBJ-L.

Note: *IBJ-L isn't a conversational list. Only the list owner will post to IBJ-L.*

IBJ-L is intended to be very low volume in the number of postings. General informational items, press releases, conference announcements, and
so forth *won't* be posted. Items that inform subscribers of new Internet
business community resources, services, and on-line documents *will* be
announced through IBJ-L.

IBJ-L will archive unique resources relevant to the business community,
but won't mirror (duplicate) resources already available elsewhere via the
Internet.

Queries regarding IBJ-L should be sent to

> Michael Strangelove, Publisher
> The Internet Business Journal
> *Internet address:* `441495@Acadvm1.Uottawa.CA`
> *CompuServe:* 72302,3062
> *S-Mail:* 177 Waller, Ottawa, Ontario, K1N 6N5 CANADA
> *Voice:* (613) 747-0642
> *Fax:* (613) 564-6641

InterText

List address: intertxt@network.ucsd.edu (Jason Snell)

Description: InterText is a bimonthly fiction magazine with more than 1,000 subscribers worldwide. InterText publishes in two formats: straight ASCII and PostScript (for PostScript-compatible laser printers). For more information, to ask about subscribing, or for submission guidelines, mail to intertxt@network.ucsd.edu. Back issues may be ftp-ed from network.ucsd.edu, in the /intertext directory.

MEDNEWS

List address: MEDNEWS%ASUACAD.BITNET@CUNYVM.CUNY.EDU

Description: The MEDNEWS LISTSERV list is for distribution of the Health Info-Com Network medical newsletter. Distributed weekly, it contains the latest MMWR from the Center for Disease Control, weekly AIDS statistics, FDA bulletins, medical news from the United Nations, and other assorted medical news items. Submissions for the newsletter are welcome; please contact the editor if you have any questions or news-letter submissions.

To subscribe, send the following command via e-mail to LISTSERV%ASUACAD.BITNET@CUNYVM.CUNY.EDU (with the command in the message body): SUBSCRIBE MEDNEWS *Your_Full_Name* (where *Your_Full_Name* is your real name, not your userid). To unsubscribe, send UNSUBSCRIBE MEDNEWS.

Editor: David Dodell (ATW1H%ASUACAD.BITNET@CUNYVM.CUNY.EDU)

navnews

List address: navnews@nctamslant.navy.mil

Description: E-mail distribution list for the weekly Navy News Service (NAVNEWS), published by the Navy Internal Relations Activity in Washington. NAVNEWS contains official news and information about fleet operations and exercises, personnel policies, budget actions, and more. This is the same news service distributed through Navy circuits to ships at sea and to shore commands around the world. Subscriptions to NAVNEWS by e-mail are available at no charge to anyone with a mailbox on any network reachable through the Internet.

NNEWS

List address: `LISTSERV@vm1.NoDak.edu`

Description: Network News is an on-line newsletter focusing on library and information resources on the Internet. It updates the information found in "A Guide to Internet/Bitnet."

Send subscription requests/cancellations to `listserv@vm1.nodak.edu`. In the *body* of the message, type

```
subscribe nnews firstname lastname
```

to subscribe (for example: `subscribe nnews Melvyl Dewey`), or to cancel subscription, `unsubscribe nnews`.

Back issues of the newsletter and the latest version of "A Guide to Internet/Bitnet" are available in the archive. Send the following command to get a list of what's available:

```
index nnews
```

Owner: Dana Noonan (`noonan@msus1.msus.edu`)

PSYCOLOQUY

List address: `PSYC@PUCC.PRINCETON.EDU`

Description: PSYCOLOQUY is a refereed electronic journal sponsored by the American Psychological Association. It contains newsletter-type materials (announcements, conferences, employment notices, abstracts, queries) and short articles refereed by the Editorial Board, as well as refereed interdisciplinary and international commentaries on the articles ("Scholarly Skywriting"). The newsletter sections aren't archived, but the refereed journal sections are available by anonymous ftp from directory `/pub harnad` at `princeton.edu` (128.112.128.1).

To subscribe, send to `LISTERV@pucc.princeton.edu` the following one-line message (no subject header): `SUBSCRIBE PSYC` *`Youruserid@Yournode.Yourdomain Firstname Lastname`*. If this procedure is unsuccessful, you may write to `harnad@princeton.edu` to have your name added manually to the list. PSYCOLOQUY is also available as the moderated USENET news group `sci.psychology.digest`.

Coordinator: Stevan Harnad, PSYCOLOQUY co-editor (`psyc@pucc.princeton.edu`)

PSYGRD-J

List address: LISTSERV@ACADVM1.UOTTAWA.CA

Description: The PSYCGRAD Journal (PSYGRD-J)—the Psychology Graduate Student Journal—is a electronic journal in the field of psychology. The purpose of the journal is to publish, from the graduate student perspective, professional-level articles in the field of psychology. The PSYCGRAD Journal is primarily published and written by graduate students in psychology. It is targeted for anyone interested in the field of psychology.

Volumes of the journal are each compiled by a member of an editing team. Each member is responsible for a specific topic area. All submissions are subject to the editing process. Subscriptions are open to the public.

The Psychology Graduate Student Journal is part of a larger system, called The PSYCGRAD Project. The project is broken into two main functions: graduate student discussion and communication, and graduate student publication. Related lists are

- PSYCGRAD@UOTTAWA (Psychology Graduate Students Discussion List)

- PSYGRD-D@UOTTAWA (The PSYCGRAD Digest)

To subscribe to PSYGRD-J, send e-mail to LISTSERV@ACADVM1.UOTTAWA.CA with the body containing the command

```
SUB PSYGRD-J Yourfirstname Yourlastname
```

After you subscribe, postings to the project can be sent to PSYCGRAD@ACADVM1.UOTTAWA.CA.

Owner: Matthew Simpson (054340@acadvm1.uottawa.ca)

Quanta

List address: da1n@andrew.cmu.edu

Description: Quanta is an electronically distributed magazine of science fiction. Published monthly, each issue contains short fiction, articles, and editorials by authors around the world and across the net. Quanta publishes in two formats: straight ASCII and PostScript (for PostScript-compatible printers). To subscribe to Quanta, or just to get more info, send mail.

TIDBITS

List address: `LISTSERV@RICEVM1.RICE.EDU`

Description: The TIDBITS list is a one-way list for receiving the TidBITS weekly electronic newsletter. TidBITS reports on the most interesting events and products of the week in the (micro)computer industry, with an emphasis on the world of the Macintosh. Issues are released early each week and are occasionally supplemented by special issues focusing on a single topic or product.

In addition, TidBITS issues are formatted in the straight-text "setext" format, which ensures optimal on-line readability and the capability to decode and import the issues into specially written browsers. These browsers are in progress on several different platforms by various different people around the world.

For more information, send e-mail to `info@tidbits.halcyon.com`, and a file will be returned to you promptly.

To subscribe, send the following command in the body of mail (*not* the subject) to `LISTSERV@RICEVM1.RICE.EDU`:

```
SUB TIDBITS yourfirstname yourlastname
```

Owner: Mark R. Williamson (`MARK@RICEVM1.BITNET`)

Note: This isn't a valid Internet address if your site doesn't understand BITNET addressing.

Editor: Adam C. Engst (`ace@tidbits.halcyon.com`)

Books

Although a large number of library catalogs are on-line, the number of available on-line books (full text) is relatively small. The sites in this section give you access to some of the books that have been put on-line.

Access method: `ftp mrcnext.cso.uiuc.edu` (128.174.201.12)

    `cd /pub/etext`

Description: This site maintains an archive of the Project Gutenberg files. Project Gutenberg is aimed at producing 10,000 of the most widely read books in electronic form. Some of the books already available at this site are *Alice in Wonderland, The CIA World Fact Book, Roget's Thesaurus, and Moby Dick.*

Access method: telnet library.dartmouth.edu (129.170.16.11)

Description: The Dartmouth library server offers the capability to search for text in several on-line literary works. Use the command connect dante to search through Dante's *Divine Comedy.* Use the command select file bible to search the Bible. The commands select file s plays and select file s sonnets allow you to search Shakespeare's plays and sonnets, respectively.

Access method: ftp wuarchive.wustl.edu (128.252.135.4)
                       cd /doc/bible

Description: Complete editions of the King James Bible, including cross references, are available for the IBM PC and Macintosh computers under this directory. You probably want to get the README file first to understand how to use the files.

Access method: ftp quake.think.com (192.31.181.1)
                       cd /pub/etext/koran

Description: This directory contains an electronically scanned version of M.H. Shakir's translation of the Holy Qur'an, as published by Tahrike Tarsile Qur'an, Inc. There are files for each chapter, and you can retrieve each one individually.

Access method: ftp nic.funet.fi (128.214.6.100)
                       cd /pub/doc/bible/hebrew

Description: This directory contains the Torah from the Tanach in Hebrew, the Prophets from the Tanach in Hebrew, and the Writings from the Tanach in Hebrew. Also included is a program to display Hebrew letters on an IBM PC monitor and a Hebrew quiz with biblical Hebrew-language tutor.

Note: *This last site is in Europe, so you may want to limit your file transfers somewhat.*

Index

Symbols

A

GO AHEAD. PLUG YOURSELF INTO
PRENTICE HALL COMPUTER PUBLISHING.

Introducing the PHCP Forum on CompuServe®

Yes, it's true. Now, you can have CompuServe access to the same professional, friendly folks who have made computers easier for years. On the PHCP Forum, you'll find additional information on the topics covered by every PHCP imprint—including Que, Sams Publishing, New Riders Publishing, Alpha Books, Brady Books, Hayden Books, and Adobe Press. In addition, you'll be able to receive technical support and disk updates for the software produced by Que Software and Paramount Interactive, a division of the Paramount Technology Group. It's a great way to supplement the best information in the business.

WHAT CAN YOU DO ON THE PHCP FORUM?

Play an important role in the publishing process—and make our books better while you make your work easier:

- Leave messages and ask questions about PHCP books and software—you're guaranteed a response within 24 hours
- Download helpful tips and software to help you get the most out of your computer
- Contact authors of your favorite PHCP books through electronic mail
- Present your own book ideas
- Keep up to date on all the latest books available from each of PHCP's exciting imprints

JOIN NOW AND GET A FREE COMPUSERVE STARTER KIT!

To receive your free CompuServe Introductory Membership, call toll-free, **1-800-848-8199** and ask for representative **#597**. The Starter Kit Includes:

- Personal ID number and password
- $15 credit on the system
- Subscription to CompuServe Magazine

HERE'S HOW TO PLUG INTO PHCP:

Once on the CompuServe System, type any of these phrases to access the PHCP Forum:

GO PHCP
GO QUEBOOKS
GO SAMS
GO NEWRIDERS
GO ALPHA

GO BRADY
GO HAYDEN
GO QUESOFT
GO PARAMOUNTINTER

Once you're on the CompuServe Information Service, be sure to take advantage of all of CompuServe's resources. CompuServe is home to more than 1,700 products and services—plus it has over 1.5 million members worldwide. You'll find valuable online reference materials, travel and investor services, electronic mail, weather updates, leisure-time games and hassle-free shopping (no jam-packed parking lots or crowded stores).

Seek out the hundreds of other forums that populate CompuServe. Covering diverse topics such as pet care, rock music, cooking, and political issues, you're sure to find others with the sames concerns as you—and expand your knowledge at the same time.

Excel—Only from the Experts at Que

Using Excel Version 5 for Windows, Special Edition

Ron Person

Version 5 for Windows

$29.95 USA

1-56529-459-9, 1,120 pp.

Easy Excel

Trudi Reisner

Version 5

$19.95 USA

1-56529-540-4, 256 pp.

I Hate Excel, 2nd Edition

Trudi Reisner

Version 5 for Windows

$16.95 USA

1-56529-532-3, 352 pp.

More on Excel from Que

Excel 5 for Windows QuickStart

Sharel McVey & Cathy Kenney

Version 5 for Windows

$21.95 USA

1-56529-531-5, 608 pp.

Excel 5 for Windows Quick Reference

Chris Van Buren & Shelley O'Hara

Version 5 for Windows

$9.95 USA

1-56529-458-0, 160 pp.

Killer Excel Utilities

Ralph Soucie

Version 5 for Windows

$39.95 USA

1-56529-325-8, 1,000 pp.

Oops! Excel

Michael Miller

Version 4.0 for Windows

$16.95 USA

1-56529-241-3, 300 pp.

que To Order, Call:(800) 428-5331 OR (317) 581-3500

Explore the Internet–FREE!

DELPHI is the only major online service to offer you full access to the Internet. And now you can explore this incredible resource with no risk. Join DELPHI today and get 5 hours of evening or weekend access to try it out for free!

Use DELPHI's Internet mail gateway to exchange messages with over 10 million people at universities, companies, and other online services such as CompuServe and MCI Mail.

Download programs and files using **FTP** or connect in real-time to other networks using **Telnet**. You can also meet people on the Internet. **Internet Relay Chat** lets you "talk" with people all over the world and **Usenet News** is the world's largest bulletin board with over 5000 topics!

To help you find the information you want, you'll have access to powerful search utilities such as "Gopher," "Hytelnet," "WAIS," and "the World-Wide Web." If you aren't familiar with these terms, don't worry; DELPHI has expert online assistants and a large collection of help files, books, programs, and other resources to help get you started.

Over 600 local access numbers are available across the country. Explore DELPHI and the Internet today. You'll be amazed by what you discover.

5-HOUR FREE TRIAL!

Dial By Modem **1-800-365-4636**

Press Return 3 or 4 times

At Password, enter **QS294**

This offer is for new members only and you need a credit card if you want immediate access. Other restrictions apply. Complete details are provided during the toll-free registration.

Questions? Call 1-800-695-4005.
Send e-mail to INFO@delphi.com

CompuServe.

The difference between your PC collecting dust and burning rubber.

No matter what kind of PC you have, CompuServe will help you get the most out of it. As the world's most comprehensive network of people with personal computers, we're the place experts and novices alike go to find what's hot in hardware, discuss upcoming advances with other members, and download the latest software. Plus, for a low flat-rate, you'll have access to our basic services as often as you like: news, sports, weather, shopping, a complete encyclopedia, and up to 60 e-mail messages a month. And it's easy to begin. All you need is your home computer, your regular phone line, a modem, and a CompuServe membership.

To get your free introductory membership, just complete and mail the form on the back of this page. Or call 1-800-524-3388 and ask for Representative 449. Plus, if you act now, you'll receive one month free unlimited access to basic services and a $15 usage credit for our extended and premium services.

So put the power of CompuServe in your PC — and leave everyone else in the dust.

The information service you won't outgrow.™

Put the power
of CompuServe
at your fingertips.

Join the world's largest international network of people
with personal computers. Whether it's computer support,
communication, entertainment, or continually updated
information, you'll find services that meet your every need.

Your introductory membership will include one free month
of our basic services, plus a $15 usage credit for extended and
premium CompuServe services.

To get connected, complete and mail the card below. Or call
1-800-524-3388 and ask for Representative 449.

Yes! I want to get the most out of my PC. Send me my FREE
CompuServe Introductory Membership, including a $15 usage credit and
one free month of CompuServe basic services.

Name: _____

Address: _____

City: _____ State: _____ Zip:_____

Phone: _____

Clip and mail this form to: CompuServe
                            P.O. Box 20212
                            Dept. 449
                            Columbus, OH 43220

America Online's Top Ten List

What can <u>YOU</u> do with America Online?

1. Access the resources of the "information superhighway" through America Online's INTERNET CENTER!

2. Send electronic mail to thousands of other subscribers on many different networks.

3. Read the latest issue of TIME *before* it hits the newstand.

4. Easily download files from a library of thousands.

5. Tap into computing support from industry experts at online conferences and easy-to-use message boards.

6. Have "real-time" conversations with other members, join clubs, and read your favorite specialty magazines.

7. Monitor your stock and mutual fund investments in your own personal portfolio.

8. Make airline and hotel reservations, and even do some shopping.

9. Search the encyclopedia or get help with homework.

10. Find out the latest information about the world of entertainment through Hollywood Online and Rocklink.

AND BEST OF ALL, YOU CAN TRY AMERICA ONLINE FREE!

If you've never experienced America Online — now is the time. There's a world of services available for you to discover and they're all at your fingertips! We'll send you free software, a free trial membership, and 10 FREE hours to explore. And all you have to do... is CALL!

1-800-827-6364 ext. 9468

America Online is a registered service mark of America Online, Inc. Other names are trademarks or service marks of their respective owners. Use of America Online requires a major credit card or checking account. Limit one free trial per household.

1-800-PRODIGY, EXT. 81

With the PRODIGY® service you get a fast and dependable e-mail connection to the Internet that allows you to correspond with over 15 million people worldwide, write to friends on other online services and keep up contacts at government agencies.* Plus, with the PRODIGY service you get so much **more** for your money.

FREE
PRODIGY
Software

($4.95 shipping & handling)

Plus a **FREE** *month of Membership*

■ The PRODIGY service lets you use hundreds of untimed features for one low monthly fee.
You get over 600 hours of news, sports, games and more every month. It all adds up to as little as 50 cents a day. ■ The PRODIGY service provides fast 9600 bps service at no extra charge. ■ The PRODIGY service brings information to life with eye catching graphics. ■ The PRODIGY service has fun and educational features for kids.

CALL 1-800-PRODIGY, ext. 81

(1-800-776-3449) today to take advantage of this special offer.

*This offer includes the additional software that allows you to access the Internet via the PRODIGY service. Available for IBM® compatibles only.

This offer is for Value Plan Membership which includes untimed use of Core features and a two hour allowance of Plus feature usage and 30 personal PRODIGY service online messages during the first month; usage above allowances will result in extra fees even in your first month. As of 2/94 there is a 25¢ charge for each additional online PRODIGY service message. Fees and service content are subject to change without notice. Call 1-800-PRODIGY (1-800-776-3449) for current information. Phone charges may apply. Offer expires 3/31/94.

PRODIGY is a registered trademark and service mark of Prodigy Services Company. ©1994 Prodigy Services Company. All Rights Reserved.

Complete Computer Coverage

Que's 1994 Computer Hardware Buyer's Guide

Que Development Group

This absolute must-have guide packed with comparisons, recommendations, and tips for asking all the right questions familiarizes the reader with terms they will need to know. This book offers a complete analysis of both hardware and software products, and it's loaded with charts and tables of product comparisons.

IBM-compatibles, Apple, & Macintosh

$16.95 USA

1-56529-281-2, 480 pp., 8 x 10

Que's Computer User's Dictionary, 4th Edition

Bryan Pfaffenberger

This compact, practical reference contains hundreds of definitions, explanations, examples, and illustrations on topics from programming to desktop publishing. You can master the "language" of computers and learn how to make your personal computer more efficient and more powerful. Filled with tips and cautions, *Que's Computer User's Dictionary* is the perfect resource for anyone who uses a computer.

IBM, Macintosh, Apple, & Programming

$12.95 USA

1-56529-604-4, 650 pp., 4³/₄ x 8

To Order, Call: (800) 428-5331

Que Has WordPerfect 6 Books
for All Types of Users!

All Skill Levels

**Using WordPerfect Version 6
for DOS, Special Edition**
1-56529-077-1
$29.95 USA

Beginners in a Hurry

WordPerfect 6 QuickStart
1-56529-085-2
$21.95 USA

All Skill Levels

**WordPerfect 6
Quick Reference**
1-56529-084-4
$9.95 USA

Frustrated Beginners

**I Hate WordPerfect
But This Book Makes it Easy**
1-56529-212-X
$16.95 USA

Absolute Beginners

**Easy WordPerfect
for Version 6**
1-56529-311-8
$16.95 USA

All Skill Levels

**Oops! WordPerfect
What To Do When Things Go Wrong**
1-56529-196-4
$16.95 USA

All Skill Levels

Killer WordPerfect 6 Utilities
1-56529-362-2
$39.95 USA

Intermediate-Advanced

Upgrading to WordPerfect 6
1-56529-296-0
$14.95 USA

Motivated Learners

WordPerfect 6 SureSteps
1-56529-242-1
$24.95 USA

For more information or to place an order, call: 1-800-428-5331

Learning is Easy with Easy
Books from Que!

Que's Easy Series offers a revolutionary concept in computer training. The friendly, 4-color interior, easy format, and simple explanations guarantee success for even the most intimidated computer user!

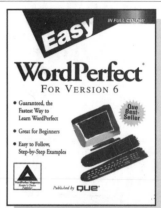

Easy WordPerfect For Version 6
Version 6 for DOS

$16.95 USA
1-56529-087-9, 256 pp., 8 x 10

Easy DOS for Version 6.2, 3rd Edition
Through Version 6

$19.95 USA
1-56529-640-0,
300 pp., 8 x 10

Easy 1-2-3, 2nd Edition
Releases 2.4

$19.95 USA
1-56529-022-4,
224 pp., 8 x 10

Easy 1-2-3 for Windows
Latest Version

$16.95 USA
0-88022-954-3,
200 pp., 8 x 10

Easy PCs, 2nd Edition
Covers IBM PCs & Compatibles

$19.95 USA
1-56529-276-6,
256 pp., 8 x 10

Easy Word for Windows for Version 6
Version 6

$19.95 USA
1-56529-444-0,
256 pp., 8 x 10

Easy Quattro Pro for Windows
Version 5.1

$19.95 USA
0-88022-993-4,
224 pp., 8 x 10

Easy Windows
Version 3.1

$19.95 USA
0-88022-985-3,
200 pp., 8 x 10

Easy WordPerfect for Windows for Version 6
Version 6

$19.95 USA
1-56529-230-8,
256 pp., 8 x 10

 **To Order, Call: (800) 428-5331 OR (317) 573-2500**

Even Beginners Can Learn To Program with Books from Que

QBasic for Rookies

Clayton Walnum

Beginner
_____
$16.95, 256 pp.

ISBN: 1-56529-235-9

Turbo C++ for Rookies

Clayton Walnum

Beginner
_____
$16.95, 256 pp.

ISBN: 1-56529-437-4

To Order, Call: (800) 428-5331
OR (317) 581-3500

Other Titles

C for Rookies	Introduction to Programming
Paul Perry	*David Veale & Lisa Monitto*
Beginner	Beginner/Intermediate
$19.95, 256 pp.	$19.95, 400 pp.
ISBN: 1-56529-280-4	ISBN: 1-56529-097-6
Que's Computer Programmers Dictionary	**Object-Oriented Programming from Square One**
Bryan Pfaffenberger	*Perry, Weisert, Linthicum, & Stack*
Beginner/Intermediate	Beginner
$19.95, 400 pp.	$26.95, 600 pp.
ISBN: 1-56529-125-5	ISBN: 1-56529-160-3

Let Que Help You with All Your Graphics Needs!

Using CorelDRAW!
Ed Paulson
Version
$29.95 USA
156529-124-7, 555 pp.,
7³/₄ x 9¹/₈

Using Harvard Graphics for Windows
Bob Benedict
Windows Version
$24.95 USA
0-88022-755-9, 555 pp.,
7³/₄ x 9¹/₈

Using PowerPoint 3
Debbie Walkowski
Through Windows
Version 3
$29.95 USA
1-56529-102-6, 500 pp.,
7³/₄ x 9¹/₈

Using AutoCAD Release 12
Morrison, Sharp, et al
Through Release 12
$34.95 USA
0-88022-941-1, 1200 pp.,
7³/₈ x 9¹/₈

More Graphics Titles from Que

AutoCAD Release 12 Quick Reference
Craig Sharp
Releases 10, 11, & 12
$9.95 USA
1-56529-024-0, 160 pp., 4³/₄ x 8

Easy Harvard Graphics
Shelley O'Hara
Version 3
$19.95 USA
0-88022-942-X, 224 pp., 7³/₈ x 9¹/₈

Harvard Graphics 3 Quick Reference
Trudi Reisner
Version 3
$9.95 USA
0-88022-887-3, 160 pp., 4³/₄ x 8

Quick & Dirty Harvard Graphics Presentations
Bob Benedict
Version 3
$24.95 USA
1-56529-089-5, 520 pp., 7³/₈ x 9¹/₈

Quick & Dirty PowerPoint Presentations
Que Development Group
Version
$24.95 USA
1-56529-289-8, 500 pp., 7³/₈ x 9¹/₈

Using Harvard Graphics 3
Bob Benedict
Version 3
$29.95 USA
0-88022-735-4, 700 pp., 7³/₈ x 9¹/₈

Using Ventura Publisher 4 for Windows
Skye Lininger
Versions 3 & 4
$29.95 USA
0-88022-929-2, 700 pp., 7³/₈ x 9¹/₈

 To Order, Call: (800) 428-5331 OR (317) 581-3500

Find It Fast with Que's Quick References!

Que's Quick References are the compact, easy-to-use guides to essential application information. Written for all users, Quick References include vital command information under easy-to-find alphabetical listings. Quick References are a must for anyone who needs command information fast!

1-2-3 Release 2.4
Quick Reference
Release 2.4

$9.95 USA
0-88022-987-X, 160 pp., 4³/₄ x 8

1-2-3 for DOS Release 3.4
Quick Reference
Releases 3.4

$9.95 USA
1-56529-010-0, 160 pp., 4³/₄ x 8

1-2-3 Release 4 for Windows
Quick Reference
Release 4 for Windows

$9.99 USA
1-56529-390-8, 160 pp., 4³/₄ x 8

AutoCAD Release 12
Quick Reference
Release 12

$9.95 USA
1-56529-024-0, 160 pp., 4³/₄ x 8

DR DOS 6 Quick Reference
Version 6

$9.95 USA
0-88022-827-X, 160 pp., 4³/₄ x 8

Excel 4 for Windows
Quick Reference
Version 4

$9.95 USA
0-88022-958-6, 160 pp., 4³/₄ x 8

Harvard Graphics 3
Quick Reference
Version 3

$9.95 USA
0-88022-887-3, 160 pp., 4³/₄ x 8

Improv for Windows
Quick Reference
Version 1

$9.99 USA
1-56529-443-2, 224 pp., 4³/₄ x 8

Microsoft Word
Quick Reference
Through Version 5.5

$9.95 USA
0-88022-720-6, 160 pp., 4³/₄ x8

MS-DOS 6 Quick Reference
Version 6

$9.95 USA
1-56529-137-9, 160 pp., 4³/₄ x 8

Norton Utilites 6
Quick Reference
Version 6

$9.95 USA
0-88022-858-X, 160 pp., 4³/₄ x 8

Paradox Quick Reference,
2nd Edition
Version 4

$9.95 USA
0-88022-891-1, 160 pp., 4³/₄ x 8

PC Tools 8 Quick Reference
Through Version 8

$9.95 USA
1-56529-148-4, 160 pp., 4³/₄ x 8

Q&A 4 Quick Reference
Versions 2, 3, & 4

$9.95 USA
0-88022-828-8, 160 pp., 4³/₄ x 8

Quattro Pro Quick Reference
Through Version 3

$8.95 USA
0-88022-692-7, 160 pp., 4³/₄ x 8

Quicken 5 Quick Reference
Versions 4 & 5.0

$9.95 USA
0-88022-900-4, 160 pp., 4³/₄ x 8

Windows 3.1 Quick Reference
Through Version 3.1

$9.95 USA
0-88022-740-0, 160 pp., 4³/₄ x 8

WordPerfect 5.1
Quick Reference
Version5.1

$9.95 USA
0-88022-576-9, 160 pp., 4³/₄ x 8

WordPerfect 6
Quick Reference
Version 6

$9.99 USA
1-56529-084-4, 160 pp., 4³/₄ x 8

WordPerfect for Windows
Quick Reference
Version 5.1 for Windows

$9.95 USA
0-88022-785-0, 160 pp., 4³/₄ x 8

 To Order, Call: (800) 428-5331
OR (317) 581-3500